CHARLES HARRIS

TRIAL & ERROR

A Judge's experiences, in it

Mereo Books

Mereo Books 2nd Floor, 6-8 Dyer Street, Cirencester, Gloucestershire, GL7 2PF
An imprint of Memoirs Book Ltd. www.mereobooks.com

TRIAL AND ERROR: 978-1-86151-940-5

First published in Great Britain in 2019 by Mereo Books,
an imprint of Memoirs Books Ltd.

Copyright ©2019

Charles Harris has asserted his right under the Copyright Designs and Patents
Act 1988 to be identified as the author of this work.

The address for Memoirs Books Ltd. can be found at
www.memoirspublishing.com

Memoirs Books Ltd. Reg. No. 7834348

Typeset in 10/16pt Sabon by Wiltshire Associates Ltd.
Printed and bound in Great Britain

CONTENTS

Dedication

Acknowledgement

Preface

To Carol, Roger, Hugh and Kate

ACKNOWLEDGEMENT

Many thanks to my two sons, both quick readers with a good eye for the inappropriate, who firmly suggested a number of desirable amendments. I took much of their advice, but not all of it.

PREFACE

There are just over 100 High Court Judges, roughly 600 Circuit Judges, and slightly fewer District Judges. There are many thousands of barristers and solicitors. Circuit judges deal with nearly all the serious civil and criminal work. I spent 24 enjoyable years as one of them, most of that time as a member - and latterly the most experienced member - of a group of thirty who specialise in civil litigation, dealing with every kind of person, and virtually every kind of dispute. The variety was stimulating, though the daily routine sometimes lacked glamour. For a time, I found myself President of the Council of her Majesty's Circuit Judges: a grand title, but with no power and little influence. About half this book is about what that career was like. It describes life as a barrister, becoming a judge, judicial personalities, how judges operate, such progress as I made myself, and how harmful complexity has deliberately been inflicted on those all who might need to litigate. As it is civil law - not criminal - which provides the structure of our country, its health and utility are important to everyone.

But legal matters - however important – do not invariably entertain. It seemed therefore a good idea to set them against the background of my life and other activities. I wondered about writing both a legal book with polemic flavour, and a memoir; but I hope that the fusion of the two has produced something of greater interest and more variety. There are accounts of childhood and education, university, politics and standing for Parliament, travel, alpine skiing, flying in balloons and other aircraft, sport, deerstalking, encounters in Africa, how to run firework displays, and family and social life in Oxfordshire. To say that there is something for everyone might be over optimistic, but I hope there is interest for most.

Charles Harris
Westcott Barton, October 2019

Chapter 1

Genesis

I was born in my parents' house in Staffordshire on 17th January 1945, at the climax of the Second World War. Allied generals were competing to cross the Rhine. The Russians were sweeping bloodily through Poland, and V2 rockets were landing on London. In Northern Europe, all was savagery and destruction. But I had security and peace.

The house, called Hawthornden, was built on a ridge near the Black Country village of Sedgley. Behind it, to the west, was a farm (owned by my grandfather, but let) and beyond that open country stretching towards Shropshire. In the opposite direction, at the bottom of the drive, was the main road to Wolverhampton, with a council estate on the far side. Next door to us, in a house called High Croft, lived my mother's father – Frederick Charles Wesson, a widower, with his housekeeper-companion Eulalie, to whom he twice unsuccessfully proposed. Born in 1876, he had suggested Hawthornden to my parents shortly after they had married (which they did on 1st October 1940, in an anxious pause between the Battle of Britain and the Blitz) so that my mother, his only child, would be close by. I thus had two adjacent gardens in which, as time went by, to climb trees, make dens, fish for newts, ride bicycles, and use a BSA air rifle.

My first memory, unprompted by photography, is of being led along a trench in the snow to see a double-decker bus on the main road, buried to its upper windows in a drift. This was in the great winter of 1947.

For a long time I believed that my father, Geoffrey Hardy Harris, was in the RAF, because he kept its blue uniform in a wardrobe. During the war, too old to be a pilot, for he was born in 1909, he had served as a navigator in Wellingtons, and then at the Empire Air Navigation School at Shawbury in Shropshire. Navigating a bomber early in the war was demanding work, involving attempts to get fixes upon stars while flying through the night at 200mph. After demobilisation in 1945 he was for a while a stockbroker in Birmingham before founding one of the earliest unit trusts, the Commonwealth Group. Richard Dimbleby sat on its board. Work often took him to London, where he stayed at the RAC club. Before the war he had run a small dance band as a hobby, and when I was young would often wander round the house playing the clarinet or tenor saxophone.

He expressed himself quite forcefully, especially in matters of politics, but was essentially mild mannered and generous, quick witted, good at figures, and had a repertoire of simple conjuring tricks. A slim man of about 5' 8", bald above dark hair, he made quite ambitious pieces of oak furniture, with complex, perfect joints. He was a capable mechanic too and restored a Corgi foldable motor scooter (designed to be dropped by parachute) for me to ride when I was about eleven. For two years he occupied our playroom with the construction of a wooden boat. This vessel only had one outing, propelled by a little Seagull outboard motor, on a canal near the Boulton Paul aircraft factory. He also put some energy into playing golf with a man who made Bilston enamels, and rather more into local government: he was for many years chairman of the finance committee of Staffordshire County Council.

My mother, Joan, was dark haired, brown eyed, of middle height and bore, some said, a slight physical resemblance to the Queen; a similarity spoilt by her habit of continually smoking Craven A cigarettes, from flat red boxes with a picture of a black cat in the centre. Trained at Studley agricultural college in Worcestershire, she knew a lot about cattle, and was fond of a breed of small ones called Dexters. While my sister Elizabeth and I were young she read us Beatrix Potter and Alison Uttley. The former had better illustrations, the latter better story lines. Six years younger than my father, she was artistic, and painted small portraits of her dogs. She ran the village meals-on-wheels service, and I heard her occasionally making confident speeches to women's organisations. Every night she insisted we said prayers before getting into bed. Her mother, Grace Price, who was partly Welsh, had died when she was only six and as she had no brothers or sisters, her childhood must have been less than perfect. Some was spent with farming relatives in Gloucestershire near the banks of the Severn. One of her ancestors was Daniel Pontifex, a silversmith active and fashionable during the Napoleonic war. She was also distantly related to Basil Liddell Hart, the military expert and historian. My mother could be forceful at times: when 17, I once tried to overtake her car at a point she regarded as unsuitable, so she pulled dangerously into my path and remained there, waving me back. I followed her home incandescent, we argued on the stairs, and I kicked out a banister strut in anger, hurting my foot.

Help in the house was provided by Mrs Fellows and Mrs Pearson, who, in tidy print aprons, cleaned, scrubbed and polished. They were kind, frugal people who budgeted to the last sixpence. As a teenager Mrs Pearson had worked in a nail factory, beating out its product with a hammer on an anvil, and was paid by weight. With us, she turned a large mangle to dry the washing, which came from a sink not a machine.

My mother's father, 69 when I was born, and generally known as Charlie, was a shrewd and benevolent man, who exercised regularly (but in private) in white combinations with a pair of Indian clubs, now in my study. A Methodist and considerable charitable donor, described as an ironmaster on my parents' marriage certificate, he ran the Victoria Ironworks at Moxley, known as William Wesson and Co after it had been purchased by his father in 1898 (the year that Gladstone died and Enzo Ferrari was born). I was taken there sometimes, and saw men in leather aprons handling glowing ingots with metal tongs. Coal arrived in barges, which penetrated the factory on a Stygian little canal in which swam the occasional rat. The men all spoke with a strong Black Country accent. This, unlike those of Liverpool, Newcastle, or East London, never became fashionable or heard much on the radio, except in the case of the comedienne and actress Beryl Reid, whom we saw occasionally in pantomimes at the Grand Theatre, Wolverhampton where my parents used to take a box, which the performers always subjected to special ribaldry. We twice saw Norman Wisdom there. A victim of paternal brutality, then flyweight army boxing champion in India, his act, though popular, was limited – consisting of singing plangent, melancholy songs and falling over. I also recall an Australian artist called Shirly Abicair, who played a zither

Gramp, as we called my grandfather, was a keen motorist and used to take us on weekend 'runs' in his large black Daimler. These outings were often for tea at the Royal Worcestershire Hotel in Droitwich, next to the Brine Baths, a spa in whose tantalisingly buoyant water children were not allowed to swim.

My only other living grandparent was my father's mother, Lily, who was born in 1872 and died in 1956 (her life exactly coinciding with that of Max Beerbohm). She was a very small person, one of ten children, and generally dressed in black. Her maiden name, Harris, had matched that of her husband, a cabinet maker whom she had married in 1901. At one stage he lost a good deal of money, and she had brought up their five children with some difficulty. This may explain why my father was never prepared to borrow, even for business or investment purposes. We saw little of his two younger sisters and two elder brothers. My mother's family, on the other hand, the Wessons, seemed to be everywhere, in various branches. There was much coming and going between their houses. One of these relatives, Leonard, a keen sailor, former soldier and a Bletchley Park code-breaker, had a glamorous Turco-Egyptian wife, Aliette. When I was about 16 she gave me a gold silk dressing gown: rather unsuitable for me to wear, but good to own. 'Every young man should have a presentable robe' she said delphically, in her faint but exciting French accent.

My first formal education was at a little school run by Miss Brassington, a bony spinster of some resilience, in the front room of her house in Sedgley, to which from the age of five I walked a mile, back and forth, unescorted. Sedgley was not a big place, but it had an ironmonger, chemist, Lloyds bank, church, doctors' surgery, cinema, barber and magistrates' court. Its centre, revealing a rough past, was called the Bull Ring. The largest house was owned by a friend of my father called Anthony Hickling, who manufactured snuff.

There were about twelve children at the school, of whom three were my friends: Graham, David and Christopher. David was very clever, Christopher was not. We ran around in corduroy shorts and blue sweaters, amicably fighting and no doubt being a nuisance. I quickly learned to read and write, and can remember thinking and then saying, without originality but entirely truthfully, that this opened up a completely new world. I have read avidly at every opportunity ever since. Early favourites were the Just William stories by Richmal Crompton, and Wild West adventures. I graduated in due course, via Robin Hood and Francis Drake, to English history and then to Pan paperback war stories about escaping from Colditz, flying warplanes or being a commando. It was some time before I appreciated stylish literature.

Books are remarkable value. For the price of a bottle of wine you acquire forever a product of immense labour, providing information, entertainment, stimulus or solace. They have now of course been replaced for some people by television, or social media, but until 1953 I had never seen a television. In that year, because of the Coronation, a set arrived at home. It was a brown wooden cabinet about 2' 6" high, and within its upper half, behind small doors, was a screen perhaps 8 inches by 6. On this, black and white pictures of imperfect clarity appeared. There was much parental adjustment of knobs marked 'contrast' and 'tone'. We all sat close to the screen, and the commentators and presenters spoke very distinctly. We watched the Queen being crowned, which was moving but did go on for rather a long time. At one moment of mild tedium I went outside and ran down the drive to the main road. I waited at our gate for about five minutes, and there was not a vehicle to be seen. When I got back the Queen was getting into the state coach, and my parents produced a Britains model of this, complete with postillions and outriders. These models are now very valuable if in good condition and complete with the original box. Sadly, although our box remains in excellent condition, the coach, horses and postilions all require major repair. At much the same time news came through of the conquest of Everest, but without any models of victorious mountaineers Hilary and Tensing.

I had a sister, Elizabeth, always called Isa. She had blonde hair worn in pony tails, a mild and pleasant nature, and wore attractive smocked dresses. We did not play together much, as she was four years younger than me, and not interested in soldiers, cowboys or climbing trees, preferring a large set of farm animals. We did however co-operate when our parents had drinks parties and would lower a small basket down on a string from the landing into the hall. Guests would fill it with canapés and pieces of cheese on sticks.

Every summer we went on holiday, always during the last week in August and the first in September. This was usually to Minehead in Somerset, where there was an extensive acreage of slightly muddy sand when the tide was out. It could take ten minutes to walk to the waves, which were generally small. My father swam a business-like crawl, my mother a slow breast stroke, wearing a white rubber hat. I flailed a little, until I got cold. I have never much taken to water – generally chilly, and with dangerous inhabitants. We stayed at the Metropole Hotel, on the sea front, but I longed to go to Butlins, half a mile to the east, behind whose gates there seemed to be a paradise of playgrounds and pleasure. I was told that appearances could be deceptive, and that we were better where we were. After a few years, while Butlins remained open, the Metropole closed and was made into flats, so we transferred to Dunster, a nearby village beneath a domesticated castle and equipped with a photogenic yarn market and cobbles (recently under threat as a safety hazard). Its beach consisted of oval grey stones, pounded smooth by the gentle but perpetual waves of the Bristol Channel. Amid the stones were set disused concrete pillboxes. A precaution against German invasion, these looked exciting to explore, but always turned out to have an unpleasant smell inside.

We often went riding, on ponies provided by the strangely-named Llamacraft stables. The family all wore proper jodhpurs, of thick twill with flared thighs, and tweed jackets, even on hot days, and we were taken on hacks lasting two or three hours around the edges of Exmoor by a girl of about 14 (or possibly a succession of girls of about that age). Once we were led in heavy rain down Porlock Hill, a steep terror to early motorists, on which the metal shod hooves of our horses slipped and scraped and slewed alarmingly. The girl in front did not seem worried. On these rides my mother often told us to watch out for the Doones. They were a tribe of Scottish vagabonds who had terrorised the district in the 17th century and whose leader shot Lorna, heroine of RD Blackmore's book, at the altar on her wedding day.

Much time was spent damming streams and exploring woods. My father kept a Gurkha kukri in his car, with which to slash the stems of ivy which slowly strangled the trees in glades at Horner and Cloutsham. At the time this did not strike me as strange, and I have his kukri, but it was an odd thing to do, and I would pause before wielding it in public on other people's trees. Kukris are, incidentally, a diminished version of the curved heavy-bladed Macedonian sword used by the soldiers of Alexander the Great, who reached the Himalayas in 328BC.

After some years my parents grew tired of Somerset, and changed to Dartmoor. For some reason they always took two cars; my father drove via Bristol, and my mother went via Bath. There was no M5. My sister and I took it in turns, and watched, while playing 'I Spy', for the salutes of RAC men on their motorcycle combinations. Our destination was a large grey pile called the Manor House Hotel, surrounded by a golf course. My sister, when running an interior design business 30 years later, got a contract to redecorate this hotel, whose sombre decor had remained substantially unchanged during the intervening period. Its owners now call it Bovey Castle – though it is not a castle – after a nearby village, where we hired horses from Mrs Brackenbury' stable behind a pub called the Ring of Bells. When I was about 12, I met a girl there who lived near Wimborne in Dorset. We walked around the golf course together and I thought her most attractive, but dared not tell her so. We may have held hands briefly.

Every January there was a family expedition to London. We stayed at the Cumberland Hotel at Marble Arch, whose lobby was lined in shiny sponge-like stone. The highlight of these trips was usually a very long taxi journey to Haringey arena to watch an ice show. The swerves, leaps and cascades of particles of ice struck me as spectacular, and I asked for skating lessons. My mother obliged, boots were purchased and I started to learn, at an ice rink in Birmingham. But I never mastered skating backwards and periodically fell over, once being quite badly concussed. I stopped wanting to skate. Many years later my wife took our daughter to the rink at Oxford for lessons, where she did so well that a suggestion was made that she should seriously pursue the sport. Fortunately she did not, for the life of child athletes is rarely happy.

There were also occasional holidays in North Wales at Easter, where it was always wet. We often visited Portmeirion, designed by Clough Williams Ellis. Its pastel variations on the architectural theme of an Italian fishing village were damp with continuous rain, and wistful, I now feel, for Latin sunshine.

My father would have liked to travel more extensively, and after my mother died in 1979, aged 63, of a brain haemorrhage brought on by a strenuous game of table tennis, he did. (Often to Canada, where a wartime RAF friend had become mayor of Calgary). During my childhood my mother usually insisted that our dogs came on holiday with us – at one stage a Clumber spaniel, then a neurotic collie called Bramble, and later three hunt terriers – so that had ruled out 'abroad'.

At home, while my sister played peacefully with her farm animals, I was occupied with what became quite large collections of model soldiers – modern khaki, Napoleonic, Unionist and Confederates, and knights-

and-Saracens. I bought two or three figures each week from my pocket money, at a toyshop called Millers in the arcade in Wolverhampton. These were all preserved, and later augmented by many more bought for my own children. They are unobtainable now. The Crusaders caused a recent frisson. A grandson who had been playing with them was asked at school what battles he was recreating. He answered accurately 'Christians against Muslims'. I was also fond of Meccano construction kits, and Dinky cars and aeroplanes. These outstanding, sturdy models are not sold now either. All is brittle plastic.

As a child I had some occasional awareness of events in the greater world. Rationing, for example. I could not run to Mrs Timmins' nearby sweet shop to buy humbugs or barley sugar from her tall glass jars without coupons or 'points'. (In 1949 the meat ration was reduced by Stafford Cripps, Labour's semi- Marxist Chancellor of the Exchequer, to less than it had been during the war which had ended four years previously. Bread, astonishingly, was rationed for the first time). In Mrs Timmins' shop was a large model of a square-rigged galleon, which made me long to experience such a vessel. Years later I did, when an Australian replica of Captain Cook's *Endeavour* came to England and I signed on for a short passage. Climbing out on a yard swaying 90 feet above the Irish Sea, holding on with chilly hands, made me wonder how such ships rounded Cape Horn without shedding half their crew, or how they were controlled in battle, with shouted orders inaudible above the cannon fire.

Occasionally we rode on trolley busses, which had arms on their roofs to connect with a tangle of overhead electric cables, from which they sometimes parted, stranding everyone. Wars occasionally intruded into my childhood consciousness. I was aware of the 'Glorious Gloucesters', an English regiment which heroically resisted hordes of Chinese in Korea. Our television carried pictures of paratroopers and Canberra bombers at the time of Suez, when my father explained that we had invaded Egypt, a place of which my only knowledge related to pyramids and pharaohs. The long French campaign in Indo China also caught my juvenile attention, and I recall a headline in the *Daily*

Sketch in 1954 announcing that Dien Bien Phu had fallen, after a siege involving dismantled artillery carried nocturnally through the jungle. The French used the romantic Foreign Legion, whom I envisaged in képis. A lot of the legionnaires were in fact German, and they wore helmets.

Every November we had a bonfire party. We always made a lifelike Guy. Bangers could be thrown about with pleasing results, and impressive high-altitude rockets streamed into the sky – the sticks could be found the next day in surprising places. One reached a quarter of a mile to Mrs Timmins. I carried my enthusiasm for fireworks into adult life, and for many years put on large, close-range displays at home, very popular with our guests and very unpopular with my wife, who always feared disaster.

Every Christmas Eve there would be a visit from my godmother, Peg Wesson, a kind-hearted, energetic, outspoken, tweed-clad altruistic eccentric, who would arrive with things she had cooked, sewn, or painted as presents for us all. Her fiancé had died in the First World War, and she never married. She worked for my grandfather, to whom she was related, and invariably, over the half century I knew her, kept her hair in an untidy grey bun. She drove the same Morris Minor for 25 years. I was once, as a teenager, in a hotel dining room with her where the service was slow. She was being ignored. She picked up a plate, held it for a moment above her head, and then dashed it to the floor, where it broke with gratifying volume. Two waiters hurried over immediately, and we had no further difficulty. I spoke at her funeral, and have always regretted not having done so on her 80th birthday, when she could have heard what I had to say.

Our other regular visitors at Christmas were Group Captain Neville Henderson – known as Whit – Roma, his Australian wife, and their two boys. With sleek black hair and slightly narrowed eyes, he was an authentic RAF war hero, for he had the DFC and bar, and had completed two tours flying Halifax bombers over Germany. A large proportion of those in his squadron died. (Bomber Command was the most dangerous of the services: 57,000 were killed from a total strength of 124,000). After the war he took part in the Berlin Air Lift, which defeated the Russian investment of that city. He never talked about his sorties or lost friends but was otherwise easy-going, amusing and fond of a drink. He went on to work for BOAC, and piloted the first panda to fly from China to England. He gave me his old leather flying helmet, which I cherished. Also two pairs of boxing gloves, with which I challenged a friend called Nicholas Holloway, who lived close by. He turned out to be a determined opponent, and after about five minutes I retired with a surprisingly sore face.

I cannot remember ever feeling seriously worried or unhappy when a small child, even when, or rare occasions, I was ill and kept in bed for a day or two. I had an ambition to own a beech wood when I grew up – which I have in a very modest way achieved. Life seemed very secure. In my bedroom was a 'wireless set', made of curved cream Vulcanite with a green tuning screen, where appeared romantic names like Luxemburg and Hilversum. I listened most evenings to programmes such as *Ray's a Laugh, Round the Horn, Take it from Here* and *The Goon Show*.

In 1953, when Churchill was back as Prime Minister, Eisenhower was elected President of the USA and I was seven, I went to prep school. This was Birchfield, a small establishment of about 75 children in Tettenhall, a smart suburb of Wolverhampton. My uniform was obtained at Halls, Tailors and Outfitters, whose premises were equipped with a system of tubes and compressed air into which cash was put in a small cylindrical cartridge and shot to some central location, whence a receipt was fired back with agreeable hisses and thunks. The school, where we wore grey flannel shorts, green blazers and caps embellished with a yellow griffon's head, was I think a good one, and I certainly enjoyed it. It was run by two unmarried men, very unlike each other. The Headmaster, Mr Brown, was short and fat, with a knitted waistcoat straining round his middle. He always wore brown suits, or possibly the same brown suit, with a faint vertical stripe in its material. He used a small Morris car, made permanently lopsided by his weight, to travel the 200 yards to the cricket pavilion from the school's front door. He was a cricket enthusiast, and in summer used to take the dozen or so boarders – one of whom, when eleven, I later became – to Edgbaston to watch Warwickshire. He did this in his other car, a large Austin Princess limousine. We children spent much of the time racing around excitedly behind the stands and saw very little of the play.

I have always felt cricket to be an unsatisfactory spectator sport, because without television you cannot appreciate what the ball is doing before it is struck or missed. Slow motion replays often reveal remarkable swings and spins and turns, quite invisible to the watching crowds, who only see whether and how far a batsman has succeeded in hitting a particular delivery. Perhaps for this reason attendances at ordinary county games are now negligible.

Mr Brown's partner (in the business sense and I am quite confident no other) was Mr Watson, a tallish, slim man of serious aspect, always in a buttoned-up grey flannel suit, rather like that of the TV character Doc Martin. He taught history in an excitingly vivid way, once describing a visit to a Roman legion which came about, he said, when he fell through a hole in the ground into an 'older world'. There he coped quite well, he explained, because he could speak Latin. He told us, accurately, that Roman troops could march up to 25 miles a day, and then construct a small fort in which to pass the night. They did this sometimes for weeks on end, which makes one wonder how they had any energy left to fight. Mr Watson's car was a smart little Riley.

The staff at Birchfield were, I suppose, characteristic of such schools at the time. The Latin master looked like a ratty version of Field Marshal Montgomery, with shabby suede shoes and a brown corduroy jacket. He smoked a curved pipe throughout the day, in class and out. So we called him Kipper. He was fond of confiscating our catapults and pen knives. He was also fond of an attractive dark-haired young matron called Miss Williams. She supervised us changing before and after games, and was discomfited when the small boys surrounded her, chanting 'Miss Williams, Miss Williams, we adore you, so pull down your knickers and let us explore you'. Eventually she became engaged to Kipper.

One or two of the masters were quite unable to keep order, and must have had a terrible time when form after form with insolent laughter refused all instruction. Mr Muggleton, much liked, resembled the comedian Tony Hancock, and would make jokes at the expense of any potential troublemaker. He was so amusing that he had no difficulties. Another master was rather too interested in the children under his control, and, I subsequently learned, made advances to several – one of whom later became both a judge and a priest.

There was much emphasis on PT, which we did in competitive callisthenic 'drill squads' of about eight boys who jumped and waved their arms and crouched and stretched and touched their toes in unison. In 1956 I won the prize for best section leader. This, apart from an English cup, was my only school prize. There were several games involving running and avoiding. In 'chariots', two boys holding hands had to rush across a football pitch without being touched by a team of interceptors. This was oddly exciting, and very gratifying if one got through uncaught. We were allowed to construct dens in trees or unused areas of the grounds, in which we pretended to be snipers, bandits, red Indians or escaped slaves. We played soccer in the winter, in stiff heavy leather boots impregnated with aromatic dubbin and shod with dangerously large studs, and cricket in the summer.

As I had no coaching, I was no good either at bowling or batting, but I was recruited for my last two years into the First Eleven as a specialist fielder, because I could run fast. I was put far behind the wicket at third man, or fine leg, and was expected to sprint round to cut off boundaries when balls got past the slips or the wicket keeper. Though I was generally able to intercept the ball, my throwing range was poor so that the batsman could often get his four by running. In one match our wicket keeper was struck on the nose by a quick ball, and fell as though pole-axed to the ground. We fielders gathered round and urged him to remove the gauntleted hand which he had clapped to his face, so that we could have a look. He did, and a jet of blood like a spurt from a miniature oil well sprayed all over our cream flannels and his white shirt. Not an unduly timid child, I concluded then that cricket was dangerous. This was confirmed a few years later at my next school, where the son of friends of my parents was carried unconscious from the wicket when hit on the head by fast bowling. Taken to the sanatorium and left to recover quietly, he died later that afternoon from an undiagnosed haemorrhage. His father was a doctor, and he was an only child.

Lessons never seemed especially hard. I particularly enjoyed English, History, Geography and Geometry, but was poor at French, to the sporadic annoyance of Mr Watson, who seemed to regard it as a very straightforward subject. It was taught with some strange textbooks including one which had as its hero a Monsieur Souris, who used to strut about 'avec un fusil'. Even for someone brought up on an agreeably anthropomorphic diet of Peter Rabbit, Jemima Puddleduck and Squirrel Nutkin, it seemed odd that French mice should carry rifles. Though Tommy Brock did have a spade.

Of those who were in the top form in my last year the two cleverest never achieved anything which came to my attention in later life. The injured wicket keeper, Chapman, who sat behind me in the Third Form, became a successful Midland solicitor and then a District Judge. He became president of the District Judges the year after I became president of the Circuit Judges. One boy, Richard Barr, who was, with Robert Hamilton, my 'best friend', became a serial adventurer, exploring underground cave systems, disturbing leopards in the Himalayas, driving over especially desiccated deserts, and, most notably, crossing the North Sea in a large balloon. He also helped to construct a full-sized trebuchet, a mediaeval war machine which could project upright pianos or dead pigs about 100 yards. Both forms of ammunition burst most gratifyingly upon hitting the ground. (I wrote to *The Times* about this after an academic historian had asserted from a study of old pictures that such weapons could not have worked. It created a very gratifying correspondence). There was also a boy called Pollard, who grew up to become Chief Constable of Thames Valley Police when I was a judge at Oxford.

Dayboys were generally driven to school. My journey was some seven miles. There was a rota of local parents and some prestige attached to their cars. One neighbour of ours, Mr Rhodes, had a Humber Super Snipe, a big, heavy vehicle which he found difficult to get through the school gates. It had an aura of substance, dark leather and wealth. At the other extreme, Mrs Holden, whose husband brewed Holden's Best Bitter, a popular beer in the West Midlands, picked up six children in a cheerful baby Fiat 500. This necessitated an amusing proximity which we young passengers much enjoyed. Unlike the Humber, the Fiat was never late.

At the time of the Suez crisis there was a petrol shortage which my mother dealt with by buying a Morris Minor convertible, presumed to be economical. This too was very popular with schoolboys, who, unencumbered by seat belts, were able to sit up in a row on the folded open hood, waving and shouting at the traffic. Policemen often waved back.

One parent had a Jaguar, in British Racing Green. I urged my father to get one, but he bought instead an MG Magnette, which though in some respects superficially similar was generally regarded, and accurately so, as a lesser vehicle. He kept a heavy paving stone in the boot to help with traction in the snow, which fell for a week or two most winters.

Occasionally the school runs were seriously, but pleasurably, obstructed by very thick fog, or 'smog' as it was known, a result of severe atmospheric pollution. This caused cars to crawl about at walking speed, and we wore scarves over our faces like terrorists. Such days were highly satisfactory, as we would arrive late after a small adventure and had to leave early. We did not worry about our lungs at all.

We acted in form plays, and in one I appeared as Robin Hood with a fine fringed green velvet tunic skilfully created by my mother (and in which my elder son was to appear about 30 years later). In another production I was Odysseus, complete with satisfyingly sturdy round wooden shield and a three-foot wooden sword. In both plays the action was more important than the limited dialogue. There may have been something latent in the genes though, as my three children were all good actors, and the younger two performed at the Edinburgh Festival to some acclaim. Perhaps this talent came maternally, though my wife denies it.

During the holidays my mother would sometimes take us to Dudley Zoo, housed in avant-garde architecture in the grounds of a decayed castle. There lived (if life it was) two sad, yellowing polar bears and an even more miserable solitary tiger. You could ride on a tuskless elephant, if patient, for there was usually a long queue.

We often went shopping in Wolverhampton. There I enjoyed Beattie's department store, spaciously arranged over several floors connected by a huge curved cream stone staircase. It was later to be taken over and ruined by House of Fraser. In the record department you were allowed to select up to three choices and take them into a little kiosk to try them out before purchase. There was a large radiogram at home, on which I played *My Fair Lady* so often that I could repeat all the lyrics word perfectly. My favourite was *On the Street Where You Live*, whose strains of hopeful melancholy I still enjoy. I have never been able to understand why this, and other fine musicals, do not qualify as opera – a quirk of snobbish taxonomy which musical friends are quite unable to explain.

I was once taken to a 'literary lunch' in Beatties' restaurant, addressed by George Cansdale (an Attenborough of his day). He produced two seven-foot pythons and called for volunteers to carry them round the tables. None of the lunching ladies were keen on this but two boys of about eleven stepped forward. I was surprised to find that the snakes were not slimy or cold, but smooth and pleasant to the touch – rather like expensive muscular handbags. Their eyes however were not friendly. I suppose they were terrified, for a Wolverhampton department store was far from their natural habitat.

I always felt Birchfield was a pleasant place, and even when I became a boarder in my final year I did not feel lonely or unhappy, though I do recall moments, usually during morning prayers, when I was very anxious lest one of my parents should suddenly die. Boarders enjoyed special privileges; we were taught how to play billiards and how to drive the large Dennis lawnmower which kept the pitches trim. When there were snowball fights in winter it was boarders versus day-boys. The former, though heavily outnumbered, usually prevailed by spirit, organisation and aggression. I suppose this was a lesson in life.

In my last year I enjoyed a brief period of celebrity because – dogs notwithstanding – the family visited the USA, where my father had financial business in Philadelphia. This meant that he qualified for some foreign currency, at that time severely restricted. In 1957 most transatlantic travel was still by ship, and we went from Liverpool on a Cunard vessel, the *Media*, sailing to New York. She had been launched in 1947, so was younger than me, and was the first new transatlantic liner built after the war. She had sturdy classic lines and a single red funnel with a black band. The voyage was about as exciting an experience as a 12-year-old could imagine. There were some tremendous seas. I can remember walking steeply uphill as the ship climbed the slopes of mighty grey-green swells, and then stumbling downhill as it plunged into huge valleys of what looked like seething liquid marble. Great waves rolled and roared and foamed across the foredeck and seethed through the scuppers. There were frames on the dining room tables to restrain the crockery for the few who tried to eat. I was quite confident that we were safe, because I had been told that if you were born in a caul, as I was, you never drown. My mother was not so sure, and very seasick. The lifeboats creaked and rolled reassuringly upon their davits, but were never called upon. Over two days we grew used to this turbulence, but then felt the silence strange as the waves grew mild and calm.

Every so often another ship would be sighted in the vast grey waste of ocean, and there would be much ceremonial hooting and saluting, especially if she was another Cunarder.

In less than a week the *Media* arrived at New York. We steamed in past the Statue of Liberty, with her right arm raised in welcome, holding what Michelle Obama was to call a 'hopefully hoisted torch'. I was told the figure was French made and so large that people could stand inside her head, which was hard to believe, but true. In the city my sister and I gazed in envious amazement at urban skaters waltzing on an ice rink at the foot of the Rockefeller Centre. We were taken to the top of the Empire State building to survey a vista of canyons made of stone and glass, and in a coffee shop there I stole a dime from a saucer. In the streets below we stared fascinated from the sidewalks at the gusts of smoke or steam which billowed up through gratings from the underworld. The taxicabs were big, yellow, and dirty inside; their drivers friendly. We always had breakfast at a little diner called Prexy's, sitting on chromium bar stools in an exciting adult manner, and ordering eggs to be cooked in strange ways, such as 'up and over'.

We went to Detroit, where three interesting things happened. The house where we were staying was in an elevated position, and early one evening I looked out of a window and saw the writhing black coil of a tornado approach us, flinging out pieces of roof, advertising hoardings and other large debris with awful velocity. It moved along as though live and purposeful, like something out of *Paradise Lost*, and very menacing. But when perhaps 400 yards from us, just as it was giving rise to real anxiety in the household, it veered suddenly to its left and vanished to terrorise some other district.

Next day our host, Frank Hendy, who was the brother of my grandfather's companion and a chiropractor, loaded us all into his bench-seated Pontiac and took us for a drive. This at one stage went through an area apparently entirely populated by black people, of whom, in England, I had seen very few. Many sat in relaxed and jovial attitudes on elderly verandas, but others stood in minatory clusters by traffic lights. Our host seemed very aware of these, and did his best never completely to stop the car. I absorbed an atmosphere of some apprehension.

The third thing was more personal. I had a bad attack of hiccoughs, unrelieved by holding my breath, drinking water from the wrong side of a glass or pinching myself. The chiropractor asked if I would like help. I nodded and he touched one side of my neck quite lightly. The hiccoughs immediately ceased. He then told me that if he had touched some other part of my neck I would have dropped dead. I found this

Chapter 2

A school in Derbyshire

Though it does not occur to children, running a school during term time must be one of the most demanding of all professions. A headmaster or headmistress has to cope with at least five separate groups of people: governors, staff, children, parents, government bureaucrats, and probably contractors too. It will be rare for all to be tranquil simultaneously. A head is never truly off duty. In independent schools there is often some large fundraising effort afoot, in order to construct yet another prestige facility with which to impress those considering spending £40,000 or more, every year, on about 34 weeks of tuition, board and lodging for their children. With subtraction for holidays, half terms, days out, and weekend exeats, the time during which the children are actually being accommodated, trained and fed probably amounts to about 220 days a year. It is very remarkable that even with a substantial number of wealthy parents from abroad, private schools are still both popular and viable. When I was being educated, and for some time thereafter, these schools were accessible to any reasonably prosperous middle-class family. They are no longer. In 1975 Eton charged £990 p.a. Adjusted for inflation, that is a present-day value of about £8,500. Current fees are about five times that.

My father had gone to Wolverhampton Grammar School, founded in 1512. In 1958 I was sent to a younger establishment, Repton, founded in 1557 by a gentleman called Sir John Port on a bleak and damp spot between Burton on Trent and Derby. 'Not near any enticing towns' as a later headmaster was to say. I think this school was chosen simply because my godfather, a Birmingham doctor, had been there. The school and village which contained it were close to the river Trent, described in the school song as 'staid and silver' but in reality dismal grey. The towers of Willington power station loomed high beyond its banks, which sometimes flooded. In 873 Danish Vikings had arrived in their longboats, seized a monastery in the village, built a substantial earth fortification and overwintered. They would probably have felt at home, because Repton was often very cold, and I was grateful for my thick blue woollen duffel coat, with a hood and horn toggles, in which, above my uniform herringbone tweed suit, I could shelter from the sleet on the 500-yard walk from my House (Brook, now abolished) to the school buildings. This was a walk I took thousands of times, about which I particularly remember two things: a permanently parked white Sunbeam Alpine sports car, which seemed a most desirable object, and encounters with a small, bruised woman, missing several teeth, always pushing a shabby pram and accompanied by two small children. I failed to realise it then, but she was clearly a 'battered wife', in need of help and money, for whom the droves of suited schoolboys must have seemed creatures from a world of incomprehensible security and comfort.

Not that we were immune from violence ourselves. House prefects could 'swish' or 'flap' fags (junior boys made to do menial tasks) for any perceived imperfection in their duties – dusting, putting Blanco on webbing belts and gaiters, or shoe polishing – by hitting them on the bottom with gym shoes. Housemasters could, and sometimes did, beat with canes. This licensed assault happened to me once, though I cannot remember why. It was very painful. Such manifestations of moderate barbarity were less in my time than they had been before, and diminished considerably while I was there. On the whole one was not often frightened. I came across little evidence of homosexuality.

You enter Public school as a nervous child, and emerge five years later, without really noticing the change, as a confident young adult. In my first year I was the junior person in a study of five boys of varying seniority, the oldest of whom was Graeme Garden, later a well-known radio comedian, but at that time taking biology A level and painting a frieze depicting the characters in *The Archers*, including a salacious caricature of John Tregorran. (Garden has lived for many years in the next village to mine in North Oxfordshire, and I used to see him commuting to work from Charlbury. Somehow commuting seemed inappropriate for a comedian). At Repton each study member – there were five or six boys to a room – had a small table to himself, which he fortified, personalised and embellished with little bookcases, shelves and a lamp. I got on well with another new boy, Bill Scott, whose mother ran a restaurant near Thornton le Fylde in Lancashire, popular during party conferences at Blackpool. Otherwise my peers in Brook House, while pleasant, did not become close friends.

The house used to echo to pop music, played on small gramophones, which were possessed by most studies. The favourite artist when I arrived was, by a large margin, Buddy Holly, though Elvis Presley and Billy Fury also had their advocates. The song I liked best, and which always strongly reminds me of my mid teenage years, and adolescent parties, was *Poetry in Motion* by Johnny Tillotson, 1960. I had the 45rpm record, on the Cadence label. Tillotson is still alive, at 81 only seven years older than me. He has managed to live a lot longer than Holly and Presley, though his music has not. I did not much enjoy the Beatles when they arrived around 1963, and I have got little pleasure from pop music ever since, except for *The Push Bike Song*, which throbbed though the Krazy Kangaroo mountain bar in St Anton a decade later. I may lack some demotic instinct. Perhaps there will be a renaissance of catchy tunes with interesting lyrics, but it seems a long time coming. I became a Light Programme listener, but that was abolished in 1967, when it and I were both 22.

Repton was perhaps just in the top dozen public schools at the time, along with places like Charterhouse, Rugby and Shrewsbury, but it was, I later discovered, better known for Christianity and sport than for academic achievement. Two headmasters, Fisher and Ramsey, had become Archbishops of Canterbury. Old boys included CB Fry and Harold Abrahams. Len Hutton sent his sons there. The school did very well at cricket, hockey and association football. When I arrived in 1958 the headmaster was Lynam Thomas, who had been teaching there since 1927, the year Trotsky was expelled from the Communist Party. He retired in 1961, the year the first man travelled in space. He too became ordained. He described the school to his successor as 'a place for the beta-query-plus boy', which he had not sought to alter. My housemaster, JD Eggar, himself probably beta-query-plus, was broad and swarthy and primarily interested in sport – particularly cricket – but also in Fives, an exciting game which involved hitting a small hard ball with a gloved hand around a three-sided stone-walled court, a dangerous manual version of squash. He had a son, occasionally seen scurrying around the house, who was sent to Winchester, and later became MP for Enfield and President of the Russo-British Chamber of Commerce. Eggar was a friend and rival of Dick Sale, who ran a House called Priory; they vied perpetually for sporting rather than academic success.

I do not think that JD, as my housemaster was known, was very fond of me, especially after I instituted a food committee to criticise the quality of what we were given to eat. The dormitory windows were kept open every night, including (indeed especially) throughout the winter, about which I also complained. My lack of enthusiasm for cricket will not have helped. He did on one occasion compliment me on doing well in a cross-country run, a five-mile canter around local fields. It was called a Long Milton, after a nearby village. On this run there was a dog which rushed out of a farm to harry and sometimes to nip the boys. One of us resolved to deal with this danger, and ran in track running spikes. When the dog next attacked he stuck out his foot, and the dog's head was impaled. It fell dead, and the boy got into some trouble. I think his father was persuaded to pay for a new dog.

RM Charlesworth, dark, cheerful, balding and scruffy, taught English, and arranged and directed school plays. He was an excellent schoolmaster who divined what might interest and stimulate his pupils, and taught with a good balance of engagement and exhortation. He encouraged me to read and understand both Beowulf and Evelyn Waugh, as well as the more traditional authors of English literature. Stuart Andrews, neat, aquiline and later headmaster of Clifton, taught history, and was very rigorous about the attribution and exactitude of any quotation. Dennis Hawkins, a large, black-bearded man, clad always in messy corduroy, presided with benign energy at the art school, a large mediaeval stone barn just inside the school entrance arch, where he encouraged self-expression, with modest emphasis on technique. I specialised in cartoon faces, also birds and churches carefully depicted in black ink, coloured with water paints. I was better at drawing than painting, but foolishly have neglected in later life to keep up this interest.

Hawkins had, apart from great enthusiasm and considerable popularity, a particular gift. There was an institution nearby which we called a lunatic asylum, where people with serious psychiatric conditions were treated. He used to visit this and developed a useful diagnostic tool. If an inmate painted a house with no door, he was, Hawkins told the staff, likely to be suicidal. Likewise, a path which meandered out of the picture without a depicted destination was a sign of less serious self-harm. In later life, when I became a member of the Parole Board, I wondered whether some similar tests might be a useful way of predicting dangerousness in prisoners.

Two years before I left, we had a new headmaster, John Thorn. He was a young man, in his thirties, with quite limited teaching experience but style, ambition and clarity of thought, who tried hard to improve the school's intellectual standing. Though we schoolboys were not to know, he had a difficult time, which he described in his 1989 book *Road to Winchester*: 'The O.R. Society... had never found me the headmaster of their dreams... my last two terms at Repton were far from easy... the boys were not often very subtle... the staff were for or against things and mostly said so without concealment... Problems were big.' He was I think fighting some pretty sturdy philistines, and he also had to contend with the highly conservative Lord Fisher of Lambeth as head of the governing body. 'By 1966' he wrote, 'I had decided I wished to leave'. Two years later he was chosen for Winchester, after considering whether to become a wine merchant in Bristol.

Thorn taught History to the Upper Sixth, of which I was a member, and sometimes took us in his Ford Zodiac to visit local places of historical interest. He was a pleasant and uncondescending man, whom I met again years later towards the end of his time at Winchester, to which I was considering sending my sons. He either recognised me or gave an excellent impression of having done so. Some schoolmasters are remarkably good at this.

I usually came about fifth in classes of some 12 to 14 boys. This level of achievement was in fact a bad thing, since it meant that I was high enough not to be chivvied or much criticised, but performing at a lower level than I might have done if encouraged or threatened. Education should always involve stimulus of one sort or another: preferably inspiration or interest, but failing that, anxiety. I was still fond of History, English and Geometry, but never got far with maths or, particularly, chemistry. It was very hard to understand how elements could be shown by algebra to combine or fissiparate under various conditions and turn into something else. How could one possibly prove by processing letters and figures that one gas became another? And why was it that whenever I asked for the chemical formula not of metal or carbon or hydrogen, but everyday things like wood and leather, or even chocolate cake, I never got a satisfactory answer but was simply told not to be silly?

Many boys used to spend a lot of their time in the tuck shop, the 'Grubber' as it was known. It was run as a small cafeteria, and egg and rather soft chips was the favourite order. I never went there much, preferring privately to eat the Mars Bars which my mother used to send in large brown wholesale boxes containing two dozen. This was not a route to popularity, for they were too big to give away, but it did save money.

Healthier activities were available. A housemaster called Townsend used to take small groups of us to the Peak District to learn rock climbing on Stanage Edge and other outcrops. He was accompanied by his Pyrenean Mountain Dog, Louis, who was the size of a slim bear. We learned to use ropes to protect ourselves and fellow climbers and how to belay and abseil, and were introduced to the classification of climbs, from 'Diff', which in a typical English way meant 'very easy', to 'VS' (very severe), which would not have troubled an alpinist but might be tricky for us. I found climbing very enjoyable, even in the heavy corps boots which we wore, and relished the feeling of moving over exposed but sound rock by toe hold, balance and fingertip. It seemed a proper progression from my earlier fondness for tree climbing, at which I was quite daring. I enjoyed the sensations of height. We used to return from climbing weekends in the school bus on Sunday evenings, and stopped for evensong at Ashbourne's fine church, filing in to the mild interest of the congregation wearing khaki fatigues.

One of our climbing expeditions was led by George Lowe, who had played a major part in the successful British led ascent of Everest in 1953 and taken a teaching job at Repton in 1959. He was a quiet man, naturally greatly admired. It was not until many years later that I leaned that his work, pathfinding on the Lhotse face, was absolutely critical to the outcome of the expedition. He had spent many hours at altitudes above 23,000 ft without oxygen, which other climbers simply could not manage. When I met him at the Travellers club a few years before his death I asked about this, and he replied that he 'supposed he had quite good quality lungs'. In 2013 he wrote an attractive, simple book, *Letters from Everest*, in which he said 'Our achievement, I hope, will last as long as there are adventurous hearts... as long as people still raise their eyes to the summits, and take on a challenge in the simple way that we did – slow and sure, head up, just one step at a time'.

Also in the Peak District, near Hathersage, and sometimes in the

North, there were cadet camps. Every boy belonged to the CCF, or Combined Cadet Force, and each Friday there was a parade and some modest military training (mostly drill, but also more excitingly how to fire a Bren gun). On speech days the whole contingent, a battalion, marched smartly through the village with rifles on our shoulders, and a band playing patriotic tunes. I used to pretend we were liberating Paris. There was a summer camp, lasting a week. These camps were fun. We slept in sturdy khaki ridge tents, which cosily kept out the rain, and tried with a portable radio to follow the fortunes of Jaguar and Aston Martin at the Le Mans 24-hour road races. In groups of four, each carrying a frame rucksack weighing about 20lbs, but no rifle, we were sent out to navigate around the local hills and lakes, and make our way back to base by dusk. A few cheated by thumbing a lift or calling a taxi from a phone box, but mostly, with maps and compasses (no GPS or mobile phones existed) and a bit of common sense, we got where we wanted to go. I grew increasingly fond of high places, and ever since have enjoyed hills and mountains, rather scorning terrain that is flat.

Once we had 'night ops', an exercise on Yorkshire hills near Catterick which involved attacking, or being attacked by, another school in the dark. This of course was very hard for those in charge to control, and rapidly became confused. I did not like the feeling of crouching vulnerable in the gloom, even with blanks in my rifle, waiting to be captured by the enemy. Nor did the others in my section. So we decided to attack. By this we meant move forward without instructions. In due course we were found by the master in charge, Tim Fisher (son of the headmaster-archbishop), who was wearing camouflage rather than his usual corduroy, and he told us that we had been captured, or would have been if we had stayed where we were supposed to, but were at liberty to escape. We ran off into the dark and became lost. I do not think we were missed at all, and when dawn broke at about 5am we could see where we were and wandered back to camp. On the way passing the very amusing sight of Fisher in the turret of a scout car he had been lent by the local TA which had got irretrievably stuck in some sort of mire. We cheered no end.

Fisher was the master who had three years before rescued me from the school swimming pool during a swimming test. I was not a good swimmer, and had for a few moments been aware that though I was progressing forward, I seemed to be doing so under the water, rather than upon it. This made for difficulties in breathing, but despite some apprehension I was determined not to give up. The next thing I knew I was on the paving slabs at the side of the pool, being wrapped in a towel and hit on the back. Nobody had noticed my underwater progress until Fisher saw a child in obvious difficulty and jumped in. I discussed this episode with him many years later when we went to look at Swanborne prep school, where he had become headmaster, but he did not remember it, or even pretend to.

There was another quasi-military activity in which I took part at Repton: rifle shooting. In the 1950s the nation was keen on this. *Country Life* magazine used to set and sponsor an annual small-bore competition (and publish the results), with landscape targets in which enemy figures were concealed. We practised for this every week in a small indoor range underneath the gymnasium, next to the school armoury, which held the pleasant tang of recently-expended ammunition. There was also, on a much grander scale, an annual public schools' competition at Bisley. For this Lee Enfield.303 rifles were used, equipped with aperture sights. These were surprisingly accurate at ranges of up to 500 yards. One afternoon a week during summer term, instead of playing cricket, about a dozen boys got into the school's vintage maroon charabanc and were driven to 'The Butts', an old rifle range grazed by cows, near Burton on Trent. There we took it in turns to shoot, and to mark and patch up targets which we hauled up and down from within a concrete-lined trench. Firing took place from 200 and 500 yards. There was no hearing protection. The object of the exercise was to get into the school 'eight' to go to Bisley to compete with scores of other schools for the Ashburton Shield. This I enjoyed. Bisley was a sort of wooden colonial village in Surrey devoted to rifles and pistols and shooting, with all sorts of interesting characters in strange hats with ammunition, slings, holsters, spare magazines and spotting scopes. It still exists, though now without the pistols. There was a stirring and unusual competition called the Marling, which involved starting at 600yds, running with your rifle to a firing point at 500 yds, firing, then running to 400, 300 and 200, shooting at each point. This was quite spectacular, with all the school teams doing this at once, and the whole range alive with the sound of continuous fire. Aiming accurately became increasingly hard as one got out of breath. It was far more entertaining than cricket. I became a reasonable and confident rifle shot. We did not however win the Ashburton Shield.

I quite enjoyed football, where I was always put on the right wing, and had to outwit the opposing full-back. My only sporting prowess however, if that is not too strong a word, was at sprinting. I found it easy to run pretty quickly over short distances – 100 yards or 220 yards – and sometimes won competitions in these events. About 25 years later when staying in Scotland I ran a race against Sinclair Bonde, a well-connected Swede of about my age who had been at Eton. He told me that he had been that school's quickest runner, and we competed on a lawn in front of a castle. I was pleased to discover that though he was taller and stronger than I was he could not run faster. This was a source of great satisfaction, as the first low foothills of middle age were by then visible on the horizon.

It should be noted that Repton was not an entirely culture-free establishment. During my last summer term, after exams had been taken, it was possible to do various things as part of a sixth form course. I chose to write a paper on Palladian architecture, which I did together with another Brook House boy, Anthony Johnson (who was totally unsuited to the school, being very intelligent, arrogant, lazy and unprepared to take part in any sporting activity at all. I do not think that he ever had paid employment in his adult life, mostly spent in France). The chief pleasure of the project was that those taking part were allowed out of school. Johnson and I planned carefully. He would go down to London, where I believe his father had a flat in Lowndes Square. While there he would inspect Chiswick House, and make a short visit to Mereworth Castle in Kent. I, on the other hand, having borrowed my mother's Standard Vanguard estate car (a sturdy vehicle, desert sand in colour) would travel to the south and west, and visit Wilton House, Prior Park and Stourhead. I did indeed visit these places, pausing only for a short time at each – though sufficient to appreciate the many virtues of their genre – before going to stay for a day or two in a small hotel called the Lambert Arms at Aston Rowant, on the edge of the Chilterns, convenient for Headington School at Oxford, where my then girlfriend was being educated. Very remarkably, her house mistress allowed her out with me more than once, for quite long periods. I bought a book on Palladian architecture, and studied Palladio's villa at Vicenza, one of the most attractive of all domestic buildings. (I did not actually visit it until I was about 60, when a little disappointment at its setting – it is surrounded by roads – did not spoil my appreciation of its style and symmetry). I found it curious that prosperous Venetians were busy building fine villas at a time when they were liable to be invaded by hostile Muslim Turks. Johnson and I collaborated on a paper about English Palladian notables, in particular Burlington and Campbell, and were commended upon our industry and perception.

There was one feature of the school which I believe affected everyone, though in different ways. Each morning there would be a short service in the school chapel, also matins and evensong on Sundays. The great feature of these was hymn singing. I have always been given to understand – though I do not entirely accept – that I am unmusical, but many of the hymns we sung were deeply agreeable on several levels. They were performed at good speed and volume, and under the direction of the music master, a small Welshman, who somehow combined playing the organ with conducting the choir. His hands and feet would dart deftly about the keyboards, stops and pedals, and every few moments he would gesticulate, while all the time himself singing lustily through his perspiration. There was a full repertoire of what is best perhaps described as sturdy Victorian music. This was not so much religious, though of course an element of this was present, but patriotic and historic: 'And o'er each continent and island, the dawn leads on another day... The sun that bids us rest is waking our brethren 'neath the western sky,' brought to mind flags being raised or lowered and bugles sounding throughout the Empire, into which I had, after all, been born. And so did 'From earth's wide bounds, from ocean's farthest coast', for, however distant, the Royal Navy would be there. And there were simple lines of great beauty – 'beside the Syrian sea', 'the heats of our desire', 'thy justice like mountains high soaring above', 'The golden evening brightens in the west'. The rolling minatory cadences of 'For those in Peril on the Sea' were frankly frightening. I have generally since found that the most moving and satisfactory church services are those in which the majority of the congregation can sing the hymns without having to read them. The words swell effortlessly from the memories in which they have reposed since youth, and their simultaneous confident reproduction is evidence of a powerful bond of common experience and attitude.

I did have one brush with serious religion, during preparatory classes for confirmation, a rite afforded to most of the pupils more or less automatically. After a few weeks of instruction from the chaplain – a dry, uninspiring man – my adolescent views about the possibility of eternal life in some form tended towards a slight probability. But not long after my confirmation, by, if I remember rightly, the bishop of Lichfield, this modest degree of conviction began to ebb. There is simply no sound evidence; and while many people profess to have faith, this normally amounts to believing something because they want to think it true. And it can hardly be correct that only that proportion of the world's population who are Christian can achieve heaven. A lot of humans had lived before Jesus did, and even more before the arrival of Mohammedanism, whose followers also claim, with greater ferocity, sole rights to paradise. I now put the prospect of life after death at no better than ten percent.

As my time at school came to an end, consideration was given to a university. I had two A/S levels, in English and History. Now, any intelligent child is expected to get at least four, but I was thought bright and at Stuart Andrews' suggestion was entered for a history scholarship at Trinity Hall, Cambridge. There were no family connections of any kind at Cambridge or indeed Oxford. My parents, neither of whom had been to university, simply left it to the school; and so did I. I was told I was ineligible for Oxford because my Latin was poor, but this did not seem to matter at Cambridge. I duly attended for interview and examination. It was extremely cold. I had disconcerting difficulty getting into the room which I had been allotted, whose door seemed to have been barricaded. I found the questions difficult, did not write well, and duly failed. The Repton motto was 'Porta vacat culpa' (which meant the gate through which one has come, namely the school, cannot be blamed). So this was clearly all my fault. I was not even offered an ordinary place which I had hoped I would be, but was told that I could try again next year. But this did not appeal at home. My parents asked where I had been offered places and the answer was Trinity Dublin and Birmingham. My mother said morals were poor in Dublin – I have no idea on what she based this belief – and so it was arranged that I should go to Birmingham. I should of course have tried again the next year for Cambridge (as two of my children were to do, successfully, at Oxford), but at 17, coming on 18, it seemed then that the obvious thing to do was to get on with life.

I have never been back to Repton. It was not a bad school, but not perhaps a very good one. Sometimes I enjoyed myself there, but quite often I did not. I gained a love of the English language, but left unable to say anything much in French. Advanced mathematics and chemistry were never revealed to me. The boys did not have the style, charm or confidence of Etonians, the intellectual certainty of Wykehamists, nor the diligent, friendly, intelligent competence of grammar school children. I made few friends. It is now co-educational and the girls do very well at tennis and hockey. I did not send my sons there.

Chapter 3

Italian interludes

I did not have a 'gap year'. These excuses for a congenial spell of mildly camouflaged idleness only became popular a generation later. However, my parents decided that I should do something 'worthwhile' during the summer between school and university. My mother, to my surprise and without consultation, quickly arranged for me to be taken on as an agricultural labourer by the Bissell estate at Enville, to work in their forestry. My job, with two youths from the village and an experienced man of about 50, was 'tree cleaning'. This meant cutting away the long grass and other growth around hundreds of small saplings, which might otherwise be overwhelmed and die. I was given a sickle, like those which appear on Russian flags, and was expected to slash away with this from 8.30 am to 4 pm every day. The work was dull, hard and hot, but it gave rise to a certain gratification as rows of liberated young trees were steadily exposed to invigorating sunshine.

We ate picnic lunches, during which the experienced man would doze and the two youths would exchange competitive accounts of their recent sexual experiences. If these were true I seemed to be missing something, but I affected a sophisticated and tolerant detachment, and did not tell them of the limited progress that a young neighbour of warm Franco-Irish extraction and I had recently made upon a swinging garden sofa. I think the village youths felt sorry for me, especially when they discovered that I had been at a school with no girls. After about four weeks I looked like a sunburnt gypsy and had forearms the colour of mahogany furniture. The modest wage seemed very hard-earned, but I certainly felt well. I was also pleased to stop. To do that kind of work for years, and in all weathers, must be a most dispiriting fate. It was of course the lot of agricultural labourers since mankind turned to farming from the more exciting – and nutritionally preferable – hunting and gathering.

I resumed my limited social life, which involved driving over the river Severn into Shropshire and there passing time playing croquet with Paul Paterson (later for a short time a restaurateur, whose premises were so hidden in the backwoods that customers – attracted by his Good Food Guide entry – could rarely find them) and longing to see more of an attractive, dark girl of shy demeanour called Tory, who lived in a big country house near Bridgnorth. I took the prettiest girl in Shropshire, Maurice Bebb, to the theatre at Stratford, and afterwards to supper at the Dirty Duck, where some of the cast could be glimpsed. There was also Suzanne, the girl upon the sofa. She yearned for French excitement, which sadly she did not get sufficiently from me, and went to the Sorbonne, where in due course she enjoyed the barricades during the Paris student riots of 1968. Before going she accidentally kicked out one of my teeth while we were tobogganing. Mr Bond, the Tettenhall dentist, mended it so well that it lasted until I was 66. I wrote occasional poems when feeling reflective, and read *The Decline and Fall of the Roman Empire*.

Occasionally I might drive to Wolverhampton to visit a coffee bar called the Milano, where various friends sometimes met on Saturday mornings. This was a limited, and in retrospect rather pathetic, existence, not enhanced by a period during which I felt it necessary to wear only black clothes. After a while I grew out of this, and my father introduced me to his tailor, Sidney Morris, who practised in a Birmingham suburb. He was a proper tailor, who made everything himself and sat cross-legged in traditional fashion upon a wide table-bench in the front room of his house. He was good at making neat, soft shoulders which did not rise into an ugly step when the wearer raised his arm. His permanent sorrow was that he could get nobody to be an apprentice and learn his craft; his son would not, other youths would not. He even tried to adopt an orphan to this end, but failed. He made me several suits over about a decade, some of which I still have – and can still wear. Eventually he left Birmingham for Felixstowe, where he was still accessible from my parents in law's house near Diss. I have retained a mild interest in clothes: jackets ('coats'), need to be a little waisted, with two vents or an inverted pleat, very slightly flared cuffs, sleeves which are not too long, have three front buttons with only one ever fastened and never reveal any shirt stomach when buttoned, trousers either with no pleats or only forward-facing ones and military bottoms (lower at the back than the front). One garment which Morris made at my request was in retrospect not a good idea. That was a double-breasted, Prince of Wales check, velvet-collared, calf-length overcoat. In it I looked like Jeremy Thorpe.

It was now time for the next experience. One of my father's city associates was an Italian lawyer who worked in London. He arranged for me to be billeted in Florence as the paying guest of Princess Clotilde von Auersperg. The object of this was to attend lectures at the British Institute, learn Italian, and pick up some acquaintance with the Renaissance. The Princess had a complex Austro-German ancestry and her family must have fallen upon hard times, probably a consequence of the outcome of the Second World War. She had four or five lodgers, including two amusing English girls, one quite forward who was quickly taken up by various Florentine lotharios. Clotilde, sturdy but not beautiful, was a friendly hostess who had few rules in her establishment and spoke many languages. However, her preferred order was German, French, English, and only then Italian, and conversation round her table was rarely in the latter. If it had been, the visitors' contributions would have been vestigial and staccato – except from the forward girl, who seemed to learn very fast.

The Institute, founded at the end of the 1914-18 war, was granted a Royal Charter by King George V in 1923, for, amongst other things, 'the promotion of good understanding between Italian and English-speaking people by providing opportunities for intellectual and social intercourse and for the English to study Italian language, art, history and philosophy.' Quite a bit really, and I only had two months, not the year or more of civilising which was common for those on the Grand Tour in the C18. At the time I was there the Institute was based at the austere Palazzo Antinori. It had an impressive and valuable library, which is now in another palace, the Lanfredini. At one stage Anthony Blunt, the spy, was a governor. In 2000 the Duchess of Cambridge attended as part of the gap year which she enjoyed.

The language classes were not rigorous but moved faster than I did, and were less devoted to imparting some immediate conversational facility than to providing a detailed structure for the Italian language, which though simple at an elementary level is a lot less so later on. Most of the questions were asked by a tall, mature American lady, well dressed and serious, and much concerned with pluperfects and subjunctives. I tried, as a joke, to interest her in gerunds one afternoon, but she was not amused. I did not make as much progress as she did, which was not entirely a surprise as it had taken me two attempts to get Latin O level, despite many years of tuition, and extra hours with BK Workman, a classics master at Repton and author of *Daily Life in Ancient Rome*.

It was however most agreeable to wander the alleyways and piazzas of the city, and to climb to the top of the tower of the Palazzo Vecchio, which overlooked the spot at which Savonarola was burned to death in 1498, and which would, I felt at the time, have been an excellent place to commit suicide. (When I last visited Florence three years ago, access to the tower was forbidden: perhaps others had had the same idea). I used to browse daily in the Uffizi, and tried hard, but without success, to appreciate and admire Botticelli's Birth of Venus. Venus leans so far to her left that were she not a goddess, she would lose her balance and fall over. The three androgynous, diaphanous girls in Primavera are not a patch on Canova's C19 three Graces. There was often something a bit deliberately odd about Renaissance art, I felt: Caravaggio's Bacchus, for example, combines the face of a plump oriental girl with the shoulders of a prop forward.

On the whole I found the sculpture and architecture much more remarkable and attractive than the Renaissance painting. It was the Medici Venus which led Gibbon to observe that 'the chisel may dispute the pre-eminence with the pencil'. He was quite right. I still do not understand what techniques enabled a sculptor like Bernini to produce a delicate tracery of leaves, or fold of translucent cloth, or an elegant little finger, with the coarse violence of a hammer and chisel.

The contents of the Pitti palace also received my consideration, and seemed to reflect the fact that their building had been designed, constructed and used as a family palace, whereas the Uffizi, wonderful as it is, was built as municipal offices.

In some ways, in my untutored and heretic view (and this is a bit like saying I prefer *The Boy Friend* to Wagner, which I do,) many of the most interesting Florentine pictures are those painted by visitors from England. I can look for ages at the skilful complexities of Zoffany, an anglicised German sent out by the wife of George III to paint the Tribuna of the Uffizi. He had been preceded some years before by Thomas Patch, a prolific and fascinating painter of Florentine personalities, scenes and activities.

I spent a good deal of time wandering in the Oltrarno and walking, often solitary, in the colonnades of Santo Spirito, and up the ascending levels and glades of the Boboli gardens. William Beckford wrote of these: 'I ascended terrace after terrace, robed by a thick underwood of bay and myrtle. Above which rise several nodding towers and a long sweep of venerable wall, almost entirely concealed by ivy. You would have been enraptured with the broad masses of shade and dusky alleys that opened as I advanced, with white statues of fauns and sylvans glimmering amongst them, some of which pour water into sarcophagi of the purest marble, covered with antique relieves. The capitals of columns and ancient friezes are scattered about as seats.' I cannot put it better.

Other seats, more regularly occupied, were to be found in the cafes at the Piazza Michelangelo, on a plateau above the city, reached by a curving road which every evening echoed to the squeal of Pirelli Cinturato tyres upon hot tarmac as young Italians rushed up the hill in their Fiats, Alfas and Innocentis to enjoy the view, the passegiata and a drink. Among these drivers was an English youth called Hector, with whom I had a slight acquaintance and sometimes a lift. He owned a black MGB convertible, and was very keen on girls – though himself neither amusing nor attractive to look at, being heavy-faced and greasy-haired. He was however single-minded and importunate, and armed with his glamorous car he would motor up there several times a week on a speculative prowl. He spoke to any female under 30 who looked at him, asked if she would like a ride, and then if she would come back to his room. Nine out of ten refused, but, he said, if you ask ten people a day, 'all is well'. He was a lesson in the rewards of thick-skinned determination.

Several of us, driven in a Fiat Cinquecento by the girl who was not forward, went to see the Tuscan tombs, San Gimignano with its jumble of unstable-looking competitive towers, and spent two days on Elba. This was the tiny private kingdom from which the exiled Napoleon escaped when his guardian, Colonel Campbell, went to Florence to visit his mistress and his doctor. (Napoleon, incidentally, not being properly French but Corsican, spoke in Italian until he was about twelve. He was an example of an interesting phenomenon: Stalin was not Russian, he was Georgian; Hitler was not German, but Austrian. It is curious how tyrants come to rule lands in which they are not native).

Contemplation of the history of the Italian City States led to the conclusion that corruption and crime are not incompatible with art, culture or indeed what we think of as civilisation. Many of those prominent in the Italian cities of the 15th, 16th and 17th centuries were, while poisoning, torturing or defrauding, still people of taste, style, and discrimination. Today, few of those who kill or steal seem to be people of gracious accomplishment, but they often were in Renaissance Italy.

It could get very hot in Florence, and from time to time a few of us would go to a swimming pool. On one occasion I went with a girl wearing earrings. Since she wore little else, she soon acquired a following of Italian teenagers with whom she played in the water. After a while she announced loudly that one of her earrings was lost. This produced a frenzy of ecstatic consternation, and the youths plunged about to find it in an effort to ingratiate themselves with this stimulating English blonde. They were all dark and hirsute, and for a while there was an amazing scene as their pelted backs and shoulders rose and fell in the water like an extended family of large otters. After a few minutes I noticed the earring caught in the girls own hair. I shouted 'here it is', or some approximation in Italian. A great cry went up around the pool: 'trovata, trovata!' and the otters gathered around the object of their enthusiasm. I got no credit at all.

While in Florence I went to no nightclubs – out of shyness; ate in few restaurants – often lacking anyone to eat with; and avoided the many luxurious shops – out of penury. Towards the end however I thought I might take back a present for my girlfriend (the one educated at Headington) and so I went to the Pucci emporium, in fact a minor palace, in search of a blouse in one of their vivid colour combinations. I wandered in, very unsophisticated, and was approached by a faultlessly turned-out woman, perhaps aged about 35, who radiated both elegance and a scent evocative of something unidentifiable but most agreeable. 'Buon giorno. Vuol parlare Italiano?' She gave me a moment's consideration and summed me up in a trice, 'forse Inglese'. She then inquired delicately as to the height and build of the lady for whom I was making a purchase and gestured, with a slim wrist lightly embellished with gold, towards a trio of girls of different sizes and ages. I selected the one most like the person I had in mind, and she modelled four or five blouses, one of which I chose. Only when I was asked how I would like to pay did it occur to me to inquire about the price. This was a figure which I regarded as about right for a week in a reasonable hotel. I managed a bleak smile, and the paradigm of lustrous style took pity on me. Would I perhaps, after all, prefer to buy a scarf? Even that took all I had in my wallet, but a few days later it was very well received. I met the recipient about 50 years later at a party in Gloucestershire. She was wearing a Pucci blouse, and introduced me to her fourth husband.

I have been back to Florence several times since. It is too popular a place. Shortly before we were married, Carol, then my fiancée, and I were driving through Tuscany to Greece and arrived early one evening only to find that there was a shoe fair being held in the city. I could locate no accommodation after a dispiriting two-hour search, and so after dinner in a pavement restaurant, serenaded by the rasp of Lambrettas, we pressed on south, pausing to rest briefly in an autostrada layby. It is not easy to sleep in a Triumph GT6, and not what she had bargained for, or I intended. The journey had already been both a delight and a disaster. We had crossed the channel by putting the car in a Bristol freighter which in the late sixties flew a splendid air ferry service from Lydd to Le Touquet. This it is now impossible to do, and the pleasures of a £25, ten-minute leap in a capacious but rather primitive aircraft are lost for ever. (Our air hostess, who had opened a small valise of duty free to give us some in-flight service, quickly dissolved into tears, and when I asked why she said, 'I joined British United to fly VC10s to Rio, instead I go to France five times a day – I try to make it a proper flight, but it just isn't, I am so depressed').

We landed and set off across France. Just beyond Amiens there was a worrying chinking from the six-cylinder engine of which I was so proud. I telephoned the RAC in England, without much confidence. Astonishingly, within an hour, a Citroen breakdown truck with authentic corrugated flanks arrived, and towed us back to Amiens, where at a Triumph garage, at 5pm on a Friday evening, a small team of mechanics took the top off the engine. "You need two new soupape [valve] guides," said the manager, "we have none in stock, but I have rung a contact at our depot in Paris, and if you go there by train in the morning they will be supplied." They were. Meanwhile he took us to a pleasant small hotel. His men worked on Saturday morning, and we were on our way. I have often wondered what would have been the fate of a French motorist stranded in England in similar circumstances.

A nephew, Henry, married in Florence a few years ago, and the reception was held on the terrace of an antique building just below Fiesole. At the wedding the congregation were asked to join in with short extempore tributes to bride or groom, and my sister in law's husband, Philip Vallance QC, distinguished himself with a delightful short speech in which he lauded his wife in most touching and sincere terms. At the reception he sat in the shade and did not circulate, but was universally regarded as charming. 'Incantevole' said one woman, to whom he was disinclined to speak. I wandered, warm in morning clothes, amongst the guests, noting an interesting group of stocky men in big-shouldered, double-breasted suits, who smiled the smiles of some grand conspiracy. Below us lay the old city, prostrate and hot, accepting the tributes of her countless visitors, who cared more for ice cream than for Lorenzo the Magnificent.

In 2011 a party went out from The Inner Temple, led by the then Treasurer of the Inn, Heather (now Baroness) Hallet, one of the few women at the top of the English Judiciary. The determined daughter of a policeman, but easy company, she was tired after a long trial and left some of the socialising to her suave and agreeable husband, Nigel Wilkinson QC, who was keen on Tuscan refreshment. The theme of the visit was crime and punishment in Renaissance Florence and mediaeval Siena. It seemed mostly to be punishment, of various inventive kinds. We learned that any accuser had to be tortured before his evidence would be taken seriously. This must have cut down the incidence of reported crime quite significantly. There was some emphasis on sodomy, for which both Cellini and Botticelli were fined. We spent much enjoyable time being expertly guided round the art and architecture, and visited the attractively faded, book-furnished house of a charming elderly Florentine academic, whose son, when he opened the gates for us dressed in old corduroy, might just have emerged from a country house in Herefordshire. We were also taken to Siena where we listened, first patiently and then impatiently, to an erudite but interminable American expert explaining the Lorenzetti frescos in the Palazzo Pubblico which illustrate the charms and horrors of good and bad government.

I was already somewhat annoyed. We had been entertained in the headquarters of one of the Contrade, organisations best known for their sponsorship of horses in the annual Palio race around the central Piazza del Campo. There are 17 Contrade, bodies which seem to blend some of the characteristics of a livery company, a Masonic Lodge, a small clan, a touch of laundered crime and a horse racing syndicate. Our host was the Contrada Della Lupa – the She Wolf. Its lair was, on the surface, an elegant Sienese building of a suburban classical type, but underneath had been excavated a large luxury catacomb like the den of a James Bond villain, in glossy black modern taste. We were addressed by a charming lady and invited to buy a souvenir. I chose (again) a scarf or large silk handkerchief, with a handsome wolf printed on it. This I put in an external jacket pocket. Within ten minutes of leaving the building it had been stolen from me without my noticing. So when I got to the American's lecture my mood was less receptive than normal. But with sun and wine it soon lifted.

My time as a teenager in Florence did not give me fluent Italian, nor deep knowledge of the Renaissance, nor any memorable experience with warm-hearted girls. But it did instil a strong fondness for antique architecture basking under warm and timeless sky, watching the generations of mankind come and go.

Chapter 4

Redbrick

Chapters about university in many memoirs tend expansively and tediously to record every conversation, indiscretion, friendship, conquest, rejection and achievement, not to mention supposed milestones of intellectual development. In my case it will not be found so extensive. My time as an undergraduate was not especially formative, and all the knowledge I possess outside the law has come from subsequent, unstructured, random reading.

Birmingham University, proposed by Joseph Chamberlain as a 'great school of universal instruction', was established in 1900 outside the city centre, in the comfortable suburb of Edgbaston. It was the first English university to be built upon a 'campus', and the first to incorporate a medical school, a faculty of commerce and a women's hall of residence. Much of its original architecture was by Sir Aston Webb in what has been described as Byzantine-Gothic, though it is not easy to detect either of these influences amongst the ubiquitous red brick. Webb also designed the Victoria and Albert Museum, and re-fronted Buckingham

Palace, so he must have been a good appointment. The university is flanked by a large teaching hospital on one side and the remarkable gallery of the Barber Institute of Fine Arts on the other, the latter in rather incongruous proximity to the students' union building, which was not, while I was there, by any means an outpost of civilisation. It was grubby, noisy and full of small posters, with a faint smell of stale food and a strong whiff of juvenile socialism. At the centre of the campus, sitting dignified and confident beneath a tall clock tower named after Chamberlain, was the faculty of Law.

I had decided to read Law. English and History did not seem to be of great practical application, and I had done quite a bit of both. Law was a subject which was fresh, wide and useful, did not involve algebra, and might lead to a career. Inquiries revealed that Birmingham had a reputation for teaching law well. Perhaps, I thought, I could become a barrister, though at school I had been nervous about public speaking, never rising at a debate without minutes of preliminary mental trembling. It took some time to master this. The Bar would have the added advantage that one did not spend most of one's time in an office, as I believed solicitors tended to do. There was a touch of potential glamour and romance in advocacy – I had once read a book about Marshall Hall KC – and I thought it should be possible to earn a reasonable living. But apart from a visit to Sedgley magistrate's court when I was 12, I had never been inside a legal building, or knowingly met a lawyer.

When I was 14, the family had moved to North Worcestershire, near the village of Kinver. Because it was only 17 miles from Birmingham, and as the student digs (a word of uncertain provenance, possibly connected to the 'diggings' of prospectors) seemed unattractive and expensive, and the halls of residence both scruffy and gloomy, I chose to live at home and drive in daily by car, like a commuter. This was not really a good way to make or nourish friendships and it meant that I stood a little apart from the full texture of student existence. Not that I minded that at the time.

The law faculty at Birmingham was excellent. Most of the lecturers were authoritative figures with sound academic reputations. Professor Hood Phillips, Dean from 1949 to 1968, was one of the country's leading constitutional and administrative lawyers; he gave friendly tea parties at his house in Heaton Drive, and some quite challenging lectures. Why was it wrong, for instance, to cut off the hands of thieves if this penalty resulted in virtually no theft? Discuss. Gordon Borrie (later Sir Gordon Borrie, Director of Fair Trading), was a rising star, and Robert Pennington, Professor of Commercial Law, was an influential member of a small group of scholars who made business law a mainstream academic subject. Chamberlain would have been proud of him. Pennington had been an undergraduate at the university himself and once foiled a bank robbery by observing a pistol which was pointed at him when he walked into his local branch, and loudly declaring it to be a fake.

I found the most effective of several excellent lecturers to be Joseph Unger. He was a German who had come to England from Hanover in about 1935, and taught law at Aberystwyth. Made Barber Professor at Birmingham in 1960, he remained there until his death in 1967, the year I was called to the Bar. He was a most popular lecturer, and indeed had been so liked in Wales that his students had petitioned the university to prevent him leaving by giving him a Chair. Happily he escaped, and established himself in a town house in the centre of Warwick, between the court and a silversmith. He was a book reviewer for the *Modern Law Review*, a publication which he had kept alive during the war when it was threatened by paper and printing restrictions. Keen on emphasising the everyday importance of his subject, in the early fifties he had published a paper on the law applicable to self-service shops, then a new feature of the urban scene. The grounding that he gave me in Contract was quite invaluable, and I often found myself recalling his observations and approach when deciding cases as a Judge. For example, in 2015 I tried a case involving a man who had been told by a well-known luxury car dealer, Stratstone, that it was selling him a brand-new car, although it had been manufactured two years earlier. The plaintiff bought the car, and used it for 15,000 miles, despite serious unreliability. Eventually, his patience gone, he asked for his money back and sought to rescind the contract. The dealer said he had no remedy, as the car, being unused when sold, had properly been described as new, and anyway it was too late to rescind. Professor Unger would not have thought the dealer was right; nor did I, and nor did the Court of Appeal.

There were lessons in Roman law, and we were taught what a worthwhile man was Justinian – a late Emperor based in Constantinople who had codified it all. I became interested in Justinian (who had a wife who performed lasciviously in public) largely because of his relationship with Belisarius, one of the greatest generals of the ancient world, who time and again thwarted the Goths, ejecting them from Rome in 536, then defending Rome in a subsequent siege and recapturing Ravenna. He also kept the Persians at bay in Asia Minor. Justinian was jealous of Belisarius, confiscated his treasure and disbanded his household. Fresh adversity in Italy prompted Justinian to re-appoint him. Yet again, he was shorn of his dignities in 562 after a triumph over the Huns threatening Byzantium. Justinian was not a pleasant individual, whatever his contribution to Roman law.

As well as lectures we had tutorials, when three or four students attended a tutor in his private room and analysed each other's essays. These were not as rigorous as had been the discussions led by Stuart Andrews in the sixth form at Repton. Criticism was muted and diffident, and the attitude towards imprecision of language was gentle and forgiving. Language should generally be regarded as an instrument of thought, not a contribution to the atmosphere, and sometimes I said so, probably irritatingly. After a while I grew more tolerant, or less rigorous. But I still cannot avoid a feeling of strong annoyance when people do not say what they mean, or, much worse, when their use of English is simply incorrect and they should know better. Some years ago a High Court Judge wrote a pamphlet of 'Guidance' for new judges. In it he wrote that it was fundamentally important never to appear disinterested when in court. As disinterested means impartial, he could hardly have been more wrong.

My fellow students were very varied. Inigo Bing was one of them.

He was the son of Geoffrey Bing, a left-wing Labour MP who later became Attorney General to Kwame Nkrumah, the less than democratic ruler of Ghana. (Bing's biographical book, *Reap the Whirlwind*, was devastatingly reviewed by Tibor Szamuely in *The Spectator* in 1968: 'it omitted almost everything of importance'). Inigo was an entertaining and amusing character, far to the right of his father, though somewhat to the left of me. We were walking up Fleet Street together when Kennedy was assassinated. Bing had an unusual sharp face of many angles, and was energetic politically, in due course exchanging membership of the Labour Party for the SDP, before joining the establishment by becoming Chairman of the Reform Club, a stipendiary magistrate and a Circuit Judge. We have bumped into each other pleasantly as time has gone by and are now Benchers of the same Inn. Like me, he never got into Parliament. I am not sure how hard he tried.

John Gray was a curious character. He was tall, spare, bespectacled, and rather awkwardly reserved. We went climbing together in Derbyshire. He was keen on this sport, but not very good, being lanky, not agile, and once he fell off. The belay held, and when he finally scrambled, relieved but ashen, to the top where I was attached to the various ropes, he strode up and shook hands with the enthusiasm of one Victorian Englishman meeting another in the wastes of central Asia. He too went to the Bar.

James Newell, was a year older than me, much brighter, and better adjusted to the world. He invested all his many activities – sporting, social and academic – with skill and enthusiasm. He became a solicitor, practised from an address close to the Temple tube station and acted for me on occasion at generous rates. He died in 1979, and I went to his funeral. The large church was overflowing, the tributes prolific, and there were people there of every kind and every age. He was the first person to die whom I knew well, and I could not help feeling that if the funeral had been mine, there might only be a few dozen in attendance. I made his son a wooden fort.

There were several interesting girls in the law faculty in my year. Anita Piper, with whom I first became friendly, came from near

Woodbridge in Suffolk and was dark with wavy hair, freckles and a firm wiry figure. She was very bright, quick and combative in conversation, and was equipped with an old AC saloon car, a classic vehicle, which added to her popularity and shared her initials. She got on very well with my mother, and the two of them discussed my various drawbacks and failings in some detail with mutual satisfaction. We went once to North Wales together, where we argued, and it rained, continuously. By contrast, on a trip to Torquay, we both got badly sunburnt, and had great difficulty finding a place to stay. The only place with any room was the best hotel. But Anita would not come to Greece with me when invited, which was a pity. She became a solicitor in East Anglia, and came to our wedding in Norfolk in 1970. I have not seen her since, though for a while she went out with a cousin of my wife.

Because Anita would not come to Greece I went with a prep school friend, Robert Hamilton. Dark with saturnine good looks, he was amusing and quick witted. We set off in my Triumph Spitfire, first crossing France at an average speed of roughly 60mph to Vevey on Lake Geneva. There at about 10 pm we went to a restaurant near the shore, and as we began to eat, curtains parted on a small stage and a man in a purple dinner suit announced 'Maintenant nous avons l'étoile du soir, votre charmante chanteuse – Vera'. On came an attractive woman who faced her audience and sang several numbers. She then turned around and walked slowly backstage, revealing that she was wearing only the front of a dress, and had nothing at all on behind.

We thought this an excellent eating place and, suitably refuelled, set off to cross the Alps by night. This was perhaps a mistake as we missed the views over the Grand St Bernard. We were indeed lucky to stay on the road at all and arrived at Aosta exhausted in the early dawn. There we had breakfast at a Supercorte Maggiore before taking the autostrada south. I do not remember why we felt in such a hurry, as we had no reservations of any kind anywhere, but it seemed essential to get to the ferry at Brindisi as soon as possible.

On we went, passing evocative signposts to Parma, Mantua and Bologna before arriving dusty and sunburnt (for the roof was down) on the Adriatic coast at Rimini. Pausing only for petrol, we raced on down a dull, hot, straight road through Apulia to Brindisi docks, where we arrived at a moment of maximum confusion. Scores of people were besieging two small ticket windows and shouting lustily for attention. The ferry was moored with its ramps invitingly open. After about forty minutes waiting to get to a window I heard an announcement that the ship would depart in half an hour. I was still some way from the guichet. It looked hopeless, and I returned to speak to Robert, whom I had left sitting in the car. He was there, but not the car. Seeing the difficulties, he had driven up to the ferry, told a sailor that I was following with the tickets, tipped him five dollars, and managed to install our little sports car behind various internal partitions from which, as the vessel filled, it could never be extricated before we left. So we caught the ferry.

After pausing briefly at Corfu, which lay utterly beguiling in tranquil sunshine, and calling at Igoumenitsa, just below Albania, the ship eventually arrived at Patras. Still infected with a strong but pointless sense of urgency, we set off at dusk for Athens, which was about 100 miles away. The road was busy with large trucks with dazzling batteries of powerful lamps, and small donkey carts without any lights at all. The silencer fell off between Corinth and Megara, which at least meant that the donkey drivers had plenty of warning of our approach. The only hotel I had heard of in Athens was the Grande Bretagne, so I drove there, and happily it found us a room. It was indeed very grand, and very expensive too, and served an outstanding gin fizz. The next morning Robert announced that we could not afford to go on staying in hotels like that, and he would prefer to sleep on beaches. So, on the whole, that was what we did thereafter, which saved a great deal of money and was surprisingly comfortable and convenient, though it sometimes left one feeling a little sticky or salty. In that way we saw most of the classic sites of ancient Greece. It was perhaps just as well that Anita had decided not to come, though if she had I doubt we would have got beyond Corfu.

Rosemary Williams was Welsh, and sounded it. Plump, dark and intellectually bright, she did not flaunt her extensive knowledge. I often sat next to her in lectures, where she giggled and talked and was excellent company. Rosemary got a good degree. I saw a little of another dark-haired girl who asked me to a Jewish wedding. This was an event which lasted a long time and involved a lot of energetic dancing. Sturdy well-dressed women in late middle age, with substantial well-supported busts, seemed to be especially enthusiastic performers, twisting and swaying with energy and stamina. Occasionally one would come up to me, pause thoughtfully, and say 'Are you one of us? I can't be sure'. It did not seem to matter at all that I was not.

Of much more personal significance was Fiona James: bright, fun, black-haired, sparkly eyed and with a cheery and upbeat manner. She was effervescent and most enjoyable company. Her father, a High Court Judge, was to be very helpful and encouraging to me. Fiona and I once went to Longleat Wildlife Park in my Spitfire. We drove through the lion-proof gates. The idea was that visitors, with their windows firmly closed, would cruise gently around the park admiring the wild animals. The most troublesome of these were generally believed to be monkeys, said to attack windscreen wipers. Only after 20 minutes did it dawn on me that we had been allowed in driving a car fitted with a removable fabric hood, and not the neat metal hardtop which sat in the garage at home for use in the winter. The detachable hood was flimsy and thin, and could have been torn open by a weasel, let alone a lion. We looked at each other, she in mild reproach and me in apologetic dread. The choice was to stop the car, blow the horn, and await rescue by the so-called Rangers in their zebra-striped Land Rovers or drive gently on, hoping for the best and thinking it unlikely that the lions, who were lying down eating large chunks of horse, would regard us as sufficiently interesting to justify getting up and bounding over to have a look at our roof. We chose the latter, mainly out of embarrassment, and were in the event untroubled even by monkeys.

There is something inexplicable about the behaviour of large carnivorous animals near motor vehicles. Thousands of people are driven in open Jeeps or small spectator lorries around wildlife areas in Africa and India, and stop close to panting leopards, salivating fly-irritated lions, or tigresses with cubs. They are never attacked. But vegetarians like elephants or rhinos do sometimes attack motor vehicles containing people. It is very odd that carnivorous animals (unless they are polar bears) ignore cars with live potential food in them, yet grass-consuming creatures attack them, though they contain nothing to eat. Perhaps David Attenborough could explain this.

Anyway, Fiona survived, as she survived later trips with me from Judge's lodgings in Yorkshire to Scarborough, Fountains Abbey and Rievaulx. In due course she qualified as a barrister, thought better of it, and became a solicitor with a successful criminal practice in the West Midlands. She occasionally brightened the court when I came to sit in Warwick, and was every bit as sparkling and cheerful as she had been at university.

I generally worked in the law library at Birmingham, and often found myself on the same sun-dappled gallery table as a tawny-blonde German girl called Geshe Bramley, a little older than me, who wore suede skirts, exuded a business-like air and had an agreeable smile, exposing two teeth which were attractively crooked. Her English was perfectly fluent, but one would always have realised from her lilt and word order that she was not from this country. Her father was a judge in Schleswig Holstein. We got on excellently and used to drive off for lunchtime picnics with a cold chicken to a wooded outcrop in a rural beauty spot. We did this over quite a prolonged period, but nothing serious came of it. We watched the 1966 World Cup final together on her television. We met again about 15 years later on a prep school skiing party in Val D'Isère, when I found that she had a new husband, a master at Summer Fields, who had appointed Roger, my eldest son, as captain of the school rugger team. His name was Stephen Cox. I now think of Geshe, of whom I was fond, as Mrs Apple, having been married first to a Bramley, then a Cox.

There were some car enthusiasts at university who organised rallies around the emptier parts of Shropshire, and they persuaded me that a car I had (before the Spitfire) would, if modified a little, be very hard to beat. What it needed, they said, was a negative camber rear spring.

They duly set about my car, a Triumph Vitesse, which was really a humble Herald fitted with a powerful 2-litre engine, and changed the transverse rear spring. This had the effect of giving the rear wheels quite noticeable negative camber, supposedly of assistance when cornering. In fact the car simply looked as though it was squatting because there was too much in the boot. Thus equipped, and with some extra spotlights, I attended at a garage near Stourbridge at 10 pm one night. There were pennants and flags. This was the start. Everyone else seemed to be in Minis, with an occasional Ford Anglia. Our navigators were issued with a route map, and the cars were flagged off into the night. I drove very quickly, in emulation of what I thought was the style of Timo Mäkinen (a Swede who had won the Monte Carlo rally). We went round corners quite well, though certainly no faster than the Minis, despite the negative camber. We were however quicker than a Mini in a straight line, because my engine was twice their size, and we overtook some on the few open stretches. But after a while I noticed, near a signpost for Clun, that there seemed to be no other cars about. I turned to my navigator, who looked at me with a mixture of anxiety and hate, and then vomited. He did this inside the car, not out of a window. It almost looked deliberate. He said that my driving had made him ill and he had no idea at all where we were, and nor did he care. I was not impressed by this, as he was a man who drove an Austin Healey 3000 (of which I was most envious) very fast indeed, and so far as I knew never felt nauseous doing that. Still full of competitive enthusiasm, I was reluctant to stop, but after a while I realised that our chances of victory, or indeed of finishing, had gone. We tried to clean the car, but had nothing to hand to do this with, so, with the windows open to alleviate the smell, we drove in what we imagined to be an easterly direction (my preparations had not included the acquisition of a compass). At about two in the morning we thought we recognised some gates we were passing, and drove through them up to a large house with a lot of parked cars outside. This was a party, given by a slight acquaintance, to which we had not been invited. I felt that this was an emergency, and so we went in, to find a number of intoxicated young people lying about on sofas and rugs. One girl was dressed only in a blanket. We were offered a drink. My navigator collapsed onto the vacant end of a couch otherwise occupied by two people who were very close together, and fell asleep.

That was the end of my career as a rally driver. The car never recovered either, and broke down in France that summer on the way to the Costa Brava, its rear wheels moving further and further apart. Four of us (Anne Fisher, April Harding, Nigel Copeland and me) were, as it happened, travelling with a couple in a Mini. We drove from Tours to Spain with me alone in the expiring Vitesse, and five people and most of our luggage in the Mini.

Many of the Birmingham students spent a good deal of time in the pubs of Edgbaston. It was at this time that I came to feel that the typical urban English pub was not a very agreeable place. It was not the occasional alcohol-fuelled aggression that struck me then as disagreeable – though it did later when I was a judge – but the whole rather squalid concept. When you go to a bar or café in, say, France or Italy or Germany, you sit at a table, chat agreeably with your companion, and a waitress or waiter comes and asks what you want; you tell them and they bring it. After a while you might feel like another drink, you raise an arm or catch an eye, and the fresh drink comes. When it is time to go you get the bill and pay. By disagreeable contrast, in a pub in England you are expected to do all the work yourself: go to the bar, leaving your companions behind, and wait for as long as it takes while other people are served or until the barman or barmaid is prepared to attend to you. You give your order, and still stand there, waiting, while it is poured, drawn or prepared. You may be jostled by people around you. There is likely to be spilt beer on the bar or on the floor. When your drinks are on the counter you are then expected to pay for them, then and there. Having paid you will be expected to struggle back to your table carrying all the drinks you have bought. The only assistance the pub offers might be to lend you a tray, which you are expected to return. When anyone wants another drink, the whole process has to be gone through again. Your empty glasses will normally be left on the table. Occasionally, someone might appear to clear them. If you ask this person whether she would mind getting you another drink, she will tell you unambiguously to go and get it yourself. The whole concept is uncivilised and unpleasant and proceeds on the premise that what is important is not pleasure for the customer but profit for the owners of the pub, who do not want to pay staff to serve and do not trust their customers. Some establishments are full of people standing up, holding glasses and shouting at each other for hours, while taking it in turns to queue up at the bar. Sometimes they stand in the cold street outside. It is inexplicable that this can be considered a pleasant way to spend time. It seems that this view is at last becoming more widely held and public houses of this kind are now closing down at a brisk rate.

During one vacation I took a job in the menswear department of Rackham's department store. This was thought the Birmingham equivalent of Harrods. My task was to sell men's overcoats. While doing so I made an interesting discovery. Customers decide in advance whether they are going to make a purchase or not, regardless of what might be available. A man might ask, for example, for a grey herringbone coat. I would produce one. 'Ah, but does it have interior pockets?' 'Yes.' 'But what about the length?' 'Well, it is just below the knee, which is normal'. 'Do you have it in blue?' 'We do, here you are'. 'I am not sure that I like the shoulders'. 'It has raglan sleeves, which is what you said you were after'. 'I will think about it'. Exactly what he said he wanted was available, but he would not buy. On the other hand, a customer might come in and say that he desired a camel coat. I would explain that we did not have any. 'Very well then, have you a brown duffel coat?' 'I am sorry, we don't.' 'Perhaps you have a grey Crombie?' 'No, but we do have a black one.' 'It must have two internal pockets.' 'I am afraid it only has one.' 'Very well, I will take that.' It was most curious. Either a person was in buying mood, in which case he would buy, even though he could not get what he wanted; or he was not, even though we could provide precisely what he asked for. No doubt a psychiatrist could explain this phenomenon.

Every summer there was a Rag Week. This was an excuse for the students to dress up and go out of the university campus and behave amusingly or outrageously in public in order to collect money for charity. The medical students were particularly keen on this, and produced flyers and simple magazines full of remarkably filthy jokes and cartoons for general distribution. Many of the females went about in agreeably revealing fancy dress. The high point of the week was a parade of floats through the centre of Birmingham, down New Street and up Corporation street. In my second year the law faculty decided upon a theme which I think might have been the Development of Justice. It involved herding a number of slaves through the crowds, and I recall striding along equipped with an army officer's four-foot ceremonial sword, made by Wilkinson, which I brandished at the slaves. The police completely ignored this. These were the days before 'knife crime' and stop and search.

It was at Birmingham that I first began to take real interest in politics, as described in another chapter, and wrote occasional articles for the student newspaper *Redbrick*. One or two of these, on the themes that individuals are what count and that socialism is usually a recipe for inefficiency, injustice and national impoverishment, still seem to me to read quite well.

In my last year at Birmingham I entered a library competition. The idea of this was that the undergraduate with the most meritorious collection of books would get a prize. I had by then started to collect political biographies, the best of which was undoubtedly David Cecil's life of Lord Melbourne, to which and to whom I had become greatly attracted. The book elegantly tells the story of a handsome and talented man, intelligent and ironic, whose life was blighted by a mad wife, but was at the end redeemed and inspired by his relationship with the young Queen Victoria. Cecil had some wonderful descriptions. Lady Oxford: 'a tarnished siren of uncertain age'. Byron: 'melancholy, detached and scornful, his heart turned to marble by a career of sin and sightseeing in every part of Europe, stood out in melodramatic silhouette against the sublimities of nature and the wreckage of empires'. This was far from Edgbaston. I had a number of other good books as well, including Blake's *Disraeli*, and Duff Cooper's *Talleyrand* (of which Harold

Nicolson wrote: 'he has woven his tangled material into tissue of silken smoothness... it is without question, a deliberate work of art). In all I suppose I had about 15 volumes, which was modest indeed, but they sufficed to win a book token. I now have over 1,700 books, and great difficulty accommodating them.

Near the end of my time at Birmingham I had an interview with a career advisor. I had wondered about applying for a Short Service Commission, probably in the Air Force. I also pondered over the attractions of Advertising (there was some amusing stuff about at the time, in particular 'the Esso Sign mean happy motoring', sung to a West Indian calypso tune), but said that I thought my career would be at the Bar. In that case, said the advisor, you had better get on with it rather than messing about. I took that advice, but on later reflection I do not think it was very good. Nobody much wants a young barrister of 22, who, however bright and promising, has little authority and no experience. A short time in the forces gives responsibility and practical knowledge, and can produce, at 24 or 25, an altogether more mature and authoritative person.

It might also give some ability in self-defence. There was an occasion in 1965 when six of us went out for an Italian dinner one evening in Shrewsbury. On emerging from Sidoli's restaurant to walk back to our cars, about 200 yards away, Paul Paterson noticed a large youth scratching a line down the sides of the parked vehicles with a screwdriver. He shouted and ran towards him. I set off in support, but was conscious of not running quite as quickly as I might. As I went to pass a shop doorway a loutish youth emerged, stood firmly in my way, and said 'I would not go down there if you know what's good for you'. Or words to that effect. Instead of dodging round this person, hitting him, or pushing him aside, I found myself saying 'You do realise that talking to me like that can itself constitute an assault? You must not threaten people in a public place'. He was mildly taken aback at this ridiculous remark, but did not get out of the way. The person who reacted best was Paul's wife, who bypassed me, ran up to the youth with the screwdriver who was threatening her husband, and kicked him repeatedly with her almond-toed court shoes. Her aim was good and he fell into the road moaning. She gave him another kick, to keep him down, and we all jumped into our cars and drove off. Had I had some military training I like to think that my response would have been more satisfactory and less craven. (Although one cannot be sure about this. Years later when I was a judge sitting at Oxford, I had a trial involving a bar fight between soldiers from Bicester Garrison and rugby players from the local club. Several soldiers had been beaten up. I observed at one stage that this was surprising, given their military training. One of the victims said: 'We did not stand a chance, your Honour. Our job was to manage munitions, they were rugger players, trained to fight'.)

After three years of quite interesting academic study, at an undemanding pace, and some modest late revision, I obtained a 2.2 degree, which was not distinguished. I felt I could and should have achieved more, and tried rather harder to overcome a streak of slight laziness. If I had been urged at school to come higher than fifth, I might have done so. Fiona and Rosemary certainly did better. Our degrees were formally conferred by the University Chancellor, Anthony Eden, a figure of tired elegance and polished manner. 'Well done' he drawled as each graduate ascended the stage on which he stood, to receive a diffident diplomatic handshake from a hand which had clasped those of many of the world's leaders. Eden was a man of extraordinary talent, who spoke several languages including Arabic and Persian. He had lost two brothers in the First World War, in which he won both an MC and remarkable promotion. His elder son was killed in Burma at the end of the Second. He had been Dominion Secretary, Foreign Secretary three times, War Minister and Prime Minister, and had recovered from serious illness. He was perhaps a paradoxical person to dispense degrees at Birmingham University, since the student body was at that time so irradiated with socialism that it could scarcely bring itself to contemplate anyone to the right of Harold Wilson. But he was my last contact with that institution.

Chapter 5

Becoming a barrister

I was now keen to become a barrister. To do this you have to join an Inn of Court. There are four: Inner Temple, Middle Temple, Lincoln's Inn and Gray's Inn. It does not really matter which you choose. These institutions are old, and have changed considerably over time. Now they superficially resemble a cross between an Oxbridge College and a Livery Company. Each has a large dining hall, a library, gardens and other ancillary buildings. Gray's is a bit remote and architecturally undistinguished; Lincolns is magnificently Victorian; Middle has a fine Elizabethan hall. The Inns let premises, called chambers, to groups of barristers. Increasingly they interest themselves in training students. Inner has its genesis in a 'New Temple', consecrated in 1185, established by the Knights Templar, who in the 12th century had the primary but awkward task of defending Christians from Muslims in the Levant. They built the Temple Church, of interesting part-circular form, which stands just South of Fleet St. The Templars' property was seized by the crown in the C14, during a Europe-wide wave of ruthless antipathy to them, and was then given to another organisation: The Knights Hospitaller. These Knights let it out to lawyers. After a short time, small semi-collegiate legal communities were established, run by 'Benchers', or Masters of the Bench, where barristers (lawyers who pleaded 'at the bar' in court) were trained. They had to keep terms by being physically present. In 1608 James 1 (while overseeing his new bible translation) granted the Masters of the Bench of Inner and Middle Temple the freehold of all the property they occupied. They have held it ever since.

Teaching was interrupted during the Civil War, but resumed to a modest extent thereafter. In the 1840s it occurred to the government that there was in fact no regularised system of qualification or instruction for barristers and a Select Committee suggested that the Inns of Court should 'resume anew' their original objects and provide a 'proper course of instruction'. A Council of Legal Education was set up to provide lectures and examinations. By the 1960s, though instruction was provided by the Council, or by a private enterprise supplier, Gibson and Wheldon – often thought a little smarter in both senses of the word – there was still a vestigial requirement for student barristers to keep terms by regular dining at their Inns. This is to stimulate collegiality and introduce foreign students, of whom there were and are many, to English manners and customs, as well as to encourage familiarity with the law.

I joined the Inner Temple as a student in November 1963 because it had the best car park and attractive views over its lawns to the river, and at the time it was said to have the best food. Dining involved attendance at formal dinners in hall, sitting at benches on long tables. We had to wear dark suits and ate in 'messes', or groups, of four. For each mess the Inn provided half a bottle of sherry, a bottle of claret, and a half bottle of port. It was considered tactically sound to join a mess with one or two Indians, Pakistanis or Africans, in the hope that they might prove to be Muslims and so non-drinkers. One evening a friend and I sat down with two large young men, jovial, friendly and from Ghana. As soon as grace had been said the bigger of the two seized one of the bottles: 'I don't know about you chaps' he said, 'but I like to start with the port.' And so he did.

I duly attended lectures at the Council, which had premises on the outskirts of Gray's Inn, and where the quality of instruction was significantly less good than it had been at University. In due course I managed to pass Bar Finals, an exam in many parts, some of moderate difficulty. During the year I attended this course I spent a lot of time in and about the Inn, ate in Hall and went to moots and talks and to the theatre with fellow bar students and people a year or two more senior. Most of them had been to Oxford or Cambridge. It was a pleasant and interesting social life.

At one stage I thought I was going to start a magazine. I had bumped into Richard Compton Miller (later to be known as the tousle-haired gossip columnist and partygoer Compton Miller). His father, a lawyer, had a sober flat in Crown Office Row, where three or four of us used to meet to plan our publication. We could agree upon nothing: title, contents, format, price, printing arrangements, or (save ourselves) contributors. How anyone gets a new magazine off the ground I do not know. We were quite incapable of this achievement. 'Obiter', as I thought of it, was conceived over many cheerful evenings, but was never born.

It was time to contemplate pupillage; that is, getting a place in a set of barristers' chambers in order to work with, accompany to court, and learn from an established practitioner. It was and is still, an apprenticeship. In due course, if you performed well, and were agreeable, the hope was that you would be offered a tenancy in your pupil master's chambers, where you could work and practice on your own account. Barristers are freelance, and, unlike solicitors, do not employ each other; they merely share premises and facilities. They jointly employ clerks, who handle negotiations with the solicitors who wish to engage them, and other ancillary office staff. Clerks now tend to be given titles such as Practice Manager, but their work remains the same. Typists, vital when I came to the Bar, are now extinct.

These days the process of Pupil application and interview is highly centralised and organised. It is not permitted to make a personal approach to a particular member of the bar. The idea of this is to take away any advantage of personal connection, and to provide for fairness to all. Chambers committees interview candidates with scrupulous impartiality, and indeed forbearance. Many questions which were once considered relevant are now regarded as unacceptable, especially those about marriage and coping with young families.

I was called to the Bar on 21st November 1967. At that time things were very different, and for some like myself who were lucky, a lot easier. I have already mentioned Fiona James. Her father, then a High Court Judge, later to rise to the Court of Appeal – and who, when at the bar, had prosecuted the Great Train Robbery – offered to take me as his Marshal. A Judge's Marshal is a vestigial remnant of an ancient role: that of helping to protect Judges as they rode from Assize to Assize through dangerous English countryside. By the 1960s a Marshal had become a sort of unpaid assistant, of marginal use to the Judge. But to be one was a very valuable experience for the young barrister, who would go to court every day, watch the cases from the bench, and have the opportunity to discuss everything he saw. A Marshal would see the advocates at work, and understand how and why they won or lost.

Most High Court judges, then and now, go out of London about half their time to the main court centres in the country, usually in large cities. This is called 'going on Circuit'. Oddly enough the next judicial rank down, that of the Circuit Judge, does not go on circuit. They are already there. (Nor does the judicial rank below them, that of the District Judge, sit in any area known as a District). These days Circuit Judges do most of the work which thirty years ago was done by High Court judges, but are not paid accordingly. Then, the work of a High Court judge on circuit mostly involved trying personal injury cases (people suing their employers for unsafe working conditions, or the victims of traffic accidents suing other participants), and the occasional murder or rape. Murders, though of course serious crimes, are not especially complicated, and were fairly uncommon. They often involve people living together who lose their temper. In 1967 there were only some 400 murders in England and Wales. By 2017, 50 years later, this had risen to 768.

In the summer of 1967 Mr Justice James was going on the North

Eastern Circuit for two months, to sit at Durham, Newcastle, York and Sheffield, and I went too. We stayed in Judges' Lodgings. This sounds like modest accommodation but was in some cases quite grand. At Durham, we lodged in the Castle, an 11th Century Norman building which stands on high ground above the River Wear. The castle was adjacent to the cathedral, whose foundations were at the time giving cause for concern. There were three Judges, and the retinue included their Clerks, who organised the lists of work and provided behind the scenes intelligence, a full time travelling male cook, and me. There was sometimes a housekeeper.

When we moved to Newcastle a 'travelling day' was set aside for the journey of some 17 miles, about right for a horse. Crockery, cutlery, and other essentials travelled with us in wicker hampers, as they would have done in the C18. The three Judges, in order of seniority, were Geoffrey Veale, a Yorkshireman who was a fine pianist, despite the loss of one thumb; Arthur James, an able and ambitious lawyer whose home was in Sutton Coldfield; and Henry Brandon, formerly an Admiralty practitioner from London. The first two were Queens Bench Judges, who did most sorts of work as needed. Mr Justice Brandon, younger than the other two, highly intellectual and even more highly ambitious – he ended in the House of Lords – sat in what was then called the Probate, Divorce and Admiralty Division. He had an MC, and had served, unusually, in Madagascar. Though an expert in shipping law and nautical insurance, his task that summer was to deal with divorces, which his intellectual speed and impatience did not ideally suit. He did not make himself popular with the local Bar either, by upbraiding its Leader – a well-liked man much older than him – for appearing in court with a hand in his pocket. I was sent down to London to drive his wife up from their Regents Park house to join him. She – formerly Jeanette Janvrin, named by a magazine 'England's perfect secretary' in 1953, and only 36 years old – was good company, and our long journey, broken by a short picnic on a dry-stone wall, passed very quickly. We discussed nothing legal at all.

Every morning, after a full and excellent breakfast prepared by the cook, the judicial party would climb into a Daimler provided by the Under Sheriff, and set out across the city to the courts. The Judges wore their colourful robes of scarlet and ermine, and wigs, and I wore morning clothes consisting of a black jacket – or coat, as my tailor called it – waistcoat and striped trousers. The judicial car was accompanied by police motorcycle outriders who swept us through any red traffic lights. On arrival at court on the first day of the Assize at Newcastle, eight trumpeters or buglers were drawn up on the steps, and they erupted into a lusty fanfare as the Judges alighted. A substantial crowd looked on with interest and no obvious annoyance. A few cheered. At lunch time the entourage swept back to the lodgings to eat, returning at 2.15 for the afternoon work, and then back again for tea. After tea Veale J would play the piano in sedative or stimulating fashion according to his mood, and in the evening there would probably be a dinner to attend somewhere.

By the time I retired in 2017, any High Court judge who came to Oxford would drive, in his own modest car and civilian clothes, down a back street, past an amiable group of mildly inebriated occupants of a hostel for the homeless, to a car park behind the court building. He or she would enter like a surreptitious tradesman through a shabby side door, unpainted for two decades. One energetic judge used to cycle several miles from the lodgings and would arrive damp with perspiration and needing a shower, the facilities for which were not available. Rather as with bishops before them, the prestige – not to say purchasing power – of the English Judiciary has been in steady decline for several generations. It is an unfortunate development for a nation founded on the rule of law.

During our second week in Newcastle we were joined by the Lord Chief Justice of England, Lord Parker of Waddington. He travelled with his wife, a strong character who had been instrumental in restoring the church in Smith Square, Westminster. He had come to see that business was being properly despatched in the North, but found a backlog. 'The courts will sit on Saturday' he decreed, with all the ancient authority of his office. Counsel grumbled, solicitors objected, litigants re-arranged their commitments, court staff complained while making ready. But the courts did not sit on Saturday. This was because the shorthand writers, who made a vital record of everything, were freelance people who could not be given orders. This was an early example for me of the limitations of power. The Lord Chief (as we lawyers called him) was thwarted by three stenographers. Now stenographers are extinct, instead computer failures sometimes thwart the sittings of a court. These tend to happen without notice.

One day I was told it was my duty to accompany Lady Parker on a boat trip up the Tyne. I carefully checked the arrangements, which included the Under Sheriff meeting us at our destination a mile or two upriver. The outing went quite well. We saw various bridges and other sites of putative interest, and she was chatty and appreciative. But as we closed on the jetty at the end, no car was apparent. There were of course no mobile phones, and catastrophe loomed. She would not be happy. I could hardly walk her two miles back down river, and it was beginning to spit with rain. My future was clearly in peril, and the next few moments were a nightmare from which I could not wake. Lady Parker was beginning to look suspicious, if not severe. I wondered whether to pretend to faint. No sight has ever been so welcome as the prow of an old grey Daimler inching tardily around the corner of a warehouse.

On another occasion I went with the Lord Chief to a meeting with a large number of local magistrates in Northallerton. He began his remarks: 'I feel rather like the fourth husband of a Hollywood film star – I know what is expected of me, but I don't know how to make it any different.' They all laughed a lot, but at the time I thought this pretty racy from a man in his position.

It is one thing to become a barrister, but it is another to succeed. One of several necessary qualities is the ability to be persuasive in court – the art of the advocate. Oliver Popplewell, an outstanding generalist High Court Judge, has written that what is needed is intelligence, hard work, personality, good judgment and a bit of luck. You also need determination, fluency, focus, and to be attractive to solicitors and clients.

It was during that summer of 1967 that I learned about advocacy. Today there are umpteen training facilities, quasi-academic classes, courses, video sessions, mock trials and practical exercises, and the Inner Temple is about to ruin its fine library to install a little amphitheatre in which to teach the subject (though no court in England is an amphitheatre). When I came to the Bar you hoped that you had some aptitude, but you picked it up as you went along, mainly by watching others, and then by doing small cases of modest importance yourself. Later you would hone and perfect your technique by appearing in cases with Queen's Counsel, known as Leaders. I do not think that despite all their training modern advocates are any better than those 50 years ago, and they often lack practical experience because fewer cases are contested.

To be able, as a young Marshal, to watch day after day the cream of the Bar of Northern England conducting important or difficult cases was experience of the most valuable kind. Perhaps the best advocate that I saw was Peter Taylor QC, later himself to become Lord Chief Justice (and another good pianist). His technique was to be quietly but firmly affable, questioning in a brisk, brief but conversational tone, though with a relevance not always readily apparent to the witness. Only occasionally, a trap sprung, would he pounce with some acerbity. Some of the cases involved causing death by dangerous driving, and when I drove home at weekends having listened to him cross-examine, every junction, almost every gear change, seemed fraught with possible danger. There was also a remarkable criminal advocate in Newcastle, Wilfred Steer, who never took or consulted a note throughout his cases, which typically lasted three or four days. When he addressed the jury at the end, he would recapitulate the exact words used, as I verified from my scrupulously accurate blue notebook.

It was best to be pleasant, quiet and friendly in questioning, and not hector, bully or bluster. In cross-examination it was most effective first to ask a series of questions in a form to which the witness would agree, so as to achieve a rhythm of acquiescence which might well carry through into more contentious areas. With expert witnesses such as medical specialists, engineers or surveyors, it was essential, by previous hard work, to have some mastery of their area of expertise. These witnesses of course knew what the barrister's questions were designed to achieve and fencing with them could be fascinating.

One of the tasks which was delegated to the Marshal was saying grace at formal dinners hosted by the High Court Judges. The Judges received quite a lot of hospitality and needed to repay it. Warned about this, I had bought an anthology, appropriately entitled *Benedictus, Benedicatur* from an ecclesiastical bookseller. This contained a wide selection, many quite unsuitable, including Chinese, Lutheran and Jewish. I took some pride in finding graces I had not heard before, some of a little length. One evening I embarked upon a fresh choice, in Latin. I got through five lines quite well, but then found I could not recollect the next. There was, of course, a pause. A pause terminated by the Bishop of Durham booming 'Amen' from the other end of the table. After dinner, when the guests were departing, he came by me and said 'I think that was rather an ambitious grace, Marshal'.

Before one of these northern dinners I found myself standing alone, watching the assembled Great and Good. A figure appeared at my side: 'You must be Arthur's Marshal. Come and meet a few of the chaps from Leeds'. He walked me over to a large group of men and women who pulled back deferentially. This was the legendary Melford Stevenson, a High Court Judge with a reputation for being right wing, fierce, intolerant with the Bar and severe with the prisoners he tried and sentenced. He lived in a house called Truncheons. He was an outspoken man and somewhat feared, but was kindness personified to me, whom he had noticed looking isolated and in need of introduction. Some years later a similar thing happened at a Sheriff's party in Oxfordshire, when the Lord Lieutenant, Sir Ashley Ponsonby, collected me into his circle. I do not think of myself as socially backward, but gestures such as this do underline the good nature of those responsible in a memorable way.

The day before we left Newcastle to travel to York I was taken out to dinner by the Circuit 'Junior,' a youngish barrister who helped organise Circuit events and answered to the Circuit Leader, whom he assisted. The junior was Humphrey Potts (later Mr Justice Potts, who in 2001 was to try Jeffrey Archer for perjury and sentence him to four years' imprisonment). He took me to an Italian restaurant, gave me an excellent meal, and dropped me back outside the lodgings at about 12.30 am. All was locked and dark. I had no key. 'You had better climb up that drainpipe', he suggested. 'The bedrooms are on the third floor, and you should be able to get into the window by the rainwater head.' I quite liked scaling things, and did not demur. Potts drove off, and I scrambled up. Drainpipes are in fact quite easy to climb so long as you can get your fingers behind them, and, of course, so long as they do not come away from the wall. The trick is not to lean backwards. I climbed up and jumped through the window onto the bed below. What Potts had not told me (perhaps he did not know) was that the bed was occupied by the cook.

Many years later my elder son Roger was a Marshal in Sheffield, where one of the judges was Mr Justice Potts, but he did not make him climb anywhere.

It was in York, in lodgings in a Georgian house – now a boutique hotel called imaginatively 'The Judges' Lodgings' – when Arthur James turned to me one evening and asked whether I had pupillage arranged. I had not, though I had been to see a rather smooth man in Kings Bench Walk, but felt that he had little evidence of much work. 'What are you looking for?' 'London Chambers on the Midland Circuit' I said. This meant chambers whose premises were in the Temple, but where there was a substantial amount of work on the Midland Circuit, which at that time stretched from Grimsby to Gloucester and included Lincoln, Nottingham, Birmingham, Stafford, Shrewsbury, Warwick, Northampton, Leicester, Bedford, Aylesbury, Oxford and Worcester.

He paused for a moment, his rather chubby face working a little. He picked up the telephone. 'Bernard, Arthur here. I've got a young chap with me as a Marshal. He is reasonably intelligent. Likes our Circuit. Will you fix him up with a pupillage?' It was a request rather than a question.

Some weeks later, I attended at I Harcourt Buildings, in Middle Temple Lane, a narrow thoroughfare, Dickensian at the top, which connects Fleet Street with the Embankment, and separates the buildings of the Inner Temple, rebuilt after bomb damage in the war, and the Middle Temple, much less damaged. Bernard Caulfield QC was head of these chambers and he had a pleasant ground floor room facing gardens which led down to the Thames. Quite a small man, with a sharp, alert face, he came from a humble background for his father had been, I was told, a Lancashire miner. He was, I later discovered, a most formidable cross-examiner, whose technique involved intently watching a witness give evidence and sensing from his demeanour any areas of vulnerability. He did not over-prepare and would rely on his Junior for any necessary information which he did not have in his head. His submissions to the judge were pressed with intensity, and difficult to resist. He later became a High Court judge himself, which he did against the wishes of his wife, who promptly left him. Thereafter he was a somewhat lonely, not to say eccentric, figure. Perhaps his best-known trial also involved Jeffrey Archer. This was the first trial, in which Archer lied and won £500,000 damages from the *Daily Star*, and in which Mr Justice Caulfield asked the jury whether they did not find Mary Archer 'fragrant'.

Caulfield interviewed me for about ten minutes in rather an alarming way, firing off a succession of unrelated and sometimes irrelevant questions. How old was my mother, what was my father's occupation, did I enjoy school, how many suits did I have, did I go to Scotland very often, could I afford the rail fare to Birmingham, did I speak Spanish, was I thinking of getting married? I could think of nothing to do but simply answer each inquiry as shortly as possible. After a while he said 'You can go to Dennis Barker', and then lifted the phone to speak to Barker, who apparently occupied the next room. A moment later he appeared, a compact, balding, strongly-made man, with a broken nose and a pipe. He had played for the Harlequins, could speak Japanese, and was yet another pianist, who had to choose between music and the bar. He clearly did not want a pupil, and said so: 'But Bernard, I have applied for Silk' (Silks, that is QCs, do not take pupils). 'Well you won't get it this year' said Caulfield callously. 'Anyway, Arthur James wants you to have him.' At this he capitulated with quite good grace, mollified by the fact that he would get £500 as a pupil fee. That was a lot of money then, worth perhaps £7,000 now. (Pupil fees have since been abolished, and pupils are themselves paid large sums, often well over £50,000, by their chambers during their year of pupillage.)

And so I began my career at the Bar. I attended daily at Harcourt Buildings at about 9 am, wearing my black jacket and striped trousers (though never a bowler hat, as a few barristers then still did) and sat at a small table in Dennis's room, with a window to the garden by my left shoulder, examining sets of papers bound in red ribbon. These were requests for advice, for pleadings to be drafted, or 'briefs' – that is, instructions to go to court to conduct a case, together with the documents containing the evidence. Dennis was very busy, and in court often, which was very satisfactory, but his appearances were often far out of London, which was less so. I spent many hours and many pounds driving to Nottingham, Lincoln, Northampton and Birmingham to watch him in action. He was an economical advocate, who targeted his questions very well, and was never embarrassing to sit behind. He did however settle quite a lot of cases, which was, after a long drive, disappointing. It was mostly personal injury work – commonly involving an injured factory worker hurt by contact with machinery. The witnesses would be the plaintiff, various workmates, a foreman, a couple of medical witnesses and two engineers. These 'expert' witnesses were carefully selected for reliable partiality to the side employing them.

One of Barker's regular opponents was Brian Appleby, a large and amiable figure, so substantial that the stripes on his trousers ran horizontally for some of their length. Brian and Dennis were both tactically astute and sometimes got away with calling no evidence from their own side – which meant that there could be no cross-examination of their witnesses. You could wound your opponent, but he had no chance to wound you.

On occasions, especially in Lincoln, it was necessary – and expensive – to stay the night. There, close to the mighty Gothic cathedral (begun in 1192 and built unusually with asymmetric vaulting) the White Hart Hotel kept a stock of wine owned by the Circuit, and served it to us in a private dining room. This convivial vestige of the past has now died out. The lodgings for the Judge at Lincoln were nearby, just outside the walls of the castle in which the court was located. Every morning the Judge, instead of walking the necessary 200 yards, was driven in a pre-war Rolls Royce. This must have been as bad for the health of the car as for that of the Judge.

When Dennis was not in court I would attend chambers and work on his papers until around 11 am, when some of the other barristers would take me off with them for half an hour for morning coffee at a café in an alleyway called Devereux Court. Nobody ever seemed in any great hurry or under much pressure. Looked at in retrospect, that was probably a bad sign.

There was one other pupil in chambers, a rather tongue-tied chap called Graham, whose three-piece suit consisted of three garments each in a slightly different cloth. Bernard Caulfield used to tease him rather unattractively. The other 'young' men were all tenants, and all very friendly. The oldest in this category, then about 33, was David Morton Jack, then a bachelor with long dark hair, some Irish property, and a mews flat in Holland Park. He drove a Triumph Herald convertible, and I thought him tremendously dashing. He was not quite as busy as, given his talent and remarkable memory, he might have been, and occasionally he paid his clerk's fees from his wallet. We became friends, and in 1970 he and I both bought houses in North Oxfordshire. David and his artistic and highly industrious wife Rosemary twice invited us to Classiebawn Castle, Edwina Mountbatten's coastal house near Sligo. This was equipped with many signed photographs of the former Viceroy with the Queen, and also with a hirsute maid, the hair on whose legs I mistook for black stockings. It was from this house that Mountbatten was to put to sea in the boat in which the IRA murdered him in 1979. David in due course became a Circuit Judge, and after some vicissitudes in courts in Aylesbury and Slough, was able to come to Oxford. Always arriving at court a nicely-calculated few minutes before he was due to sit, he was a tribunal with considerable presence, whose style was not informal. He is a knowledgeable amateur historian. Rosemary remains a whirlwind of estimable energy, and after a career teaching at Headington, is now an enthusiastic bridge player. Time spent in their company is always agreeable.

In the late sixties David shared a room with Alexander Bradshaw, a keen Catholic, with a large nose and flowing, if seriously receding, blond hair. Bradshaw was after a wife, and hunted with a fellow barrister from other chambers. They were keen on minor European royalty, but in the end he married Suzie Eisenhower, granddaughter of the former President. They lived initially in a small flat in Lincolns Inn, but she was ambitious to get into American politics and after a while insisted on returning to the USA. Bradshaw went with her, and gamely qualified for the New York Bar. They settled in Rochester, N.Y. with three children. Sadly Susie in due course left him and married a Republican politician of some sort.

Bradshaw was friendly with her sister, whose divorce from, I think, a Mexican, he handled. Carol and I met them one day in New York at an American Bar Association conference. After dinner she asked if we would like to go on to her club. I had visions of a glass of whisky in a leather chair, and we took a cab to the Upper West Side, stopping outside a brownstone mansion. The entrance to the club was steps down to a basement, where we handed in our coats. Our hostess and Bradshaw then vanished, and I found myself standing at a bar. I asked for a gin and tonic. 'I cannot sell you alcohol' said the barman. 'Why not?' 'Because, sir, in the state of New York nudists cannot be served alcohol'. This was a disconcerting response. I pointed out that I was not a nudist. 'But you soon will be' responded the barman, 'look'. I turned my head and through a mist of theatrical smoke could make out a dance floor on which couples were dancing perfectly normally, save that many were indeed quite without clothes. It turned out that the club was Plato's Retreat, a well-known location for *dévergondage*. The facilities there included a Mat Room, which could only be entered, naked, by couples or single girls; a swimming pool, quite well occupied but with little swimming going on; and a lounge or sitting-out area in which amiable people wandered round introducing themselves. The atmosphere was not tacky or unpleasant, but after a while Carol and I slipped away, it not being what we were used to.

Bradshaw obtained a divorce (very difficult for a Catholic, and involving the fiction that he had never married), went to Italy, where he qualified as a priest, and then returned to the United States to run a parish. The parish to which he was allocated was Rochester, NY, where lived the wife whom in the eyes of God he had never married, and his children, whom, presumably, in the eyes of God he had never helped to conceive. This would have seemed far-fetched in a novel. We lost touch and I heard nothing of her thereafter until she was interviewed on the radio for the 2019 anniversary of the D Day invasion, which her grandfather had been in charge of.

We saw a good deal of Ian Schmeigelow, who had a smart flat in Seymour Place and a very attractive wife who was to die tragically prematurely, as also did his second wife. It seems often to be the case that serious misfortune strikes the same people repeatedly. Ian – a tall, blond Scandinavian with perfect manners, and related to the famous Lunn skiing family – was an entertaining man whose heart was not in the Bar: he left to pursue a business career and moved to Hampshire.

Another young tenant, who worked hard to build up a practice, was Nicholas Chambers. Son of the man who had run the Rootes Group car rally team, he is a big and generally cheerful person who, while not highly athletic, enjoyed arranging and playing in cricket matches. Ambitious, hardworking and determined, he stayed late many evenings reading the Weekly Law Reports, hoping that a brief might come in. He read libel for *The Times* (once ruling some Bernard Levin text inappropriate: he was told not to do that again). His tenacity paid off. He began to prosper, acquired some banking work, and armed with that, and warned by a solicitor that our clerk was not good to deal with, made application to Brick Court, the leading commercial law set in London. He was taken on there and did well. We were sorry at his departure. In the end he became a Senior Circuit Judge and the

Commercial Judge for Wales – an attractive position, if geographically rather testing. When he retired from that he took up arbitration – much easier for a High Court judge to do than a Circuit Judge. We, our wives and two of my children once went on a riding expedition together in the Wyoming Rockies where he revealed himself as an outstanding watercolour cartoonist, producing delightful pictures of grizzly bears peering round pine trees. He too moved to North Oxfordshire. He is married to Sally, a strong-minded woman from Worcestershire, a rider, artist and outstanding gardener with firm views about most subjects. Both are very kind people. Nick and I have remained good friend for some 50 years, though he did once tick me off very fiercely indeed, for voting to leave the EU in the 2015 referendum. But I have forgiven him.

Our chief Clerk, Harry Charlwood, was a slim, dark and mildly lugubrious man. He was a Mason, and an ex-sergeant in the Eighth Army, with which he had fought his way along North Africa and then up Italy – a country to which he always returned for holidays, at Lake Garda. Harry was in some ways a good clerk of an old-fashioned kind, which meant that he took an interest in matching the talents of his barristers with the requirements of the solicitors who came to chambers, but he did not believe in 'touting' – actively seeking work through social intercourse – and his reserved manner was not every instructing solicitor's cup of tea. Nor indeed, less happily and even more seriously, did he believe in active fee collection. He never seemed to appreciate that a young barrister might like some money. Fees might take six months to a year to come in. Some (particularly from the solicitor to the Metropolitan Police) never came in at all. His wife Dorothy did the accounts, and sent out such bills as were submitted. She had very firm views about a lot of things, but particularly anaesthetics. There came a time when she needed chest surgery, but she refused all pain relief. Not surprisingly, there was difficulty finding a surgeon to operate. But finally one did, snipping swiftly in 18th century style through her ribs while she lay silent and fully conscious.

After six months, pupils, assuming that they have been formally 'called to the Bar' by their Inn, are allowed to appear in court. When I was called, the Bar consisted of about 2,500 practising barristers. When I retired from the Bench 50 years later there were about 16,000 – rather too many for all to be able to earn a reasonable living.

My first case, for a firm of solicitors called Hall, Sich and Jasper, was on the 27th May 1968, marked 5 guineas, and involved defending a taxi driver. Such cases were often tried in central London by stipendiary magistrates, who had a dull diet, mainly of trivial traffic offences and drunks. 'Stipes', as they were known, were able, but often jaundiced and impatient men; fundamentally fair, sometimes even kind, but keen to move as fast as possible through their tedious lists. Intelligent, confident, and frequently bored, they were often much readier to acquit than lay magistrates. If you had a good point and put it succinctly you might well succeed; but if you flannelled and took too long you lost all sympathy, and, often, your case. Appearing before them was good training, much better than attending courses. I was once at the Marylebone magistrates' court co-defending with Mervyn Stretfeild, an eccentric, altruistic man who came to chambers shortly after I did. A tall, benevolent person who wore loose high-waisted suits, perpetually stooped, with a glaucous eye and waspish tongue, he listened to my submissions to the Stipendiary. I finished. 'Mr Stretfeild,' said the magistrate. Mervyn stood up theatrically slowly (he was an amateur actor, and one of his sons was to become an excellent professional one). He paused: 'Mr Harris is probably right' he said, 'he sometimes is,' and sat down again. This was a risky technique, but luckily both our clients were acquitted.

For the second six months of my pupillage I was transferred to David Hunter, a man unlike Dennis Barker, who spent most of his time doing high-quality paperwork in his room. This was handy for me as I could combine appearing in small cases in London with attending to Hunter's papers. A day's work in my early days might involve three briefs. I would walk from the Temple, say, to Bow Street, opposite the Opera House, and there meet a cab driver alleged to have shot a light. The police spent, or wasted, a lot of their time watching traffic lights. 'Have you any witnesses?' I might ask. 'Would it help if I had?' 'Obviously it might, if there is evidence to support what you say.' 'Give me a second, I'll make a phone call'. Within a few minutes two other cabbies would arrive, ready to say that the lights in question were at the time defective.

Then on to Marlborough Street, where my case was called on. No prosecuting solicitor, barrister or policemen appeared. I asked that the case be dismissed. A lay bench hearing such an application would anguish about the desirability of waiting a bit; perhaps something had gone wrong, should there be an adjournment? 'Case dismissed,' said the stipe. 'I would like to give you something' said the happy client. This was terrifying, for under no circumstances should a barrister take money directly from a client. He had to be paid by the instructing solicitor, through the Clerk. I explained all this. The man smiled, then took two large cigars from his overcoat and slotted them into my breast pocket. I never smoked (after an unhappy experiment with an oval, pink coloured Passing Cloud) but I kept them a long time.

I only received one other present during my career at the Bar. I had won a rather difficult case against the odds, and the party I represented sent me a dozen expensive bottles of Burgundy, which were duly consumed. Nine months later the case got to the Court of Appeal, and the result was reversed.

My third case in a typical day might well be an appearance at the Bear Garden. This was the curious name given to an upper hall in the Royal Courts of Justice, a mighty Victorian building at the east end of the Strand where civil and appeal courts sit (not to be confused with the Old Bailey, which is near St Paul's, and deals with serious crime). At lunchtimes this space was a teeming mass of solicitors, clerks, junior barristers, and litigants in person. Opening off it were a number of rooms occupied by 'Masters'. These men – in the 1960s they were all men – were procedural judges who coped with applications which arose in the course of getting cases ready for trial. They were former barristers who had not taken silk, generally confident and talented but often people of mild eccentricity. They sat behind substantial tables, on the other side of which barristers, standing, would crowd and make submissions. The Masters were very short of time, and would listen, sometimes seeming alert and sometimes apparently in a coma between sleep and death, for a few moments to each sides' arguments, and then bark out their decision. There would often follow some pleasant observation such as: 'All you keen young men flooding to the bar... no future in it you know, it will all be done by machines quite soon... good day to you.' The Masters, of whom there were perhaps six or eight, and a few extra Chancery Masters (who tended to have double-barrelled names, like modern footballers) stuck together. They ate at a table in the Inner Temple at which non-masters were not warmly encouraged.

The Senior Master also accumulated a large number of other roles and titles. One such, Robert Turner, was also, amongst other things, Queen's Remembrancer, the Prescribed Officer for election petitions, advisor to the Malta law Reform committee, a member of the Notarial Board, a Steward of Westminster Abbey, President of the Institute of Credit Management, Chairman of the Sherbert foundation, and the editor of various practitioners' books. Another Master, Keith Topley, was, by contrast, really only interested in sailing.

After about eight months in pupillage, the question as to whether I would get a tenancy and become a member of chambers arose. Things had not gone badly, there was little competition, I was hopeful. One day I was taken aside by David Hunter and told that I was to be offered a place. I accepted immediately, and a day or two later a signwriter attended and wrote 'Mr Charles Harris' in white capitals on a black wooden slat which was inserted below the other names on a board at the entrance to chambers. I had arrived at the Bar. But in the light of later events I might have been rather hasty.

There was one opportunity in particular which I missed. My Inn ran an annual advocacy competition, which in 1968 I entered, and reached the final. This was held in Hall and took place after dinner in front of a large audience of barristers and judges. It involved playing the role of counsel in a civil trial. I had recently been a Marshal with a chance to see excellent advocates in regular action. It was easy to slip into their mode of argument and address. My opponent had not had that opportunity, and I won the Inner Temple Advocacy trophy. As the evening ended various eminent men – heads of chambers or senior Silks – came up to me and asked if I would like to come for a chat about a tenancy in their chambers. This was the most golden of opportunities, which most foolishly I squandered, saying that I was already fixed up. It would have been a chance to see and compare other sets and other people besides those I knew. Some of these other places would have been larger, with more members, some would have had different or more specialised work, some might have had greater prestige. It was, quite literally, a chance of a lifetime, and I made a serious error in turning down that evening's invitations. Instead, I wandered out into the darkness carrying a silver cup and returned to my flat in Ladbroke Grove feeling pretty uplifted. I raised a sash window and played a triumphant piece of Richard Strauss to slumbering West London.

Chapter 6

Life in chambers

The senior members of chambers during my early years were all men, and all with charm as well as talent. After Bernard Caulfield's elevation to the bench, Bob Purchas QC, later to become Lord Justice Purchas, took over. Slightly on the portly side of handsome, very genial and well connected, he ran chambers smoothly and skilfully as a benign dictatorship. He understood what was needed in the way of tenants, staff, accommodation and facilities and organised it all himself, later gaining the grateful sanction of the members at an annual general meeting over which he would preside as a short prelude to dinner at the East India Club. No 21st century chambers would be run like that; all now have a structure of committees, bureaucracy and various levels of devolved responsibility. But Bob's methods, and connections, worked very well, and everyone was quite content. As an advocate, he prepared sedulously, often with full notes for various contingent lines of cross-examination. He was busy and popular, though he did not quite wield the deft scalpel of Caulfield.

He was however very deft when it came to chambers membership. We were about 20 strong, then regarded as middle-sized, but in need of new blood. Bob persuaded Tudor Evans QC and Richard Rougier QC (both later to go on the High Court bench) to join us. They were a most talented couple. Tudor Evans, a friendly man with a slightly gloomy expression, worked from a small clearing in the tangled forest of books, files and papers which filled his room. He had been in the navy and suffered a head injury which left him with permanent tinnitus, which he never mentioned. He was an enthusiastic race goer who, when knighted, remained in conversation with the Queen on the subject of horses well beyond the few moments allocated. A quiet man, his technique in court was one of soft and gentle interrogation, so gentle that witnesses tended to lose their anxiety and lower their guard. One day I watched this process: useful answer after useful answer was drawn from the plaintiff until, with a fierce sibilance, just above a whisper, Tudor Evans said 'So, Mr So and So, is it not clear that on your own account you have no case at all'? The witness looked at him, swallowed, and then fainted, hitting his head hard on the witness box as he fell. I never had quite this degree of success. Tudor was not the administrator his predecessor had been when he took over as head of chambers, but we were sad upon his elevation.

While talking of horses, it might here be interposed that Bob also recruited Guy Hungerford, a stylish, fluent and powerfully-built young man, as a result of a chance meeting at Ascot one June. Guy had a well-filled mind, insufficiently exercised by his former life in advertising, and was – and remains – an engaging companion, ready to talk with confidence on most subjects, of which the law, as it turned out, was not always foremost. (He has an ancestor, Walter, who fought at Agincourt and became Steward to Henry V). His turn of phrase was both amusing and challenging. He and I were to share a room in chambers for many years, and each became a godparent to one of the other's children. He has always been excellent company, and has an attractive, mildly combative way with those he meets. For a while he looked back nostalgically to his J Walter Thompson income, and kept up an interest in racing in parallel with the Bar. In due course he was to marry the charming and extremely astute Clare. They asked us on holiday once to Ibiza, where we spent some time with moustaches drawn on our faces, which puzzled the Germans in an adjacent villa, and we also made ambitious nautical forays on pedaloes. The Hungerfords established a conference centre and hotel near Bath which became a considerable success. However, in demand and fond of advocacy, Guy remained at the Bar, in due course became a Recorder, and often sat at Oxford.

Richard Rougier, son of a QC and the romantic novelist Georgette Heyer, was rather a star. Fond of golf, cards and fishing, he looked like Rex Harrison, belonged to the Garrick, and trailed a little glamour. He had the greatest mastery of language and material that I came across in 50 years. Formidable at first instance, especially in the very difficult art of re-examination – where counsel has a chance to put back together a witness damaged in cross-examination without resort to leading questions – he was perhaps at his most impressive before a sceptical Court of Appeal. In that tribunal there are three judges to contend with. One might raise some objection to a submission, which Rougier would counter with a quotation from Shakespeare. The next might suggest that the law was not quite as he had submitted. To this Richard might reply; 'Well, your Lordship will no doubt recollect what Lord Diplock had to say on that subject in 1975'. The third: 'But was there in fact any evidence for that finding, Mr Rougier'? 'Perhaps your Lordship has not recollected the passage on the second day of the trial, at page 147 of the transcript, line H'. This ability to deploy different types of response with disarming extempore swiftness was quite formidable. It could also, I was told, be somewhat irritating to some members of the Court of Appeal. Though he was certainly my favourite advocate, I am not sure that he was theirs, though they often found in his favour.

Rougier could also disconcert his clients. On one occasion I was acting for the Co-Operative bank and had taken in Richard as a Leader (banking was neither his speciality nor mine, but two heads were better than one), and several senior executives came down from Manchester for a conference. As they were leaving, he said: 'I will see you then, at Philippi'. The bankers looked about in consternation; had they misunderstood something, what did he mean, where is Philippi, surely the trial was to be in London?

Richard did other things. He kept wicket at chambers cricket matches, and he played high-stakes bridge with men such as Omar Sharif. The stakes were sometimes too high. Tiring of his metropolitan quarters in a flat in Gloucester Rd, he had bought a country house near the Welsh border, where he enjoyed some aspects of rural life. But he lost so much money playing bridge that in order to pay the debts he had to sell the house. He camouflaged this at the time by saying he would rather have a cottage in Sussex, which was better for golf.

Unfortunately for us, his legal talents were recognised in other chambers too, and a set in Paper Buildings invited him to become their head, jointly with Harvey McGregor QC, the pre-eminent veteran authority on all matters contractual (and an Oxford academic and amateur cabaret artist). Richard felt this was a good opportunity, but it was a considerable blow to Harcourt Buildings.

The next most senior figure was David Hunter: tall, with a lined face, balding, careful, an excellent lawyer, a good golfer and a very heavy smoker, whose pupil I had become after six months with Dennis Barker. After much cogitation in a cloud of tobacco, he would draft an opinion with great care, but no great economy of words. His conclusions on law were generally impeccable, and he had a large paperwork practice. He was however by no means so masterly with live witnesses, and so was less relaxing and enjoyable to sit behind in court. In due course he became a High Court Judge in Hong Kong and later sat in the Court of Appeal there. In going to the Far East he trod in the judicial footsteps of Dennis Barker, but did not make the same mistakes. Barker became sadly unstuck. Divorced and solitary in the far East, he drank heavily and became friendly with unsuitable people. Engaged to try a vast pan-Pacific conspiracy, he inexplicably threw out the prosecution case after six months of evidence. He resorted in the end to Cyprus, where he remarried and then died in a car accident in 1989 aged 63. He had great talents, but came in the end to little. It was perhaps strange that both of my pupil masters should have gone to Hong Kong.

While I was David Hunter's pupil he also did some divorce work, amongst his banking and property practice, which often involved conferences with, and appearances for, actresses of attractive appearance. One was Adrienne Corri, about to star revealingly in *A Clockwork Orange*. I enjoyed these brushes with celebrity.

In 1970 there were three other senior juniors. Peter McNair, an amiable man from Chelsea, who had lost an arm in the war, and was in demand as a 'Silk basher', that is a barrister of some seniority, good enough to oppose leading Counsel, but costing less. Eventually he tired of this and retired to the Circuit bench. Giles Rooke, uxorious father of many children, a slight dandy, and a member of the TA, lived near Canterbury, where he had a criminal practice. He was amusing, kind and helpful, behind a mask of mild affectation. One of his talents was to be able to speak long passages in Latin. I once appeared before him when he was sitting as a Recorder in a case in which a defendant had not been delivered for trial from his prison. Slightly tongue in cheek, I sought an order that the governor be required to attend at court to explain himself. Giles was somewhat taken aback by this unusual application, and did not quite know the answer. He then delivered various remarks, at some length, in Latin, which nobody in court, including me, understood. When he stopped, I replied 'fiat justicia, fiat voluntas tua' (which means 'let justice be done, let thy will be done'): this was all I could think of. The case was then adjourned and I was surrounded by the local press, admiring our apparent learning but desperate for translation. I hurried from court, drawing around me a deceptive cloak of putative erudition.

Giles' approximate contemporary was Roy McAulay, a sound lawyer and advocate of the unflashy kind who was small, fit, neat, dark, careful, tidy and always very well prepared. I shared a room with him for some time, and he was very helpful to me. He had a busy practice, and I used to 'devil' for him, that is prepare work to be sent out in his name, in exchange for a proportion of his fees. Some barristers were not very careful to account to their devils, but Roy was always both prompt and meticulous. Though he chose to live inconveniently in Blackheath – where he was not lavish with his wine – he had an excellent practice on the Midland Circuit, and was very well thought of. He took Silk in 1978 and was clearly destined in due course for the High Court, but succumbed to cancer, quite swiftly, in early middle age, working until a few weeks of his death. Besides being an inestimable tragedy for Ruth, his wife, and his two delightful children, this was a body blow for our chambers, of which by then he was the head.

When I began to practise these chambers were happy, confident and successful. But sets of chambers tend to wax and wane, and this was especially so when they contained a comparatively small number of people. Many contemporary sets have well over 100 members, and some far more, while a lot have 50 to 70. When I was called to the Bar in 1967, a small set might be one Silk and four or five juniors. A set of 25 or so was considered quite substantial. Now such a size, unless highly specialised, would be marginal. At Harcourt Buildings we steadily lost quite a lot of people. Some, like Bradshaw and Schmeigelow, left the Bar; another, Charles Kelly (a good singer), went to Newcastle. Simon Coltart – a friend later to become known, when a judge, as Colonel Tart on account of his brisk, cheerful, traditional manner – went to Brighton. Nick Chambers, possibly seeing how the wind might blow, had gone to Brick Court. Two, in one year, died in accidents – Nick Hoffman on a motorcycle in Norfolk, Tania Pond under a parachute. Some able people joined , including Annmarie Harris, now Lady Lloyd-Jones.

One of the junior arrivals was Charles Bennett. Tallish, thin, a fencer and a Greek speaker, he was a man with a remarkably high IQ. This was almost a disability, as he often analysed the strength of his opponents' cases more highly than his own, which did not invariably endear him to his solicitor clients. He was very particular too about spoken English. At lunch I once said to a waiter 'we will all have a cup of coffee'. 'No' said Bennett immediately, 'We will each have a cup of coffee'. He did a lot of paperwork, but never achieved, or perhaps never wanted, a substantial court practice.

Another bright and well-educated man, with a taste for expensive cars, was capable, but his personality was not wholly endearing. He once threatened to report me to the Bar Conduct committee. I had given him one of my cases which I was unable to do – a 'return', normally gratefully accepted by a recipient who would thereby work and earn when he would otherwise have been unemployed – but the papers were with me in Oxfordshire, not in London, where he was. As the case was for hearing in Birmingham I suggested he should drive up to my house, where we would give him supper, a bed and a desk, and whence he could continue to court the next day. He said this was not convenient. I offered to meet a train at Bicester, via which he could travel from London to Birmingham, and hand over the brief to him there. He did not want to use a train. He asserted that I ought myself to travel to London (and back) and deliver the papers to chambers for him. In due course he left to practise elsewhere.

Francis McLeod, boisterous, cheerful and self-confident, could have developed into an excellent barrister, but decided to leave the bar for some other occupation. My strongest memory of him was when he seized a coat of mine which had a curly black sheepskin lining. He turned it inside out, put it on his head and strode out of chambers into Middle Temple Lane declaring himself to be Samuel Pepys.

With Purchas, Tudor Evans, Barker and Hunter taking appointments, Rougier leaving, and McNair going on the Circuit bench, we were much depleted, and there were no recruits at a middle or senior level. In due course Giles Rooke became a Circuit Judge in Kent. Roy McAulay assumed the leadership and strove mightily to recruit suitable people, but it did not prove easy. We considered and rejected an ex-MP, and a charming man of private means from East Anglia, alas without a practice. At least one senior Silk did not wish to join. But we took in one group of four juniors together. This was not to prove a happy step. They operated as something of a clique. One was a good lawyer, but a trace fusty and retiring. Another was a reasonable performer, amiable but not distinguished, and the other two were simply extremely difficult people. Talented enough to be mildly formidable, they seemed to have some unrealistic toxic agenda of their own.

The more aggressive of the two was a chain smoker who infected the whole premises, not just his own room, with the odour of his cigarettes.

He used a good deal of unpleasant language. At one stage the group of four agitated for us to move to expensive premises in Chancery Lane, which they claimed would attract many recruits and solve all our problems. They frequently called for a merger with another set – but there was no suggestion that anyone wanted to merge with us. Many chambers meetings descended into intemperate acrimony – a far cry from delightful evenings at the East India Club. We had two fairly senior juniors, Simon Wheatley (he had been my pupil and was talented), and Jeremy Pendlebury (similar, and avid for vogue sports like American football and cross-country cycling). They were both pleasant, capable men, but when it came to vote on various issues, were prone to abstain. Two excellent young recruits were Julian Waters and David Platt.

After Roy's death, Ray Walker, a year my senior, became head of chambers. He had joined us some years before at the request of Richard Rougier, who had led him a good deal. Ray was a resilient and competent advocate, the son of an Air Marshal. He took Silk in 1988, the year before I did. He was an unusual person. Until his arrival we had all been sociable in each other's flats and houses, taking it in turns, for example, to hold Christmas drinks parties. I do not think that Ray ever invited any of us to his Halkin Street apartment, and he certainly was not prepared to host a Chambers gathering there. He had glittering blue eyes which focused into rather an alarming gaze. He would drink neither tea nor coffee, claiming them to be unhealthy (despite this precaution he was to die prematurely in 2010 aged 65 while still at the Bar), and he was a sportsman, in particular a strong golfer and tennis player. He liked to disappear in his Daimler SP250 to Brancaster (where his funeral was held, at deterrent distance).

The situation became increasingly unsatisfactory. We drifted in a disagreeable direction. The atmosphere in chambers had ceased to be one of mutual respect and agreeable badinage and became one of friction, frustration, anger and anxiety. The premises looked a mess, and most of the rooms had been allowed to become inappropriate for the reception of good-quality solicitors with desirable clients. We appointed a two-man committee to deal with this. The results were not popular. Pendlebury sent round a circular which read as follows: 'In case it should be thought that, being one half of the chambers' decoration committee, I chose or concurred in the choice of colour to the common parts, I write this circular to inform everyone that neither was the case. In my view the colour is utterly appalling; it neither complements the carpet nor does it create a proper business atmosphere nor is it seemly... These views are only my personal views and are not those of the decoration committee'.

Some people paid their chambers expenses tardily. One of the Clerks appeared to have been taking money from petty cash, but when I suggested he be sacked there was no enthusiasm for this – he might sue us. In fact he asked for an interest-free loan of £5,000. By the early nineties we had simply ceased to be a happy ship, indeed I felt we were foundering, and chambers overall income was stagnant. When working quite hard and travelling a lot to sustain or improve a practice, you do not want to have to worry about your professional base. When I began, this had seemed fine. When I left, it was precarious.

But back to the beginning. In my first case, at the Clapham Magistrates' Court, I represented a taxi driver called Augustine, summoned under the Hackney Carriage Acts for some offence concerning his licence. My brief 'marked' at £5 guineas would have a present-day value of about £80. I arrived very early, full of anxious trepidation, and had to wait in the street for the doors to open. I had prepared my slim brief for hours, considered every question I might ask, and even debated which tie to wear. (In magistrates' courts barristers did not robe, but in the County Court and High Court they did, wearing a wig, a stiff wing collar, bands and a black gown. All this had to be carried round wherever we went). This trial was the real thing: in this modest and unfashionable forum was my first appearance after years of learning and training.

I identified and deferentially approached the Clerk to indicate my presence and inquire when we might come on (a matter of some importance and within his disposition). I watched the bench of three lay magistrates decide two cases before mine. They convicted in both. Mr Augustine was called. I asked the police witness a few careful questions. I called Mr Augustine to give evidence, which he did with a broad and friendly West Indian smile, explaining his position and conceding that there may have been some misunderstanding. At one point something he said made the chairman laugh. I earnestly submitted that there was surely some element of doubt. Due solely to my client's personality we won, and I returned to Harcourt buildings in great triumph, and waited six months to be paid.

Between May and December 1968, I had 29 cases, almost all before magistrates, though my last case that year, on New Year's Eve, was a civil claim in the Bow County Court, for 9gns. I did 138 cases in 1969 and 184 in 1970, so I was fairly busy, though with pretty trivial work. A barrister's life is a bit like that of an actor. You can never be sure of your next appearance. If the pile of papers by your desk grows depressingly small, you repine. When it grows, you exult. This is a feature of most barristers' careers

When not in court, I did some textbook writing; initially sections of a practitioners' work called Atkins Court Forms – one on Service of Process, one on Clubs – and later the section on Evidence in Halsbury's Laws of England, a multi-volume standard reference work. This latter I wrote together with Roy McAulay and Richard Inglis, another capable member of chambers, who in due course left us to practise in Nottingham where he later become a Circuit Judge. Halsbury involved much tedious work, checking thousands of references and authorities (earlier cases of relevance). The proofs were laid out on a large table in the basement of our house in Pimlico, which was occupied in this way for about a year. I used to descend to it without enthusiasm. In December 1976 I received the sum of £666.66 for my efforts (worth £4,600 now). I did not want to do another text book. It requires a great deal of patience, and it is difficult to write with much elegance or style. Furthermore, any lapse from complete accuracy can be a disaster, putting the authority of the whole work in question.

I became a governor of St Clement Danes Church of England primary school, just north of the Aldwych. I believe someone in the

Bow Group recommended me. The most interesting aspect of this was the selection of a new Head. All the candidates were so nervous that they were barely articulate, and I could not understand how any of them would have the confidence to run a school. I also took a part-time post as Secretary to the Bar Association for Finance, Commerce and Industry. I attended a few meetings, and drafted some submissions to the Law Commission, but as I knew nothing about finance, commerce or industry, it did not turn out to be a very worthwhile position.

Rather to my surprise I was instructed out of the blue in two substantial criminal cases at the Old Bailey. This, England's major criminal court, was heavy with almost tangible atmosphere. Famous Silks could be seen smoking in its spacious corridors, and a few glamorous women hung around inexplicably. I felt well out of my depth, but at one awkward moment was saved by James Crespi QC, a man of enormous girth, later to be injured in a bomb attack. He saw that I had no idea what to answer to a question from the Bench. He whispered 'simply say that you are asking for the usual order'. I did, and all was well.

The first of these trials lasted 15 days and involved drug importation, with an exotic Ethiopian connection - colourful scimitar-featured witnesses flew in from Addis Ababa. The man I represented, who lived less excitingly in Earls Court, was lucky to be acquitted. Prosecuting counsel was in one respect quite uncharacteristically inept, repeatedly asking a co-defendant where he had been at a particular time. (He had been in prison. He knew, and prosecuting counsel of course knew, that this should not be revealed to the jury). 'Out of work and on holiday' said the defendant, extemporising as best he could. 'That won't do', said counsel, who was big, bluff, charming and experienced – but having a bad day. 'Tell the jury where you were'. 'Very well then, I was in Parkhurst prison, and I claim a retrial.' The other case lasted for two weeks. I felt quite grand marching daily down Fleet street to the Bailey via Ludgate Circus. These were quite lengthy trials in those days, and by my standards well paid. I got £1,026 for the first (now worth some £12,500).

But however well it paid, I did not relish criminal work. Most of the witnesses were either policemen or crooks, and neither category was very attractive. The police gave their evidence by reading from their notebooks, which they made up in concert after the events described. This was often deeply unpersuasive as they agreed in every particular and asserted remarkable powers of recollection. They also frequently expressed themselves in curiously formulaic language, and still do. To the end of my judicial career policemen were speaking like this: 'I observed a male exit a stationary parked-up vehicle; this male then proceeded towards two persons situated in the vicinity of retail premises and engaged them in conversation.' Why they cannot say 'I saw a man get out of a parked car and walk over to talk to two people standing by a shop' I have never understood. It makes them sound robotic and stupid, but is so widespread that I wonder if they are trained to it.

The crooks of course varied a lot, but many would give perfectly ridiculous accounts to justify what they had done: 'I hit him because he looked at me disrespectfully when I was talking to this girl. I forgot I was holding a beer bottle, and he broke it with his head'. Some criminals though were pretty wily and fluent, and it was sad to see them running evidential rings around, say, a prison warder. Defendants in cases involving child molestation were often pathetic individuals, with miserable histories, but their behaviour was repulsive and they were hard to approach in an objective way.

Besides the content and dramatis personae of criminal cases, there was their relentless tedium. Everything moves at a speed deemed appropriate for the slowest member of the jury. This pace was often so lethargic as to send the jury itself, let alone counsel and the judge, into the appearance of sleep. There were many irritating exclusionary evidential rules. For me, a little crime went a long way, both at the bar and later on the bench. In civil work, there are no juries, and matters can proceed at a good pace and in a far less artificial way. The judge finds the facts for himself.

Before I took Silk in 1989 I had gradually acquired quite a lot of work in the Midlands, with several good firms of solicitors in Birmingham (notably Buller Jeffries, due to an outstanding and knowledgeable old-style unqualified solicitor's clerk, Mike Simonds, to whom I owe a lot, and whom I can never repay, and with Cartwright and Lewis, an excellent small firm); in Nottingham, with Browne, Jacobson and Roose; and also a solid connection in Hampshire whose cases went to Winchester. One good Midland firm in Leamington went by the encouraging name of Wright Hassel. A lot of my work was personal injury litigation – accidents at work often involving machinery, or collisions on the road. I was usually but not invariably for the defendant, instructed by an insurance company. I also did medical negligence, which I enjoyed. Simon Wheatley's father was in charge of legal affairs at Lloyds Bank, and he kindly put a little banking work my way when Simon was my pupil.

I had originally thought that if you won cases, that was sufficient for professional success. But this was not entirely true. Solicitors and insurers who gave work to particular barristers liked to feel that they were friends with them, on equal terms. Preferably first-name terms. I sometimes failed to recall the names of these vital people when we met before a trial, sometimes referring to them as Mr So and So, and sometimes merely by look, tone or inflexion. In retrospect, this must have been a handicap. There were many barristers who were by no means star performers but who knew all about their instructing solicitors: their houses, their families, holidays, hobbies and dogs. They talked, and indeed lunched, with them avidly. These people often had healthy practices because they were liked better than those who simply turned up and conducted a case with the minimum of social chatter. Some were actually poor advocates, but still had work.

However, if you were effective in court, capable of winning marginal cases, then this was certainly a good foundation. I did become pretty good at cross-examination, which I much enjoyed. This required a lot of careful preparation, reactive thinking and some judgment of character. Successful cross-examination is most gratifying, as it can in a few minutes completely destroy a witness's credibility or case. Badly done it is irritating and time consuming, and often confirms the reliability of the person being questioned. What worked best was a pleasant approach, as much economy as possible, mastery of the available evidential material (surprisingly not every barrister seemed to read all this) and a concentration upon relevance. When you have the answers you need, move on immediately, do not linger for emphasis, which might lead to unwanted qualification. It was sometimes possible to win cases purely on cross-examination, which was highly satisfying, though it never did to be too confident. On one occasion, at a trial in Lincoln, I got every answer I sought from a plaintiff, who in the end agreed that his injury, sustained in an ordnance factory where he worked, was solely the fault of his own carelessness. I rose to make my final submissions: 'My Lord, I rely upon the answers given in cross–examination'. 'You would be foolish to do that, Mr Harris' said the Judge, Mr Justice Pat O'Connor, a shrewd, hard drinking old-style tribunal. 'You were smiling at the witness. He was a nice man. He did not want to disagree with you. I shall pay no attention at all to his admissions.'

On one occasion I made the mistake of starting a question to a plaintiff who was a lathe operator: 'Prima facie, Mr So and So, you would expect...' 'Mr Harris,' interrupted the judge, 'you seem to be speaking in Latin. I rather doubt if the witness understands Latin.' He turned politely to the witness: 'Do you by any chance speak Latin?' 'No, My Lord.' 'I thought not, Mr Harris. Pray continue in English.' Later in the same case – I must have been having an bad day – I listened to an answer a witness gave and then repeated what he had said for emphasis. 'Mr Harris, if you are going to repeat all the evidence yourself, the case will take twice as long as it otherwise would.'

It was important to understand the Judge before whom one was appearing. Most, as might be expected, were fundamentally fair-minded, but many had a certain partiality for plaintiffs in personal injury cases, because if they did not win, they got no compensation. This frame of mind, though understandable, especially in cases of very severe injury such as paraplegia or brain damage, was quite wrong, in that a party should not win if the evidence, on balance of probability, was insufficient to establish his or her case. It could be most professionally irritating, as well as expensive for insurance companies. An example of this kind of situation, not infrequent, was when a young child ran from behind a parked car into collision with a passing motorist. There would naturally be immense sympathy for the injured child, and also for its parents, who were themselves probably to blame for failing to control the child, but rarely joined in the action and never found liable if they were. The poor motorist, often driving in a perfectly reasonable and normal way, would suffer judgment against him for failing to keep a proper lookout, or going too fast, when in reality neither was the case. The reason was that he was insured, his insurer would pay, and that way the injured infant would get compensation. I fought, and lost, quite a few cases for such defendants. One of the most annoying involved a young motorcyclist riding very fast in the wrong direction down a one-way street. He hit a car coming the other way and his leg was torn off. The car driver, who I represented, was held 70% to blame for 'not heeding his approach'.

Most of my cases, though some quite valuable, were fairly short, lasting between one and three days. It was common to have more than one listed in the same court at the same time, especially in the High Court in Birmingham. This sort of listing was potentially unfair to litigants, who would come to court and then not be able to get a trial. Often one case would settle, and one would fight. I probably settled rather more cases than I would have done if there had been fewer of them. But generally, once both sides were at court and ready for trial it would be apparent to the advocates how a case was likely to end, especially when they knew both each other and the Judge. A plaintiff obviously did not like to run the risk of getting nothing, and the insurer of a defendant would often be content to settle at a discount to what might be payable if the case was lost. The stresses involved in appearing for plaintiffs who might fail were far greater than when acting for a corporate defendant or insurer – professional litigants who were able to take a commercial view for themselves. The Bar is not a good career for those of an anxious disposition.

Each day was a tournament, often against the same opponents, who would become friends, or at least friendly. I enjoyed regular rivalry with Richard Maxwell in Nottingham and Lincoln, and Nicholas Worsley and several others in Birmingham. Maxwell often endeared himself to witnesses by slipping into their East Midland vernacular. It was rare for barristers to seek to take unfair advantage of each other, and almost all were scrupulous to reveal their authorities (relevant earlier judicial decisions) in advance, as was proper. I remember only once being ambushed by a barrister I knew quite well, with a case reported the week before.

During my thirties and early forties I was leading a satisfying professional existence: regular civilised combat with agreeable people, in pleasant parts of the country, conducted before familiar tribunals. I would drive to court, arrive early, have a bacon sandwich and a cup of black coffee at a handy café while glancing at the Times, change into a wing collar, bands and gown in the robing room, identify and talk to my opponent, my solicitor, and my client, maybe negotiate a little, and then go into court. Sometimes I won, sometimes I lost. Many of the cases had interesting aspects, often medical, requiring analysis by rival specialists, frequently people of considerable eminence. Over time one became quite knowledgeable about how the human body coped with injury and how it might repair itself, or be repaired. Industrial injury cases and motor vehicle accidents often called for an understanding of machinery, and engineering experts would be called by each side. These experts were often, when I first came to the Bar and for some considerable time thereafter, extremely partial to the side calling them. This used to provide amusing material for cross examination: 'Mr So and So, in all your 25 years as a professional witness have you ever been called on behalf of a plaintiff'? 'Oh yes, certainly'. 'How often'? 'Well, twice'. Subsequent reforms have almost eliminated this problem, emphasising experts' duty to the court.

I soon realised that there was some advantage to being 'London' counsel. You could appear anywhere on your circuit, or elsewhere, and while the local barristers' clerks would do their best to get their own cases advantageously listed, one was quite happily received by the local solicitors and barristers. But the local Bars tended to be local. For example, barristers from Nottingham very rarely appeared in Birmingham, and vice versa. This was even more evident when other circuits were involved. Sheffield (on the North Eastern Circuit) and Nottingham (on the Midland) are not far apart, but I never met anyone from the Sheffield bar in Nottingham, or indeed in Lincoln or Birmingham. Nor did Birmingham barristers get to Winchester much. People with chambers in London however were welcome everywhere without comment or criticism. Years before, there had been a tradition that a barrister going 'off circuit' would pay a 'fine' to the local bar mess at the place where he appeared, but this was dead by 1970.

By my early forties my pattern of life was well settled. In 1975 we had moved house from Pimlico to North Oxfordshire, from where, on the train from Bicester or Charlbury – the latter more comfortable but more expensive and less reliable – I could get to London in something significantly over an hour. That I did for conferences in chambers, or appearances at the Royal Courts of Justice. More usually I would drive to Birmingham (then possible in just over an hour) or Nottingham (further) or Winchester (much the same as Birmingham, but more attractive when you got there). Some days I would sit at my desk at home doing papers in the sunshine. I was earning reasonably, though but not at all spectacularly. Most evenings it would be necessary to work for three or four hours for the next day's trial. It was a stimulating and pleasant existence. Perhaps too pleasant. If you are content where you are you tend not to explore other avenues, notice shifting tides, or change when perhaps you should.

Chapter 7

Silk

There comes a time in the lives of many barristers when they wonder whether to apply for Silk, that is to try to become a Queen's Counsel, or QC – normally roughly 10% of the bar. There are various reasons to do this. Junior barristers have to draft pleadings, which are the documents in which each side states its case and indicates the extent to which it agrees or disagrees with the other. This task can become tedious, repetitive, and (though mine were concise to an extent no longer permitted) time consuming. Silks do not have to do this, so their time is freed to concentrate on writing opinions, preparing for court appearances or conducting substantial cases. Silks normally command higher fees than Juniors. They also enjoy some prestige as the cadre of England's finest advocates, suitable to be instructed in cases of great difficulty, value or importance. High Court Judges were commonly appointed from their ranks. But there is a potential downside. Clients may not be happy to employ you at a higher rate. You may not be thought of as good enough for the most important work and there is not much of it. The world of the Silk is extremely competitive. You may find that though you were busy as a junior, you have no practice as a Silk. And there is no going back.

I decided to have a go. In 1984 there were 85 Silks on my circuit, the Midland and Oxford. It was necessary to make application to the Lord Chancellor (whose office was abolished, without consultation, by Blair's Constitutional Reform Act 2005) on a very simple form, giving details of practice, income, and one's Head of Chambers. It was desirable to solicit some support from High Court Judges before whom you had appeared. This I duly did, writing or speaking to two or three. I awaited the outcome anxiously, but fairly confidently. After all, I thought of myself as better than some of my regular opponents, and so far as I could see I was as busy as most. I thought I was a respectably good lawyer too. It should be understood that a good lawyer is not necessarily a good advocate, and vice versa, but a Silk really needs to be both.

In those days the list of those who had been successful was announced just before Easter, and on 3rd April 1985 a letter arrived from Tom Legg, head of Judicial Appointments in the Lord Chancellors Department. 'I am sorry to tell you that the Lord Chancellor has not felt able to include your name among those to be recommended this year for appointment as Queen's Counsel'.

This was a bit depressing, though not as depressing as it is now when quite large sums of money have to be paid as an application fee, and still more should you succeed. But initial failure was not unusual, especially for people who had a general practice, not highly specialised. I was still young in legal terms. I carried on as before, taking care not to fall out with the High Court judges in front of whom I appeared, and occasionally, if I thought I had done well, soliciting their assistance as references. I tried to make the most of any Court of Appeal appearances, on the basis that the judges in that court were understood to be very influential when it came to the selection of Silks. I forgot that though to me appearances at that level were sometimes memorable, to the court they were simply part of an endless conveyor belt of well-conducted litigation. These judges, very busy indeed, were unlikely, months later, to recall a particular talent demonstrated before them.

At this time I also considered a move to different chambers, because as explained, my own were less than convivial and getting weaker. Changing chambers is commonplace now, and little remarked upon or criticised. It was not so in the late 80s, though the permafrost of convention that one generally did not move was beginning to thaw. There were several suitable sets of chambers where I knew a number of the members, had appeared against them, and where the atmosphere and prospects were better than where I was, but discussions were a very delicate business, and I rarely felt confident that it was a good idea to embark on them. Had any hint got back to my own chambers it would have been likely to create an even more unhappy atmosphere.

I applied for Silk twice more, and finally, in 1989, the year that the Berlin Wall came down, I was lucky. One of my referees had been especially helpful, I learned. This was Mr Justice Sheen, who had tried a case in which I appeared against Scott Baker QC, later Mr Justice Scott Baker. It was a fatal motor accident, in which an Aston Martin with an inexperienced driver managed to take off on a slip road from the M4 near Slough, fly over the central reservation and land on top of a Ford Fiesta. I was arguing that some of the blame attached to the condition of the road, maintained by the Highway Authority. I did not succeed, but the Judge, on a subsequent costs application, made some kind remarks about my conduct of the case, which I believe may have been repeated with persuasive force when my Silk application was under consideration. I was very fortunate, especially since I had tried to settle the case, and had I succeeded, would have been in no position to impress.

When the letter arrived indicating that I had been granted Silk I wandered off around our two small undulating fields, in tears of relief. I was 44, and this was a major landmark in my life. I had achieved something.

For a few days I had a feeling of elation. As I walked around the Temple I felt like a member of the elite, almost a minor god. This gratifying sensation was periodically deflated when people one bumped into failed to make any reference to my new status, or were indeed unaware of it. A few letters arrived from members of the Bar conveying congratulations. Others, less welcome, arrived from firms of solicitors for whom I had worked for years which said 'well done', but went on to add that, sadly, they would no longer be sending me work on account of my promotion. I bought a very satisfactory Silks coat from Ede and Ravenscroft, with neat shoulders, short tails and frogged buttonholes, worn with a long waistcoat. The cloth (now unavailable) was sturdy and such that you could fold and crush it into a small case, but it would come out uncreased and elegant. It was a garment of which I became very fond. Chambers gave me a dinner at the Garrick, and flattering speeches were made. But would I get any work?

It was very important to be on the best of terms with the junior bar, so that they might tell their solicitors that a particular case really called for a Leader, and that the person they would like instructed was Charles Harris. So I went about smiling in a wise and friendly – though perhaps uncharacteristic – fashion at anyone I might bump into. I am not much good at that sort of thing, but tried hard to be extra agreeable for some time. If a new silk does not get support from those within his own chambers it is very difficult to survive, let alone thrive. Here I was lucky, and two or three of the younger members encouraged their solicitors to use me, which was reassuring. I have known more than one person who has taken Silk and then sat proudly, then hopefully, then desperately at an emptying desk waiting for work which never came.

It was permissible for a new Silk to go on doing his existing cases for twelve months, so appearances in court did not simply dry up. Occasionally there was a hint of faintly increased respect or indulgence from the bench, and I had one case which, maturing satisfactorily, worked its way to the House of Lords. The facts were of modest general interest: it concerned the construction of safety regulations applicable in the Austin Rover car factory in Oxford, where a man had been overcome by fumes while working in a tank. Austin Rover had been prosecuted in the magistrate's court and convicted, we said wrongly. In those days there was a great deal of personal injury litigation concerned with accidents sustained at work, and many claims were based upon breaches of statutory duty. Very few got to the Lords. I was instructed by Anthony Henman, an Oxford solicitor who had skilfully built up a large practice and a substantial firm from small beginnings. We won in the Court of Appeal, but the Factory Inspectorate took the case to the House of Lords. Anthony was prepared to retain me despite my inexperience at this high altitude. He was a reassuring man to act for, for his demeanour never changed throughout the ups and downs of a case. (Just as he would remain inscrutable while watching his son Tim play tennis at Wimbledon). He was a most agreeable instructing solicitor, and was and has remained, a man of astonishing physical fitness, playing international hockey deep into his seventies.

I had been in the Lords once before, in 1979, led by Richard Rougier QC in a case concerning the sale of an old Reliant three-wheeler whose chassis collapsed, causing a collision in which a passenger was killed. We appeared for the defendant vendor before Lord Diplock, Viscount Dilhorne, and Lords Hailsham, Keith and Scarman. I did not have to say anything, and could watch with pleasure as these five eminent men argued with counsel and disputed with each other in a sustained and fascinating way – polite, but sharply incisive. We won, because the car had been sold 'as seen and with all its faults and without warranty'. But for my second appearance it was for me to address the court, not sit safely behind anyone else.

In October 2009 a new 'Supreme' Court was opened, opposite Parliament and next to Westminster Abbey. Until then England's top Court was the Judicial Committee of the House of Lords. This sat in a large Victorian-Gothic room, with its upper corners lost in shadow, off a parliamentary corridor, hundreds of yards and several levels from the robing room. Its judgments were delivered in the debating chamber, where advocates were placed in a small fenced-off reservation at one end. The whole building was highly atmospheric in a 19th century way. The law lords did not robe but sat in ordinary suits in a semi-circle. Advocates did not speak from their benches, reassuringly surrounded by their files and papers as in an ordinary court, but from a small central lectern which they took it in turns to occupy. There I stood, facing five of the most intelligent and formidable lawyers in the world. Five searchlights trained upon one person. But It was not that bad. Lord MacKay was presiding, was not fierce at all, and he chaired the other four very deftly. As we had won in the Court of Appeal, and they had read its judgment, and seemed to agree with it. I got a fairly gentle ride. It was however a remarkable experience, endeavouring to field a succession of thoughtful and penetrating questions without significant pause for thought. When finally Anthony Henman and I emerged into tepid sunshine on Parliament Square I felt that I was an advocate who might have a go at anything.

There was a fairly modest flow of cases of the kind I had always been accustomed to – fatal accidents of one sort or another, or, much worse, accidents which were not fatal but left someone gravely handicapped, either physically or mentally. I also had quite a few cases involving what was then known as medical negligence, but which is now called clinical negligence. Some of these were factually very grim– typically involving the incompetent delivery of a baby, which in consequence suffered severe brain damage, which might leave him or her unable to think, walk, talk or properly develop, and the parents condemned to a life of care and management which destroyed all normality both for them and for their other children. There was often evident a ghastly contrast between the lack of skilled attention at birth and the highly expert subsequent steps taken to sustain at all costs a life with no shred of quality or hope.

Occasionally I was offered something different. I was retained by the West Midlands police to defend a case brought against them by a large party of protesters, who had gone to someone's house with a view to demonstrating so violently that the police would feel constrained to arrest them. When they were arrested, they behaved badly in the police station, lied continuously, and then sued the police for wrongful arrest, and on other grounds. There were five plaintiffs, and a tremendous list of largely spurious allegations. It had been estimated that the case would last two or three months, at considerable public expense. The plaintiffs all pretended they had no assets, and they had been granted legal aid.

Much detective work had been done into the backgrounds of these people, discovering, for example that the most prominent plaintiff, who presented herself as a single lesbian without any possessions, had in fact married a foreigner, in order to facilitate his coming to England, and lived with him in a jointly-owned property of substantial value. The plaintiffs had given false names and addresses and divested themselves of all identifying belongings before their arrest. They pretended to be vegetarians to complicate their treatment at the police station. One Silk had done about four months' preparatory work, but then said he did not feel he could conduct it.

I went to a pre-trial conference in Birmingham attended by 27 people and spent several weeks preparing the case, and in particular perfecting cross examinations. In the end it settled at the door of the court. It would have been far better for my practice and my pocket to have fought it, as there was considerable press interest and a substantial 'refresher' (daily fee). I have always regretted the outcome of that litigation.

My innings as a Silk was short, and I often thought subsequently that I should not have gone on the bench when I did, as I shall in due course describe. It was some achievement to have become Queens Counsel and I should perhaps have stayed longer in that rank and tried to make more of it.

Chapter 8

Politics: the art of failure

After I had established myself on the bottom rung at the Bar, my mind turned increasingly to politics. I first became aware of elections as a small child, when our dining room became a 'committee room', stocked with piles of pamphlets, lists, envelopes and middle-aged people in rosette-embellished cardigans or blazers. Posters were put on trees and in windows, and placards thrust into hedges. Canvassers produced lists of those whom it was supposed would, might, or would not support the party. In our house the prevailing colour was blue, and I was told that our family were Conservatives, who were the most sensible and business-like. But it was also conceded that there was something to admire about 'Old Labour', many of whose supporters had jobs in my grandfather's works, and that Attlee was a very 'sound man', just as patriotic as Winston Churchill. It was also hinted to me, when I asked, that the Queen might be a Conservative, but she would never tell anyone. I asked what would happen if she came to lunch, and my mother said that that we would eat in the dining room and probably have roast chicken. I later gathered that my father was chairman of the local constituency association.

I had no particular interest in politics until one autumn term at Repton when George Brown came to the school to speak. He was at the time MP for Belper, and Deputy Leader of the Labour Party. He was also a governor of the school. Ebullient, fast talking and happy to make jokes at the expense of the Headmaster, he went down well. I later learned that he was unpleasant to his wife and often drunk, but he was attractive to schoolboys. He talked about foreign affairs (and indeed became Foreign Secretary in 1966). The expression 'tired and emotional' was coined to apply to him by *Private Eye*, but he was mildly inspirational to many who heard him that afternoon, and seemed wide awake. He made politics sound fun.

At Birmingham University I found a large and thriving Young Socialist organisation which dominated the Students' Union, and a tiny Conservative group. I wrote scornful articles about the white heat of Harold Wilson's technology for the student newspaper, *Redbrick*. I attended political meetings, and went to see Alec Douglas Home at a 1964 general election rally at the great pseudo-classical temple which is Birmingham's Town Hall. Gaunt in grey tweed, he was roared at furiously by a large and inflamed crowd. He did not flinch from this wall of vituperation, but was, as a civilised and courteous man, at the end of thirteen years of conservative rule, clearly rather shocked. Even as an anonymous spectator I was a little frightened. Most of those shouting had not the faintest intention of giving him a hearing and their only desire was to drive him unheard from the hall.

It was around this time that I came to the conclusion that I believed in free speech, individual responsibility, low taxation, strong defence, and light touch government under the rule of law. This did not preclude looking after people who could not care for themselves. But I did not see why the industrious should subsidise the lazy or improvident. So I was a Conservative. Whether I would have thought the same if I had emerged from a less comfortable background I do not know. I might have felt the same with greater conviction.

Extreme and intimidatory reluctance to listen, or engage in debate, struck me then as it does now as a powerful indictment of those responsible. Such people I felt, neither deserve democracy and free speech nor appear to believe in them. There have been many recent outbreaks of this kind of violent intolerance in American and English universities, called ungrammatically 'no platforming', and often the authorities swiftly give way with craven weakness, although the very essence of a university is of course the analysis of conflicting ideas. An allied phenomenon is that the English come in for continuous criticism over slavery – which they abolished - whereas Muslim Arab slavers, and indeed Danes (who took large numbers of British slaves for several centuries) are never impugned at all.

One well-known, if controversial, politician did brave the Birmingham Students' Union with success. This was Enoch Powell, then MP for Wolverhampton, whose early aim in life had been to become Viceroy of India (several of whose languages he could speak). He came to a meeting so over-attended that students virtually fought to get in, though determined not to hear what he had to say. His opponents were loud and semi-organised. When Powell stood up they bayed and yelled and chanted. He stood quite still, looked implacable, and slightly narrowed his eyes. His jaw twitched occasionally beneath his moustache. He did not attempt to say anything at all until, after what must have been three or four minutes, there was a slight lull. After all, it is absurd even for a mob to try to shout down someone who is not actually speaking. But then he did start to speak, at first in a low and deliberate manner, never pausing to concede an interruption. Then, with a firm mesmeric rhythm, a flat Black Country accent and rising volume, he began to pound out point after point with relentless intensity in a steady cadence, all in perfectly-formed sentences. The audience, for such it had become, fell silent, cowed by his fluency and force of character. Despite themselves they listened, as, without notes, he dissected their incoherent beliefs, illogical assertions and myopic trains of thought. Then he stopped. There was utter silence and, after a few stunned moments, some weak applause. It was beyond extraordinary.

Thirty years later, when I was sitting as a Recorder at Warwick, I went to his funeral at St Mary's Church, which was close to the Assize Court. The service, in moving traditional language, full of dignity and history, recorded his achievements as classical scholar, soldier (he rose from Private to Brigadier), philosopher, poet, orator and Member of Parliament. His coffin was carried by soldiers of his old regiment. He was a man not always justly maligned.

When I left University I went to London to read for the Bar, and divided my time between lectures at the Council of Legal Education in Gray's Inn and the tranquil library of the Inner Temple, now about to be mutilated to provide space for a little student teaching facility in place of its dignified and sun-blessed gallery. I also joined the Bow Group, an association of ambitious young Conservatives, then chaired by Christopher Bland, and later by such personalities as Norman Lamont and Michael Howard. I got to know Michael quite well through lunching with him regularly at the Inner Temple. (He once asked me whether it was prudent to become someone's fourth husband. Since the person he was contemplating was the delightful Sandra Paul, the answer in his case was clearly yes.)

The Bow Group was an organisation which said it was interested in policy, but was really designed to give a platform and publicity to would-be MPs who wished to come to the attention of actual MPs who had influence over candidate selection. It produced pamphlets and invited speakers to meetings. It took itself seriously, and was much more polished and stimulating than anything I had come across in the Midlands. I sat on its membership, home affairs and political committees, and wrote pamphlets about privacy and the reform of company law which almost nobody read. Insofar as I developed any political philosophy it was that government should be as unobtrusive as possible, but disposed and able to intervene to cope with injustice and emergency.

One curious thing was that almost all these young Bow Group sophisticates declared themselves devoted fans of a football team. I once trailed to Molyneux with Howard and Lamont to watch a match between Liverpool – Howard was adopted for a Merseyside seat – and

Wolves, which was my team because I had been to prep school near Wolverhampton, where Stan Cullis, the then famous Wolves manager, had sent his son. I still turn to the sports pages to see how Wolves are getting on, but whereas in the 50s and 60s it was a top European side and I knew the names of many of the players – notably the formidable half backs Wright, Flowers and Slater – now I could not name a single member of the team, which I believe is largely Portuguese.

I wrote an article on political language for *Crossbow*, which the editor, Simon Jenkins, was kind enough to publish. I became a member of the Chelsea and Westminster Conservative Association, and addressed it. I also embarked on a pamphlet on the subject of candidate selection. In order to gather material I wrote to a dozen front bench Tory MPs. Eleven did not reply. The twelfth, Willie Whitelaw, did. He was I think Chief Whip at the time, and by far the busiest of them all. But he gave me 40 minutes in his room at the House of Commons, treated me kindly, talked quite revealingly and left me feeling mildly important and extremely grateful.

In my early twenties I had begun to think that, along with being a barrister, I might become an MP. I had no very detailed idea of what this might involve, but had read a lot of C19 political biography. My favourites were Melbourne, Palmerston, Disraeli and Salisbury. These men were untroubled by their constituencies (if they had them), seemed to lead attractive lives making interesting decisions and well-turned speeches, and spent much of their time in agreeable country houses. It had not perhaps come fully home to me that things had moved on a bit by the mid-1960s – though not as far as they have now, when most MPs seem to regard themselves primarily as constituency ombudsmen or social workers, rather than as formulators of law and policy, which is their proper constitutional role.

To become a candidate it was necessary to get on the Central Office list. This, over the years, has become increasingly rigorously run, but when I first applied it was not an unduly difficult process, requiring only the production of a modest CV and a short friendly interview at Smith Square with the MP in charge of candidates. As I was fairly articulate, reasonably turned out and could say that I had 'campaigned' in various general elections in which I had done a few hours canvassing, I was put on the list after no very long delay. It is possible that my father had contacted Peter Thorneycroft, then influential at Central Office, whom he knew.

I began to apply for seats, starting optimistically with Melton Mowbray. I was scarcely ever given an interview, and it was soon explained to me that I was expected to fight at least one hopeless seat before being a serious prospect for somewhere safe. Desirable too would be to have more political experience.

In 1970 Jim Prior (Later Lord Prior), who represented Lowestoft in Suffolk, agreed to take me as a 'personal assistant' (affording help for which he had no need, but I was engaged to his secretary, of whom he was fond) for the general election campaign of that year. He was a large man with a fine curved nose, thick silver hair and excellent eyesight; relaxed, pleasant and popular – even with those who would not vote for him. Shrewder than he cared to appear, and to the left of the party's centre, he lived in a comfortable farmhouse surrounded by a moat with swans (later to be killed by otters). I went with him round such shopping centres as there were in rural Suffolk, small factories and fish jetties. He made short impromptu speeches, generally fairly humorous, and knew a lot of people by name. There were evening meetings in places like the Rifle Hall at Halesworth, which I would address before he arrived. Sometimes I went canvassing alone, and on one occasion made the classic mistake of accepting an invitation to go into a house. If you do this, you lose a lot of time. But the occupant of a narrow terrace house in a small seaside town was insistent. He showed me into his front room. Every vertical surface, and the ceiling, was covered in sea shells; of scores of kinds, applied in complex and iridescent patterns. He had scallops and conches, whelks and periwinkles, limpets and sea urchins. These, once focused upon within the mass, I recognised; but he had incorporated much else besides, which he explained: solzons and speckled alphabet cones, like miniature amphorae; leopard spotted junonia and, finest of all and woven into a delicate cornice, dozens of basket stars, whose tendrils were like lace embroidery, delicate as the extremities of a Bernini sculpture. He had made a large-scale work of quaint but definite beauty, if with a faint whiff of stale sea. It had taken seven years to create this domestic grotto, and it was not, he felt, wholly finished, though his wife would not let him start upon another room. He was a retired storekeeper of modest means and background, but could have been a remarkable artist or fashionable interior decorator.

The election went well from a Conservative point of view, and to general surprise Edward Heath became Prime Minister. After a year or two I started to concentrate upon finding a hopeless seat. In this quest the chances were much better. While a hundred or more would apply for a safe seat, it might be only half a dozen for a hopeless one. I also joined the Central Office speaker's panel, and accepted engagements wherever they arose, from Wales to East Anglia. These could be quite gratifying, because the audiences were grateful that I had come so far. They generally got a decent speech, or one rather better than they were used to, and there was no strain such as was involved when trying to be chosen as a candidate.

There is a lot of satisfaction to be had from the composition and delivery of a well-turned and novel speech, compounded when the audience is appreciative. On the other hand, a speech as a piece of art is an utterly ephemeral thing, which can never be precisely reproduced. Perhaps not quite as bad as the productions of a cook, which are destroyed at their moment of perfection and without the maker even seeing the appreciation of those who enjoy them; but they are things of the moment, moving or effective perhaps, but then gone with the air which carried them. By contrast a book remains a book, and a building a building. A permanent reputation is simpler to achieve for authors and architects than it is for orators.

I applied to a number of hopeless seats and some marginals, and optimistically put my hat in the ring for Powell's seat in Wolverhampton South West in February 1974 after he had abruptly left the party (though I did not travel there first class from Euston, as was reported by the Times). Most associations wrote polite letters.

But one, Portsmouth North, sent out a peremptory telegram, on 27 May 1974, demanding a response within 24 hours. Many were in unattractive places, or very distant.

In due course Central Office indicated that a constituency on the border of South Yorkshire and Derbyshire, near Sheffield, was seeking a candidate. This was Penistone, a place of which I had never heard. It was thought important when applying to a constituency to be able to establish some local connection. The seat in question was close to the Peak District, which I knew from CCF and climbing activity, and where my father in law had taken me grouse shooting (though this would need to be kept secret). I could legitimately contend that I had some legal practice in Nottingham, some 40 miles to the South and so almost local, and I had been educated in neighbouring Derbyshire. I applied. I think there were four applicants, none local. In turn we made short speeches in an upper room of the Rose and Crown Hotel to a selection committee of about ten, who sat with folded arms at folding tables arranged in a horseshoe. I was not bad at that, writing it out carefully, more or less memorising it, and then speaking apparently extempore without notes. This I found effective, but it is laborious and memory dependent. I did it for many years until, during a wedding speech for my god daughter Camilla, when I had paused for a moment of laughter, I realised that I had simply no idea what the next paragraph was. I remained silent, and fortunately the laughter continued. Just as I began to feel that I would have to extemporise, the text returned to my mind. Since then I have always had some notes in my pocket.

My remarks went down well in the Rose and Crown, and having weathered a few questions of the 'will your wife help?' kind, I was duly chosen. But there was no general election in the immediate offing, so I had to 'nurse' the constituency. I had the local papers posted to London, but more demandingly, I began to drive there and back regularly. Quite often I almost fell asleep at the wheel of my car, a Peugeot 504, which was a soft- riding, comfortable and slightly soporific vehicle. My head would sometimes jerk upright at the sound of the car thumping along the studs at the edge of the carriageway, and I would startle to a stirring scene of vivid industrial history. When approaching Sheffield along the M1 at dusk, the sky would be lit up by scores of flames. If you squinted they resembled, I fancied, the campfires of a huge mediaeval army. If you did not, it rather looked as though the city had been recently lightly bombed. More careful scrutiny revealed a late manifestation of England's metal production industry – gantries, sheds and chimneys outlined in the flames of furnace and of forge.

Past this display I drove on to Penistone, to attend a wine and cheese party or a branch meeting. I would be introduced to a dozen or so pleasant Yorkshire people whose names I would instantly forget, though they did not forget mine. I would then deliver a short and elegant speech, which they would instantly forget. I would be offered a sandwich and a drink. And then it was time to drive back 175 miles to London to be prepared for court the next day. This was of course a ridiculous and rather dangerous regime.

Central Office arranged a candidates' visit to the EU Headquarters at the Berlaymont in July. We were put up free of charge, fed relentlessly, and had discussions with a variety of eurocrats and special advisors. All were fluent in thought and expression (in English) but reluctant to get involved in any discussions which might question the premise of their beliefs. We were taken to NATO headquarters, where conversation was more robust. But undoubtedly the most amusing time was spent with Sir Christopher Soames, the first British Vice President of the Commission. Our Ambassador in Paris 1968-72, he was a hefty man, engaging, charming, and very outspoken. We were given substantial quantities of white wine with which to lubricate our consideration of his remarks. He referred to this as 'Brussels weasel piss', which put us off a little, but did not lessen the enthusiasm of the staff dispensing it.

On 10th August 1974 I attended a candidates' conference, addressed by a galaxy of top party figures: Willie Whitelaw, Peter Walker, Robert Carr, Jim Prior, Margaret Thatcher and Edward Heath. I suppose it was felt that this exposure to serious political talent would by some process of osmosis invest us with the zest and skill needed to win an election or run the country.

In October 1974 a general election was called. I felt my moment had come, and I would challenge my socialist opponent in Penistone, a Mr Mandelson, to a grand debate in which my eloquence would expose and devastate him. I wrote an election address for public distribution. It was fetchingly illustrated with a photograph of my wife wearing a large hat. Ideal for a mining area. My slogan and theme was 'Common sense for the common good'. Mandelson however, very left wing and of Polish/ Jewish extraction, was not interested in debating. In one sense he had a rather C19 attitude, only coming once to the constituency, for three days, during the three-week campaign. He made one speech, calling for free TV licences for old age pensioners – a proposal ecstatically received – and then took the train back to London. He knew just what he was doing.

I, on the other hand, went out daily, canvassing, 'meeting people' by accosting them in the streets, loud hailing from the back of an old Land Rover, and speaking at any available location every evening. My biggest audience was about fifty, in a disused cinema, but usually it was up to a dozen. Each speech was specially prepared, and they were well received by a friendly local press. The Liberals were rude and unfriendly, while the Labour people were perfectly pleasant and did nothing at all. They did not need to. Most of the people I met were amiable in a gruffly adversarial way – an approach typical in Yorkshire and one of which the inhabitants were, and still are, rather proud. Guy Hungerford, well equipped from the world of advertising, came up to Yorkshire to help. Polished and confident, he went into a pub one afternoon and bravely announced that he was canvassing for Charles Harris, the Conservative candidate who was hoping for their support. The bar fell silent, tankards were put down. One man spoke: 'Arris, I'd laike to put im dahn a man'ole...' he paused for effect, 'and then stand ont cuvver'. He then bought Guy a drink, and they discussed racing at Pontefract.

I went down a pit, clad photogenically in a helmet and dungarees. After what seemed a descent of thousands of feet in a vestigial lift called a cage, we then walked horizontally for perhaps half a mile. One of the miners turned, grinned, and said 'we've got yer where we want yer now, ant we?' But somehow I believed that if the props started to give way he would do his utmost to save me.

The mine was interesting because I had always vaguely imagined that a coal face was a wall at the end of a tunnel. However, the face was in fact the distance between the ends of two parallel tunnels between which a mechanical cutter ran back and forth, at right angles to both. The pit I visited had sufficient light and reasonable headroom (I am 5 ft 9in, the same height as was the Duke of Wellington and the explorer Robert Falcon Scott). But some seams I gathered were only 4ft high. As a working environment for 30 or 40 years a pit, however modern, did not seem an attractive place, so it was remarkable how attached to their employment these miners were. Cheerful and articulate on the whole, they could not explain their loyalty to their leader, Arthur Scargill, a hypocritical ranting man, who was soon to lead them to destruction in an acrimonious war with Margaret Thatcher, and who for many years occupied a luxury flat in the Barbican at his union's expense.

A lot of time and little money was spent designing, printing and putting up posters. I doubt if large pictures of a candidate stuck in prominent places urging people to 'Vote Harris, for your Future' persuaded many people to vote in my favour. But a good show of posters certainly encouraged me and my supporters.

My parents came up for a day to see how I was getting on. I do not think they felt that the organisation and canvassing arrangements matched those which they were used to at home, and they were unconvinced that I was unlikely to poll very highly. But I enjoyed giving them lunch at the Spencer's Arms in Cawthorne, showing them round 'my' constituency and seeing them get on well with such supporters as they met. Perhaps the one I chimed with most was Richard Marsden, a local industrialist. He was amusing, practical, and most helpful, and we were to exchange Christmas cards for over two decades.

Election day was less exciting than expected. Carol and I drove lethargically around the polling stations and the party committee rooms. Nobody seemed very optimistic. We were anxious lest the Liberals should beat us, which they had been desperately keen to do.

Eventually it was time to go to the City Hall in Sheffield, where we hung about for hours watching the counting going on for several of the local constituencies. At last the result was announced: John Mandelson, Labour: 27,146; Charles Harris, Conservative: 12,011; David Chadwick, Liberal: 10,900. Labour majority 15,135. 24% of the vote had been cast for me. It could certainly have been worse. I drove away from Penistone for the last time with a feeling of relief and mild elation.

Everyone should stand for Parliament at least once. It is an experience which teaches very quickly how little power to influence any individual has. You might talk briefly to 100 people a day for three weeks, but that only amounts to some two thousand electors, most of whom will vote as they always have. The undecideds are just as likely to take against you as to like you. Those who do like you may not vote for you. Favourable newspaper or radio coverage will not get you far in a constituency such as Penistone. In those days there were no social media. However, the campaign did take me to places I would otherwise never have seen, especially high up in blocks of grim municipal flats. There I found a mother with three small children, each by a different father, living on benefits. Her grubby flat contained little food, no books, and no husband. No doubt she would soon be impregnated again by some wandering inseminator, and her situation grow yet more desperate. There are no medals for the kind of valour which made her continue the hopeless struggle to make a home for her children.

Experience in the North, however fruitless, had not put me off politics. I spoke in Swansea West on Valentine's day 1975, and to the women of East Suffolk at Kesgrave on 6th March. I was back on a revised candidates list in May 1975, and a year or so later joined the European Movements speakers' panel (the premises and beliefs of which I have now come wholly to oppose). On 1st September 1977 I wrote expressing some pro-Common Market views to *The Times* and received a very detailed letter from our local MP Neil Marten, a member of the House of Commons scrutiny committee, which looked at EU proposals. He observed: 'it is quite clear that a highly centralised policy is being built up in Brussels which more and more is beginning to affect the lives of people in every country', and that it would take power from the UK Parliament. He was quite correct, but this was not widely appreciated at the time.

I had got back on the candidates' list after a competitive selection weekend in an hotel near Maidenhead. This was taken quite seriously by some of the applicants, less so by others. I was put into an entertaining group invigilated by Christopher Soames – son of the Ambassador – who, large and jovial, like a friendly well-dressed hippo, led discussions amongst the aspirants. The idea, I think, was to see who might show qualities of fluency, confidence and leadership. It did not suit everyone. I asked one woman who had made much of her travelling experience in Borneo what the natives did with their dead. She went ashen, had no idea, and could not answer. Her confidence was gone. I survived this modest ordeal, and back on the list, was now keen seriously to seek a safe seat.

The first attempt was at Banbury, where Neil Marten was retiring and near which Carol and I had lived since 1975. Being local, I was interviewed, and reached the final with two others. On that occasion I performed very badly, speaking about national and world politics, not matters of local concern. My views about the future of our nation, or indeed Western civilisation, were of little interest to the selection committee, who were thinking more about local housing development, and the fate of a small hospital on the outskirts of town. I recall speaking for a while about afforestation. This was an error. I came second, or, possibly third, it was not quite clear. It was a badly wasted chance.

Thereafter I applied to a wide variety of places, to a few of which I was invited for interview: like Bristol, where I had an informative conversation about garden design with Arabella Lennox – Boyd, whose husband was seeking the seat; Bath, to which I wore a dapper three-piece Irish tweed suit, probably not the best choice; Buckingham, where I got further than Leon Brittan; and Falmouth. My journey to the latter was unusual. A train was supposed to go from Oxford, but when I arrived at the station I was told it had been cancelled. Furious,

I found the stationmaster – a feat which would be impossible today. I described the urgency. He sucked on a pencil, looked at a timetable, and said 'If you can get to Newbury in 25 minutes, I'll have the train for Cornwall stopped' – something which would never be done in this century. I raced off down the A34. For some years now this highway has been a sad coagulation of congestion, road works and accidents, after which the police always seem keen to shut the road or parts of it for as long as possible. Then, it was a fast dual-carriageway and by sometimes exceeding 100 mph, I got to Newbury Station in time to see an impressive express train change tracks and come to rest just for me. On I jumped. Triumph. But there were no seats. The express had picked me up, but could not accommodate me. I trudged up and down the corridors for 15 minutes and then had to prop myself against a door until we reached Taunton. I was not selected.

That was one of my best experiences with the railways. Another concerned sandwiches. During the seventies and eighties many stations had small cafés of the *Brief Encounter* kind, where the staff made sandwiches. I like egg and tomato, which I always asked for, and sometimes got. But at Bicester Station, which I used to go to London, the attendant was prepared to make egg sandwiches, or tomato sandwiches, but not egg and tomato sandwiches. She said she would not know what to charge. I said price was not critical. She was adamant. So, as a busy barrister having time on my hands, I wrote to the Area Catering Manager. Some time went by and then a letter arrived, for me to show at station buffets, requiring the staff in them 'to provide the passenger bearing this letter with egg and tomato sandwiches, so long as both ingredients are to hand'. This remarkable passport to joy remained efficacious for about five years.

Still I had no constituency. On 12 August 1983 I was interviewed at Eye in Suffolk, an attractive rural backwater, but not chosen. Then a better opportunity arose. My wife came from South Norfolk. She had many relatives in the area, and one was John Alston, who amongst other things was President of the SW Norfolk Conservative Association and owner of an attractive, slightly Strawberry Hill-Gothic property called Bestthorpe Hall. A candidate was needed. The seat covered a large territory replete with grand houses and large estates, centred upon Swaffham. I put my name forward, and about 150 others did too, including some well-known local people. Sam Roberts, a young barrister and local gentleman whose mother occupied a family estate, and whose father, no longer alive, had been a Sheffield MP, was one. Another was a genial agricultural journalist called Chamberlain, and a third was a Norwich schoolmistress called Gillian Shephard.

The list was whittled down in some way to about 25, who were asked to a drinks party at which the selection committee might meet, look at, talk to and compare the various hopefuls. I found these affairs, of which by then I had some experience, to be awkward. It was necessary to try to exude a little charisma, and simultaneously to display, or simulate, interest, charm, enthusiasm, wisdom and reliability. It was vital to remember people's names, which I found impossible. From this process emerged a short list of three: Roberts, Chamberlain, and me. We went forward to the final, a performance before a selection committee of about 40, requiring a speech and responses to questions. The journalist, a heavy convivial type, would probably have done well in a saloon bar, but was eliminated. Roberts, although both local and a barrister, may have been a somewhat diffident speaker. By a small margin, I was chosen.

I felt that this was very satisfactory. I was approaching 40, doing quite well at the Bar, and now able to join the ambitious and dynamic Bow Groupers in Parliament. I had made it. The adoption meeting, which I understood to be a formality, as they normally are, was set for three weeks ahead, on 21st May in Swaffham. I went home to prepare.

By now we had been living in North Oxfordshire for nearly ten years, but I had told the selection committee I would get a house in Norfolk, so I began reluctant steps to put our house on the market. Quicker than vultures after a kill, people from Savills, Knight Frank and other leading agents descended on our house to press their qualifications to dispose of it. I went to London to meet the sitting MP, Paul Hawkins. He had held office, briefly, as an assistant whip and something called Vice

Chamberlain of the Household, and was an ex-auctioneer and county councillor. He had a tiny cubicle-office in the Houses of Parliament. Although polite, he was certainly not friendly, welcoming, or in the least encouraging. I should have become suspicious.

On the appointed day I drove from Birmingham, where I was conducting a case, to Swaffham. It was a tedious three-hour cross-country journey. There I found the town hall packed to the rafters, almost Pickwickian, with a surprisingly large number of people, presumably members of the local association. I was introduced briefly though not effusively by the chairman, and then spoke. The speech was quite good, though not my best. But then I had nobody to compete with.

I was asked to retire for a few minutes while the vote was taken. I waited with my wife and mother in law in an ante-room. Time went by. After about an hour and a half the chairman appeared, to announce without much embarrassment or apology that it had been decided not to adopt me after all. 'You are not a local candidate, you see.' I was given no opportunity to speak to the audience about the fairness or propriety of this. I went straight back to my case in Birmingham.

It was never entirely clear to me why this happened. I suspected, and was subsequently told, that Lady Roberts, determined and powerful locally, had packed the meeting in the hope that if I was not adopted, her son would be. A Norfolk lady who knew her told me recently that this would have been quite in character. Jeremy Bagge, a well-known local figure and sometime Sheriff, had risen at the meeting to suggest that the candidate must be local, but he had not been gentlemanly enough to notify me of his intention in advance. I have never understood why the committee ever listed me (or many others) for interview at all if it was thought essential to choose a local person, nor why the chairman did not point this out at the selection meeting. Furthermore, both the agent and the chairman, one Richard Johnston, must have known of the opposition, but gave me no intimation of it, nor any opportunity to address whatever objection there was. I suspect that many at the meeting, if asked whether this was fair, would have felt that it was not. I had many letters expressing both sympathy and incredulity, and a pleasant letter from Sam Roberts. Central Office was not interested in getting to the bottom of things. Cross-Bencher in the Daily Express said that the constituency had 'ratted on its candidate', which seemed pretty accurate.

In the event, however, Sam Roberts was not led to the podium, and the whole process was started again. This time Gillian Shephard was short listed, selected and duly adopted (although Bagge did not like female MPs either). In 1987 she was returned with a majority of over 20,000, and rose to be a Cabinet Minister. In 2005 she was made Baroness Shephard of Northwold. Might any of this, I have sometimes wondered, have happened to me?

South West Norfolk was the end of my interest in becoming an MP. If people in a traditional country constituency behaved like this, what must it be like in Westminster, thickly populated by ruthless professionals? Would I, anyway, have got anywhere once there? Would I have been able to remember the names of those I met, tolerate the tedium of low-level political events, deal with constituents' complaints and anxieties, impress those responsible for promotion, and would I have been lucky enough to have been made a Minister? In any case, all prospects would have come to an abrupt end in 1997 with the election of Blair's first Labour government, leaving me, aged 52, in an opposition party for well over a decade. Such a position is one of deep insignificance, and utterly frustrating in what should be the prime of one's career. So in the end the outcome of that meeting in Swaffham may not have been a bad one.

I have often thought it strange that while I and many of my contemporaries and friends wanted to go into politics, fewer of my children's generation seem to. Hugh and Kate both went to Oxford, and most weekends they used to appear at home with groups of hungry undergraduates. They would all eat voraciously, and argue agreeably and impressively. They were charming, highly intelligent and well educated, but seemed to regard politics as something like the weather – a background to life which might be good or bad, but about which they could do nothing. Roger, my elder son, has a well-informed interest, but not as a participant. Hugh, now a senior civil servant, regards it as better to advise ministers than to be one.

In 2001 David Cameron became our local MP. It was fascinating to watch the skill with which he operated in Witney. When he began, he was promising that Britain 'ought to have its fishing back', that the CAP needed 'drastic modification' and generally how sceptical he was about the EU. Many agreed with the formulation in his Bloomberg speech in 2013. Yet elegantly, effortlessly and charmingly as he managed his constituency appearances, as time went by and we watched the charade of renegotiation, a corrosive, let-down feeling began to seep through the association. His final position on Europe was seen as pitiful and unbecoming. My son Hugh worked as a civil servant in No 10, and doubtless for that reason Cameron was always pleasant to me. I once approached him at a party, full of annoyance about his scrapping our fleet air-arm Harriers. He saw me coming. 'Charles,' he said, smiling, at a range of about ten feet, 'very good to see you'. My irritation swiftly melted into an ingratiating grin at this personal greeting from a friendly young Prime Minister. I met him again at a constituency gathering in Lord Chadlington's garden shortly before the referendum and asked whether it would not be a fine feeling to go to Buckingham Palace and say 'Ma'am, you have your country back'. He gave me a curious and unhappy smile, and said that would be a pleasure he was prepared to forgo. Cameron was a man with an almost feline instinct for politics, and considerable style. He was friendly, approachable, deft and fluent, but his downfall was sudden and dismal, a fine example of Enoch Powell's often cited assertion that all political careers end in failure. Certainly mine did.

Judges of course have to be non-political, and I may have stretched that slightly in May 2016 when I chaired a meeting in the Oxford Town Hall, addressed by David Owen and Michael Forsyth, upon the merits of leaving Europe. The event, not properly advertised and thus not as fully attended as it might have been, was a great success in terms of its reception of the speaker's arguments. Nobody in the hall had the slightest inkling of the disaster which Theresa May was to make of the necessary steps to achieve independence. No senior legal figure rang to tick me off or call for my resignation.

Chapter 9

Where to live

Where you live, and in what sort of building, greatly affects the life you lead and the frame of mind in which you lead it. In my case not just mood but sense of identity is heavily influenced by domestic and indeed professional surroundings. Children have no option but to be where they are. But sooner or later – at least in a life of modest success – there generally comes real choice, and this will be important. It must be hard to achieve tranquillity and stability, or to appreciate beauty, if you have never experienced these qualities in your surroundings.

I was born, and lived until the age of 13, in an undistinguished Edwardian four-bedroomed, brick house. A large tiled porch protected its front door (which nobody used because it was on the other side of the house to the drive). It had an extensive rural view down sloping fields to the south west. There was a small kitchen, with a Rayburn stove which ran on coke and needed frequent attention. We ate in the breakfast room. The dining room, with its circular gateleg oak table, was rarely used. The sitting room had at one end a substantial fireplace made of little reddish-amber bricks with two flat hobs that you could sit on – a good place to be on a winter evening, for the house had no central heating. At the other end was my father's bureau desk. My bedroom had a high windowsill and a view into a big crab-apple tree, just too far away to climb to. Outside, a barn-like building was divided between a large wood store, with a hole in its roof through which I could scramble, and a garage, where my father kept his car – when I was small it was normally a Ford Zephyr or Zodiac – while my mother's, for a time a Morris Oxford, was left outside. A path of paving stones, good for tricycles and bicycles, connected our property to that of my grandfather next door.

After he died my parents decided to move. They presumably wanted somewhere larger and more rural. Many houses were inspected, and I remember being taken to a mansion called Mathon Lodge on a hillside in Malvern which they were considering. It seemed to my sister and me to be immense and had very distant views, but it would have been some way from our parents' circle of friends, not to mention ours. In the end they found an attractive secluded house, about 8000 square feet, of old mellow brick, on the Worcestershire/Staffordshire border. It stood on a slight eminence in about ten acres and was called Heathlands, perhaps because the ground was sandy and grew broom and bracken. There was a walled kitchen garden of about an acre, a decayed greenhouse and a gardener who enjoyed racing pigeons and a Dutch wife. The house lay between the villages of Kinver and Enville. My sister and I had been taken for a preliminary look. Its owner, a local industrialist with a factory at Stourbridge (whose son was to purchase it after my mother died), had the skins of zebra and lion on the floor in the hall, which I found exciting. There was a big cellar, approached through a trapdoor in the hall floor, also exciting, and a small tower with a room fitted out like the cabin of a ship, with bunks and a mock porthole. I was keen on occupying that, but my father stripped out the nautical fittings and adopted it as his study. He installed a safe in which he kept his service revolver. I was given two small rooms knocked together above the kitchen, with access via a steep back stair, and a view over the yard towards the gardener's cottage, the garages and kitchen garden. I made several bookcases out of discarded drawers turned on end, into which I fitted shelves, and quickly filled them. I liked this accommodation, which was very private. I had a new radio, on which I listened to the Light Programme, and a gramophone on which to play records by Françoise Hardy, Kenny Ball, Lonnie Donegan, John Hanson and Harry Secombe, whose song 'If I ruled the world' I rather liked. It evoked happy autocracy.

Heathlands was a relaxed and comfortable house, large enough for entertaining, though my parents did less of that than might have been expected, possibly because my mother suffered badly from migraines and often spent days in bed. It had a wing in which my grandfather's companion came to live, with her own sitting room and kitchen. There was also a 1930s billiard room extension, about 40 feet long, which made an excellent playroom and games room. One end was slightly raised, forming a low stage. Here I made scores of Airfix and Revell plastic models, mostly of English or American aeroplanes. These were more satisfying than the balsa kits I had constructed at prep school, which had needed careful, intricate and quite skilful work to cut and glue the framework struts, cover them with thin translucent paper and paint the result with strong smelling 'dope'. Some of those machines could fly, powered either by a wound-up elastic band or a tiny, waspish engine running on methylated spirits. But anything that flew would quickly crash, invariably with severe damage to the fragile balsa. The plastic planes did not suffer the same fate but sat in satisfying squadrons on the cork floor awaiting hand-held sorties, or were hung by cotton thread at dramatic angles. I also extensively deployed a large collection of model soldiers.

There was a circular drive, excellent for a go-kart which I was given. Called an Aerocart, it was powered by a 98cc Villiers two-stroke engine with a three-speed gearbox. My father assembled it from a set of parts sent from Bromyard in Herefordshire. I suppose it could only go at about 30 mph, but as one sat three inches from the ground, and there was no bodywork apart from the tubes of its frame, the sensation of speed was exhilarating. The engine howled and crackled most agreeably. I learned to slide and spin the kart on the gravelled area on front of the house, experience I felt came in handy later when driving cars on snow. It probably simply made me reckless.

The circular drive surrounded a small field or paddock, occupied by a quartet of fierce geese, which only my mother was prepared to catch, seizing their serpentine necks as they hissed in minatory hostility. The gardener observed helpfully, from a distance, that a blow from a wing could break an arm. I thought this only applied to swans. Later my mother obtained a donkey, called Tarka, to live in the same field and graze it. The geese did not take to this new tenant, and sometimes pecked him. Though normally gentle, he would then lash out with his rear hooves, and once killed one of his anserine tormentors in this way. It must have given him considerable satisfaction. I thought perhaps that we could eat the dead goose, but my mother said it was far too old. The gardener buried it, or said he did.

I became quite attached to that house; its large, sunny, south-facing wooden floored hall with a baronial stone fireplace and capacious sofas was a friendly room. It opened to a stone terrace with views over a small valley (ours) towards rising farmland and woods. There was a substantial rockery with an artificial stream and pools, and a decayed tennis court which my father refused to repair because he said nobody would play on it. My mother said that as it was nobody could play on it. I did some of the mowing, on a ride-on machine which was prone to shed its driving belts. When it did, it required the combined efforts of my father, the gardener and me to put them back.

After I became 17 in January 1962 I had five driving lessons, and took my test in my mother's white Mini Traveller (with wooden strakes), in which I had practised reversing and parking while at home. Happily, the streets of Wolverhampton did not present many problems; traffic was light, and I did not upset the examiner. I unfastened my L plates and was free.

One of the things I was free to do was to make nocturnal expeditions to the house in which Anne lived. These involved waiting until everyone was asleep and creeping downstairs and outside to the Mini, which I had left facing in the appropriate direction near the top of the back drive, which had a slight slope towards the gate. I let off the handbrake, and with the car in neutral it would then run silently down the drive. When at the road I could start it unheard and drive some seven miles by rural lanes to Wightwick (near the Manor described as a Pre-Raphaelite banquet by Simon Jenkins) where she and her family occupied a large house, full of Georgian furniture, with a flat-roofed porch. I would park the car 200 yards away and hurry up a lane to the house. The porch roof was supported by two columns, up one of which I was able to climb and somehow surmount the low entablature. Anne's room had windows opening onto its roof. I assume that neither set of parents ever discovered this. If they did, nothing was ever said.

Heathlands was home until, aged 22, I went to London to read for the Bar. There I rented a bedsitter in South Kensington while searching for a flat. It had a vestigial little gas cooker, no space for belongings, and neighbouring rooms with audible occupants. I hated it, and every day studied the *Evening Standard* advertisements for places to let.

After about two weeks I noticed a two-bedroom flat in Ladbroke Grove, Notting Hill. This was not then the fashionable and expensive quarter it was to become. Though its architecture was in parts well-painted and elegant, it was in others run-down and grubby. The flat in question was on the top floor, the fourth, of a large terraced building south of the church, with private gardens behind. Its main feature was an astonishing, somehow liberating, view over several miles of West London. Its telephone number was Park 5178, which I thought most sophisticated. I took it immediately, to share with a friend, Nigel Copeland, who worked for Whitbreads in Chiswell Street in the City. He provided a table, and I an old sofa. The rent was £12 per week (about £200 in modern terms). I travelled every morning from Holland Park tube station to Chancery Lane, at the top of which was the Council of Legal Education, and down which I could walk to the Temple. It was most convenient.

Notting Hill had many little restaurants, trattorias or bistros where it was possible to buy supper for two, including a bottle of wine, for about £5. I had no credit cards; it always had to be cash. The Ark in

Palace Gardens Terrace was one such place; cheap, narrow, crowded and enjoyable, with absorbent, checked paper tablecloths. The Good Food Guide for 1971 records that the cost of three courses à la carte there was 87p, with carafe wine at £1. This would have produced a bill of around £3 (present day equivalent £40). It was full of middle-class youth, the girls mostly pleasantly wholesome – anyway the ones I went there with.

I have always hated restaurants where they try to seat you at tiny adjacent tables where one person has (normally his) back to the room, with pedestrian traffic moving behind. This, as any interrogator knows, is psychologically disturbing, and means that the host can see neither the waiting staff nor the other people in the restaurant. I often went with Carol, both before and after we married, to La Bicyclette, in Elizabeth Street, for there you could sit side by side, and both see what was going on. But my favourite destination for many years was Au Bon Accueil, in Elystan Street. This was a place suitable for lunch or dinner with a parent, a child, an elderly aunt, a fellow barrister, or a girlfriend, fiancée, or wife, should you have any of these. It had Italian staff, but a mildly French atmosphere, and was friendly without being obsequious, efficient yet unhurried, not elegant but a long way from scruffy. Its three course à la carte in 1971 was £1.50 (£20).

Occasionally I cooked in the flat, and worked out that a good way to entertain was with a turkey. Turkeys were quite cheap to buy and easy to prepare, requiring only some strips of bacon over the top and a long time in the oven. Butchers sold ready-made sausage meat stuffing, and I could serve frozen peas and new potatoes. This was utterly simple. Anyone invited regarded such a meal as unexpected and agreeable, and there was always a lot left over. I like cold turkey, and, after providing supper for six or eight it might last up to a week. I am not very adventurous with food (I particularly dislike spices and Middle Eastern varieties of tapioca, which seem to go under many names), but do like meat, game and fruit.

Ladbroke Grove had the advantage of being very handy for Western Avenue and the A40, which was the way home for weekends in Kinver. I often preferred to go there rather than wander round London spending money I could not afford and wondering what to do on Saturday night. I always thought it rather sad to go to a cinema, for it implied that you had not been asked anywhere else. I did however sometimes go to the theatre, in particular to a musical called *The Boy Friend*. There I took every girl I knew, some twice. It was a most wonderful light-hearted show, with about a dozen amusing and memorable numbers, melodic and infectious – far more than in any modern musical. The girls sang and danced on the promenade at Nice, or in their finishing school, with cheerful brio and style, and called each other 'Chaps'. The men were droll and amusing, their long, nimble legs clad in baggy white trousers. The show always made every audience, and certainly me, extremely happy. There is something about the sound or rhythms of a 1920s dance band which switches the mind instantly to fun, and makes you feel a lot better. Something to do with synapses, I daresay. It does not require loud amplification. It should perhaps be played in GP waiting rooms. A few years ago there was a revival production of *The Boy Friend* at the Regent's Park open air theatre, to which I took a party of ten. It was every bit as good as I remembered it.

The other play of which I was especially fond was *Cabaret*, with Judi Dench, then an attractive gamine figure, with a voice like stale tobacco laced with burgundy.

One afternoon I came back to Ladbroke Grove to find Nigel gravid with excitement. He told me that he had just got engaged to April Harding, an intelligent, very attractive, sensible girl I had known since I was about 12. We had been to dancing classes together where her progress, up to and including the bossa nova, was far more impressive than mine. I congratulated Nigel. He went on, 'We thought we might live here'. This was rather less welcome news, and was unexpected. I had rather thought of the flat, which I had after all found, as 'my' flat, which we shared. However, I think gracefully, I went back to the *Evening Standard*, and quickly found another, in Queensgate Place, just off the Gloucester Road. This was on the first floor of a vaguely pompous, poorly-maintained late Victorian property. It was south facing, with ceilings about 12 ft high, tall windows and a set of musty maroon velvet curtains, which I bought from the previous occupant, a balding city man, for £15 after some negotiation in a pub near Tower Bridge. This flat had no garden, but there was a modest balcony opening off the sitting room, from which one could survey the street below. Richard Crabtree, whom I had met at university and was also just starting at the Bar, agreed without great enthusiasm to share with me. He was rarely enthusiastic about anything. He had the small bedroom, in which he smoked. I had the rather larger one, in which I utilised two sets of black sheets. I thought these pretty smart and potentially romantic, but the great advantage was that they never seemed to get dirty. There was no washing machine, and if there had been, I could not have worked it. About once a quarter I would take the sheets home and my mother would deal with them.

In 1970 Carol and I, after many weekends and some holidays together, illuminated by her cheerful and infectious conversation and happy demeanour, became engaged. Neither of us actually remember my proposing, but I do recall asking her father. He said that she had a very warm disposition. We were to get married that summer. She was not at all keen on Queensgate Place, which she regarded as gloomy, dirty and generally undesirable. These adjectives were legitimate, and as she was living with her sister Wendy and another girl in rather smart accommodation at 15 the Little Boltons – above the actor Richard Harris – I could understand why she felt as she did. Back to the *Evening Standard*.

It did not take long to locate a top floor flat in Elvaston Place, also off the Gloucester Road, one block to the south. This was comfortable and attractively laid out with luxurious thick blue fitted carpet everywhere. The kitchen was big enough to hold a table of modest size, the sitting room had a proper fireplace in which we could burn logs (carried clandestinely upstairs in a sack), and a long cream sofa on which to recline while enjoying the fire, the television or each other. It also had an internal staircase with a landing at the top sufficiently spacious to accommodate a round pedestal table at which six people could sit.

This was our dining room, unusual and quite practical. I embellished it with a home-made wooden pilaster. There was a trapdoor above, giving access to a small loft in which we once hung a brace of grouse and then forgot about them. Some ten days later a shower of maggots fell onto the carpet below, into which they burrowed. Carol spent an afternoon drowning them individually in a bucket of Dettol. The other agreeable feature of this flat was a bathroom with a large west-facing window, such that it was possible to lie in warm water enjoying the evening sunshine.

We lived there only about three years. I assigned the flat to Carol's sister and her husband, Philip Vallance, also a young barrister (I had indeed introduced them). Here I was a little naïve, because fairly soon they enfranchised the lease, and thus acquired a valuable property which in due course they sold to another barrister for quite a lot of money. He added a floor and then had a penthouse apartment worth a very great deal. I had not considered this. It was perhaps an error.

Anyway, we needed a house. Many of our friends lived in Fulham or Chelsea, both expensive quarters of London, and not very central. I had a strong, doubtless irrational, desire not to live south of the river. We cast about for a while, wondering about Notting Hill again, or Bayswater or Little Venice, but it did not take long to conclude that Pimlico would be the best choice. It was central, not unduly expensive, and had handsome streets and squares, the legacy of Thomas Cubitt, His first building was constructed in the year of Waterloo, but ten years later he set about Belgravia and Pimlico. He was an unusually altruistic man, who personally financed part of the Thames Embankment, and of whom Queen Victoria said upon his death (in the year of the Indian Mutiny): 'A better, kinder or more simple, unassuming man never breathed'. Pimlico was handy for the Temple, and also for Parliament, in respect of which I then had some ambition.

There was a house for sale in Cambridge Street, number 89. Full of my supposed skills as a barrister, I went to see the owner to negotiate. He turned out to be an elderly man called Rainbow who owned three Pimlico properties, but lived himself in Peacehaven on the south coast, in a converted Nissen hut. I noticed on its curved walls pictures of Rolls Royce armoured cars. I asked about them. He had been part of a squadron sent to Southern Russia after the end of the First World War to help the White Russians, and had driven along the banks of the Don. The armoured cars had been effective, he said, and assisted the Whites to several victories. However, after they won, it was the habit of these troops, who were brave but without discipline or much military sense, to have a celebratory party and carouse enthusiastically for quite some time. Soon the Reds got wind of this, and adopted the tactic of putting up a perfunctory fight, swiftly retreating, then returning a few hours later to slaughter their drunken opponents.

My skilful negotiation with Mr Rainbow produced the result that I agreed to pay his asking price. The house had been divided into three flats, and was not habitable as it was. With juvenile confidence and a desire to save money, Carol and I set about it ourselves. There was the splendid discovery, behind sheets of plaster panelling, of a large double door connecting the front first floor sitting room with another, smaller, room behind, suitable as a study or library. Each, beneath more camouflage, contained attractive marble fireplaces, which I disinterred with mounting enthusiasm. There was the same concealed inter-connection on the ground floor – perfect for a kitchen and a dining room. I made kitchen units out of 'two by two' timbers, sheets of dark green Formica and louvred doors purchased from a woodyard at the junction of Ebury Street and Pimlico Road. If you did not look too closely at the result, it seemed quite good. We employed a plumber to do the necessary pipework and fit central heating, and should have employed a plasterer too. But by then I was carried away with such artisan talents as I had been exercising, and set about re-plastering the walls of the sitting room myself. This did not seem too difficult, with a large trowel and a rectangular hawk on which to carry the wet plaster. Carol helped energetically, as did Suzanne Farrell, my warm-hearted neighbour from Heathlands, now back from revolutionary excitement in Paris. I thought we did pretty well. The walls were painted an attractive shade of pale terracotta. Furniture was arranged, and lamps put on low tables. As soon as these were switched on the walls disclosed not an even smoothness, but gentle undulations, hollows and even minor hillocks, a bit like looking at the surface of the moon through powerful binoculars. It was something of a disappointment.

However, we got the house ready, and moved in on 24th March 1972. When Carol had our first child, on 13th February 1973, he came back to a nursery room at 89 Cambridge Street. We had a spare room too, and that was occupied for a few weeks by Barty, the nanny/nurse who had looked after me as a baby thirty years before. Known formally as Sister Bartram, and, dressed properly in grey and white, she was an excellent person in every way, calm, knowledgeable and confident. She specialised in Jewish clients and came from Brondesbury, but where that was I never knew.

We had a basement, and I engaged an Irish builder from nearby Charlwood Street to work on this. It turned out that there were building regulations which implacably required that the front room window be enlarged, though the room was light and bright and did not need it. But the back room, rather gloomy, was acceptable with its existing fenestration. However, as the local authority was paying me a grant, I did not complain.

We installed a large bathroom and a flight of open treaded wooden stairs, which looked smart. During the course of the works scores of sacks of cement and plaster appeared in the larger room, enough for several houses, and later vanished again. After a few months, when most of the work was done, the builder, Mr Mahoney, vanished too. He sent no bill. His office premises were closed and empty. It was a mystery, but not an unfortunate one. There was nobody for me to pay.

Nothing much ever happened in the basement, save that during a period of fuel shortage I stored a plastic barrel of petrol there, thus no doubt invalidating the insurance. I also revised a large legal textbook in the well-lit front room, and kept a lookout for an insolent cat which seemed determined to use the basement area as a lavatory. Normally I prefer to deal with annoying animals with a firearm, but not in Pimlico, so I went to several chemists and garden centres and asked for cat poison. This produced a variety of results. Some of the shop assistants, possibly mishearing me, possibly not, gave me packets of rat poison. Others helpfully said they had no specific cat poison, but maybe rat poison would do the trick. A third category shot me venomous glances, said that it was illegal ever to kill cats (a proposition of law which is not accurate) and threatened to report me to the RSPCA or the police. In the end I came across a product called Reynardine. This, as the name implies, involves the scent of foxes. A little of this vulpine essence sprinkled in the relevant places worked well, and the disagreeable cat troubled us no more. Perhaps there will be a general feline retreat now that real foxes are colonising London so extensively. But foxes are not to everyone's taste either.

Cambridge Street was a satisfactory place to live. It was handy both for the Temple and Sloane Square, with plenty of nearby shops selling the things houses need, and several neighbours who were our friends: notably Sally and Charles Villiers (who used to ask us on excellent holidays, to Polzeath, Venice and the Marche) in rather smarter Sutherland Street; and the Beevors, a little further up Cambridge Street, where Cilla, a kind woman with an amusing tart manner, a sort of semi-affectionate astringency, sometimes fed me when Carol was detained in Norfolk with her awkward second pregnancy. Our house however was not ideal for little children, since a high proportion of its internal space was taken up by steep staircases, and the only 'garden' was a small yard out of which grew a large chestnut tree. It did have one rather desperate flower bed, in which once appeared the footprint of a burglar. I called the police, who in those days were prepared to attend the scenes of burglaries, perhaps even to make some attempt to solve them, and a detective constable arrived. I pointed out the spoor, and suggested he pull himself up and look over the wall – there might be a clue on the other side. He declined this invitation on the basis that he might scuff his shoes and dirty his clothes. Now of course no policeman would even attend, and their clear-up rate for burglary is well below 5% – presumably made up of thieves who, overcome with remorse, attend at police stations (if they can find one) to confess.

In 1974 we decided to move to the country. My practice took me a good deal to the Midlands, and we both felt it was pleasant for us and for the children not to live in London. We embarked upon a widespread ill-focused search in a large arc including Oxfordshire, Buckinghamshire, Northamptonshire, and, oddly, Suffolk. We studied *Country Life* and spoke to many estate agents. There were no computers to help. I suppose we inspected about thirty houses, from wattle and daub (with pargetting of course), to wood, flint, brick, or stone. We examined the evidence of many occupants: their books, decoration, furniture and floorcoverings, their kitchens, bedrooms, bathrooms and stables, their many different smells, their patina of happiness or acrimony, love, divorce, illness or death. But no house seemed to strike a chord of real enthusiasm until we came across Romeyns Court, at Great Milton in southern Oxfordshire. It had a contented atmosphere, good large rooms and a cricket pitch. Carol went to the auction, and I suggested she did not go beyond £50,000. The bidding opened at £100,000. It was sold to Tim Rice, cricket enthusiast and lyricist for famous musicals less entertaining than *The Boy Friend*. Perhaps we could not afford to live in the country after all.

She looked at one other house before retiring for an awkward confinement in Norfolk. This was a small stone manor house, in largely unspoilt country between Oxford and Banbury. It was an unusual property, built by an architect from Bath, called Manners, in 1858; clearly Victorian, but as Pevsner put it 'in the Tudor style'. By this he (actually the entry was written by an associate, Jennifer Sherwood) did not mean Shakespearean timbering but mullioned windows and quite steep roofs. The kitchen had a stone floor undulating dramatically with the erosions of use, and an iron column in the centre, supporting a sagging beam. It was raining at the time of Carol's visit, and the interior seemed gloomy and dark. She did not care for it at all, and reported back accordingly. It was to be sold at auction by a widow, Cynthia Laws (whose sister, the Countess of Ranfurly, wrote two highly amusing books, *To War with Whitaker* and *The Ugly One*).

It failed to sell at auction. I went to have a look at it myself. When

I got there it was not raining, and I liked the confident but modest solidity of the house, with its fine stone staircase (supplemented, of course, by back stairs for the servants it would never see again). It has high ceilings on the ground and first floors, with interesting and quite intricate cornices in what estate agents call the reception rooms. There is also an attic with two bedrooms with splendid views, though my sons who slept there complained that they were extremely cold in winter. More windows were needed – Victorians did not like sunshine in their houses. There was an ugly rear lean-to extension. The house was very secluded, on a slight hill, with two modest fields, a small wood and a spinney. The river Dorn, a stream about eight feet wide whose depth varied according to rainfall from five inches to five feet, defined the southern boundary, and the whole setting had something of the air of a mini-park. Charlbury Station was eight rural miles away (I did not then know how miserably unreliable were its trains, which ran between London and Worcester, liable to sporadic cancellation and extreme unpunctuality). Bicester Station was eleven miles, with a better service, but less agreeable carriages.

I liked the house, negotiated with more success than I had with Mr Rainbow, and we bought it for £50,000, completing on 11th July 1975. The modern equivalent of its 1975 value would be £425,000, but it is currently thought to be worth a great deal more.

It had to be got into shape for us to move in before the arrival of our second child. My surveyor recommended a good firm of builders (though their grasp of the intricacies of VAT was less than their understanding of construction work), and in quick time they felled the extension, opened up dummy bedroom windows, replaced the kitchen floor, and replaced the failing beam with an RSJ. This time I avoided personal involvement. The house was now light and sunny as well as sturdy and handsome.

I raced up and down from London in my Peugeot to invigilate this, and received three speeding tickets while doing so. (I was saved the normal inconvenient consequence by a fluent and unusually well-dressed local solicitor, Quentin Campbell, later a Circuit Judge, to whose persuasive charm the bench deferred most satisfactorily. He was married to Ann, also stylish, a kind but ambitious solicitor, who became first a District Judge at Oxford, where we used to spar pleasantly at lunch, and then a Circuit Judge at Reading, where she was very popular and occasionally called Queen Ann.)

Two removal vans came from SW1 to OX7 and soon after Hugh was born, in July 1975 at the Norwich and Norfolk Hospital, the house was almost ready to receive him and his mother – and indeed Barty too, who this time had much better accommodation than previously.

We had help in the house from Mrs Cross and Mrs Bassett, two very different people who lived in the nearby village. Mrs Cross, short, sturdy, and cheerful, occupied with her husband a tiny two-roomed thatched cottage about four hundred yards from us. She scarcely ever left the village, had never been abroad, and only once to London. But she had confidence and spirit and a matter-of-fact approach, and could be left in charge of things. Her son, Barry, sometimes cut a large hedge for us with hand shears. It took him six days. Now a chap with power tools does it in under 40 minutes. Mrs Bassett was a gentler, larger, quieter individual, with strong religious convictions and an air of utter respectability. Both were very good with, and I think fond of, our children, and were very much part of the background of the family. When they retired they were difficult to replace, but Margaret Cox, a woman with surprisingly wide interests, used to come to us, sometimes with her sister, and was invaluable. She would very kindly bring elevenses to my desk.

As I write, we have been at Westcott Barton for 44 years. We have put in many extra windows (about 16, plus a small garden room). I remain very fond of its privacy and solidity. My study is lined far beyond capacity with books. We use three of the open fireplaces, which are inefficient but agreeable. There are a lot of good trees, though sadly few flowers. Sheep graze picturesquely beyond the ha-ha. The pull of this house has been strong and I am most reluctant to relinquish it. Whenever I returned from court or have come back from holiday, or turn the curve in the drive after a substantial journey, to see the sturdy stone building - grey or Cotswold-gold according to the light- with its modest proportions but air of Victorian certainty, I feel a strong sense of privacy, security and satisfaction. Occasionally slates slide off the steep roofs, and I climb about, on a rope like a mountaineer, in order to replace them. But to buy it was a sound decision. It has been an excellent family house.

It was also an excellent location for a series of large firework displays which for many years we used to put on, as we always seemed to owe a lot of hospitality. The invitations read 'Fireworks, Drinks and Jazz'. We had audiences of up to 400 on the lawn, with me igniting the mortars and rockets, wheels, shells, Roman candles and set-pieces, just beyond the ha-ha. Carol and Mrs Cross had the harder task of furnishing mince pies and sausage rolls in regimental quantities. The children brewed glühwein enthusiastically in big vats. It was an excellent method of entertaining, because people felt that they were being given an extravagant display, which they were, but dividing the price of the fireworks by the number of guests produced a modest cost per head. The whole event, display, hot wine and mince pies, lasted only two hours, from 7pm to 9pm. Nobody came into the house. The secret of its success was that the audience was much closer to the fireworks than a safety expert would suggest, and could feel the thump and percussion, smell the heady scent of gunpowder, see the whooshing trails of the rockets and enjoy the starbursts of colour, like palm trees in the sky, right above them, not a furlong or two away. And there were absolutely no pauses – always something in the air. We often finished with a waterfall of light stretching above the ha-ha between two trees, and as it died away I would stand modestly in the field, with Roger, Hugh and Kate as they got older, and enjoy a grand ovation.

We stopped these parties when the government banned the sale of mortars to the general public, in an absurd over-reaction to an incident in which an especially stupid school master had decided to look down the tube of a mortar which had failed promptly to ignite. It went off while he peered in. This was a year in which there had been several fatalities in the course of three-day eventing, when riders died falling from large horses going fast over difficult and inflexible obstacles. That activity was not banned or even questioned, though undoubtedly risky and sometimes fatal, but big fireworks were no longer to be sold to the general public. A fine example of timorous interfering nanny government, which is reluctant to trust people with explosives. (My father when a child had been able to buy gunpowder at the chemist, and had, he told me, once fired a cannon in Bilston). The absurdity was magnified when I made enquiries about the detail of the prohibition. I have a friend, a former Brigadier, Charles McBean, who used to command tanks. I asked the authorities whether he, a man with intimate knowledge of the ways of powerful explosives, might not be allowed to buy mortar shells. No, came back the sanctimonious reply, not unless he works for a local authority. (He had in fact twice been in charge of my mortars, and once became so carried away with enthusiasm that he ran out of ammunition prematurely before the end of the display. This would not have done in battle).

So popular did our fireworks become that Nigel Talbot Rice, the enthusiastic, energetic and successful headmaster of Summer Fields Prep School, where our sons went, asked me to do a school display. I would like to have accepted, but it would not have been thought appropriate to have the audience as close to the fireworks as I liked, and I suspect it would have been impossible to insure. If by any chance I had managed to singe any member of the audience, both the school and I might have been vulnerable.

As I write we still live at the Manor House, and I do not want anything smaller. Several of our friends have, as they like to say, 'downsized'. But when visiting them we discover that what they have generally done is adapt some agreeable building so that it has a room fifty feet or so in length, and they cook at one end, sit in front of a fire at the other and eat in the middle; a sort of modern version of a mediaeval mead hall. Since such rooms, while impressive, are not very cosy or private, they will also have a small snug room with sofas and a television, and a good complement of bedrooms and bathrooms, boot -rooms, larders, utility rooms and quite possibly a large entrance hall and conservatory. The square footage often seems to end up much the same as the houses they have vacated. Our house certainly has the odd disadvantage – draughts, mice, moles, expensive heating, lack of roof insulation – but, to misquote Hamlet, I prefer to bear the ills we have rather than fly to others that I do know of – especially lack of space and privacy.

When my father died, I inherited some money and thought it sensible to buy a flat in St George's Square, Pimlico. This was primarily to provide a place for the children to live when they left university, but I thought it might also be an agreeable pied à terre for their parents. It was a sunny west-facing third floor flat with a large sitting room and kitchen, a small second bedroom (from which it was just possible to see the Houses of Parliament) and a tiny bathroom. There was a view over the square's gardens. It was two minutes from the tube and some useful shops. Other owners of flats in the building included a psychiatrist with an artistic wife, a female former spy, and a spinster on the ground floor who carefully supervised every arrival and departure. For a while there was an infuriatingly noisy man in the flat above, but our flat proved a fine investment, providing each child with three years' free accommodation (and the ability to have a paying lodger) and considerable capital appreciation. As time went by its value was divided among the children in a way which seemed fair at the time, leaving Kate as the final owner. She sold it several years after she was married for a sum roughly equivalent to five and a half times its original cost. It was a very fortunate and satisfactory investment. The single disadvantage was that I only ever spent three nights in it.

Chapter 10

Going downhill fast

You either like skiing or you don't. For those with anxieties about balance, painful boots, cold, heights and injury, it is an activity to be avoided. For others the gratifying sensations of rhythm and speed, the beauty of high mountains in winter, the heady thrill of steep slopes, bracing air and the smell of pine, have the opposite effect, and make times spent on skis some of the most agreeable there are. To this may be added lunches in mountain restaurants, after which, fuelled with the risky confidence of wine and food, you swoop away down the friendly slopes with remarkably enhanced skill.

Skiers are not generally dull and gloomy people; they are mildly fit, attractive, confident and happy, and keen on the different aspects of their pastime: waltzing along paths through trees, curving rhythmically down a piste, crouching streamlined on a schüss, bounding with springy but exhausting jumps through virgin snow, or trudging through a whiteout like an Arctic explorer. It may be chilly, but you nestle into the stalwart comfort of your high-tech clothes in agreeable insulated isolation. It may be hot and bright, but all you have to worry about is whether and to what extent you will be sunburnt. And riding chairlifts is mountaineering without effort.

I have skied for over 50 years, but it did not start well. I had just left school when my mother, not a skier, thought I ought to learn, and took me to Harrods to buy appropriate clothing. I had a girlfriend, Anne, daughter of some friends of my parents who also wanted to go. Her father, Welsh, fluent and affable, was one of the leading gynaecologists in the West Midlands. Her mother, Megan, was quiet, tolerant and very pleasant to me. Anne herself, then 17, was pretty in an English way with light brown hair, vivacious eyes, an excellent figure and a speaking rate of about twice normal. She was great fun, and I was fond of her.

We enrolled with Erna Lowe, then a leading arranger of skiing holidays, and found ourselves on a train to Austria equipped with a 'party' carriage. The journey took a long time, and enthusiasm for 'partying' – which meant squeezing back and forth with warm drinks in an inadequate space – soon waned. Eventually we arrived at Innsbrück, and were taken by bus to a village called Stienach, near the Brenner pass, seven miles from the Italian border. This was the birthplace of the inventor of the Luger pistol, a favourite German weapon in both world wars, but it was not much of a ski resort. There was little snow, and few lifts. The group turned out to consist of 18 girls and two boys. This might sound agreeable, but was not. The girls behaved as though it was a wholly female party.

We had wooden skis with cable-spring attachments for our double-laced boots. These had inner and outer layers of leather, which expanded and contracted continuously and differentially, depending upon the degree of damp or heat, and were, in my case anyway, always painful. We were taken by coach to some higher territory where there was a bit of snow and were trained in how to walk about and make static turns by putting one ski up on its heel and then flipping it over. Our instructor was a young lawyer from Vienna on a holiday job, and he took a liking to Anne, which within a few days she began to reciprocate. This put me in a poor position; a rather abject creature in the eyes of the other girls, abandoned by the one I had arrived with. I soon grew fed up with this, took a bus to Innsbrück, and flew home. It took all the money I had. Everybody was upset and annoyed. I had not learned to ski but had learned how wounding women can be. I had lost some confidence in females, but still had two pairs of almost unused tapered black ski trousers, with instep straps, and a grey anorak. These were not to be wasted.

Two years later I joined a university party to ski on a mountain called Cairngorm. In those days Scotland enjoyed reliably snowy winters, and various hoteliers in a number of villages stretching from Kingussie to Carrbridge raised money to build a chairlift up the mountain. Aviemore was the central village, and was not then the shoddy, downmarket development it has since become. The Birmingham University party occupied a log cabin on the bank of Loch Morlich, at the edge of an area of so-called 'primeval forest' out of which loomed the snow-dusted horns and warm muzzles of hispid Highland cattle.

We still had wooden skis, but there was ample snow, and our instructors were cheerful Norwegian girls in big knitted sweaters. The drawbacks, however, were only two runs and one chairlift, and it was extremely cold. We did gain a little skill, and mastered the snowplough turn, a basic but reliable technique for changing direction. But despite the Norwegians, the holiday was not really a great success.

Towards the end there was a musical night in the cabin, at which everyone was encouraged to perform. This was the only time I ever sang in public. I cannot in fact sing, or so I am told, but I did know the words to 'Dinah', a 1920s dance tune which was on a Temperance Seven record that I had at home. The lyrics are of a quality no longer written:

Dinah, is there anyone finer
in the state of Carolina
if there is and you know her,
then show her to me.

Ah Dinah, with her Dixie eyes blazing
how I love to sit and gaze in

the eyes of Daisy Dinah Dee.
Every night, why do I shake with fright?
In case my Dinah might
change her mind about me.
Ah Dinah, I would travel to China,
even hop an ocean liner
just to be with Dinah Dee.

This received a very short burst of generous applause, and was my last and only attempt at show business. But I do still appreciate this sort of music, which is light, graceful, witty and fun – qualities entirely absent from modern popular music. These qualities are also absent from classical compositions, such as those of Wagner, which some people like, and more pretend to. There is a country house opera in a converted barn at Longborough on the edge of the Cotswolds, quite near home, to which a party of us went one summer to see part of *The Ring*. On a stage set with a few concrete blocks and a pile of rubble, with performers in distressed denim and grey sheets, a woman woke up after having slept for hundreds of years, apparently with a bad headache. She seemed cross with a dwarf about a sword stuck in a piece of stone. On and on they wailed loudly at each other. There was no respite. Finally I got up and left, explaining to the concerned usherettes that I was not feeling unwell, just unhappy. I went up to the meadow behind the barn, sat in my car and turned on a programme called 'The Dance Band Days'. The balmy rhythms and deft seductive music of Ambrose and the Savoy Orpheans pulsed softly over the damp nocturnal grass. Below, just audible, was distant Germanic raging. I knew then, with no shadow of doubt, which was the superior civilisation.

But back to skiing. Time went by, and one evening in the late 1960s I was sitting desultorily with Nigel Copeland in our flat in Notting Hill in want of diversion, feeling rather like the bored characters at the outset of the story in *John Macnab*. I was looking at the personal advertisements in *The Times*, then a trove of wants and opportunities. One said 'Two men required to complete chalet party in Switzerland'.

Encouraged by Nigel, I telephoned the number given and was told to come to a meeting in a flat near South Kensington tube station. There, a few days later, assembled six young men in dark suits and striped shirts, and half a dozen pleasant-looking and well-spoken girls. One in particular bundled in late looking cheerful and neat, with rather elfin dark hair, a well-sculptured face and a happy smile.

It turned out that twelve places had been booked in Supertravel chalet Thomy in Zermatt. Supertravel was a business set up by three friends, David Rogers (whom I later came to know quite well as a neighbour in Oxfordshire), David Lewthwaite, who died suddenly and young, and John Chadwick, who soon left the travel business, went to the Bar and ended up in the Court of Appeal. The chalet came with three chalet girls, who cooked and cleaned but were social equals (at least) and ate and drank, often quite enthusiastically, with the 'guests', as the customers were known. Their rivals worked for a company called Murison Small, whose girls were called Muribirds. Our chalet was a bit run down, on a steep and icy path a little way from the centre of the village, but picturesque, atmospheric and jolly. We had an extremely good holiday, with ski school in the morning, hurtling recklessly about the mountains in the afternoon, and after a substantial dinner, visiting various bars and dancing places. There was dangerous but exciting nocturnal tobogganing, two up, along icy tracks. Zermatt was an agreeable mixture of quaint, twisted old chalets, black with age, set down icy alleys, and expensive fashionable hotels. Its emblem is the Matterhorn, a mighty bent pyramid astride the Italian border.

I liked the neat elfin girl, who was called Carol. One day at about 4.30 in the afternoon we took the last cable car up to Stockhorn, a high and distant crag not far from Monte Rosa, with steep skiing below it. The idea was to make the final run of the day from the highest point. She, having spent time at a Swiss finishing school, was a far better skier than I was. When we got out at the top I threw my skis down onto the snow in a flamboyant masculine gesture of confidence, preparatory to stepping into the bindings. I had paid no attention to the fact that in those days, skis did not have any braking devices. Mine shot off briskly downhill on their own, towards a distant hamlet called Gant. Drenched with shame and ignominy, I had to dart back into the departing car, leaving Carol to ski capably down with the professional who was 'closing' the piste. I watched, miserable, from the cable car.

Despite this setback, we were to get married in the summer of 1970. We have skied pretty well every year since, initially romantically on our own, then later with various combinations of children or friends.

After several clumsy years, one January morning at about noon, I made to turn on a gentle slope, and felt, for the first time, my skis moving smoothly together in effortless parallel harmony. Somehow, unconsciously, I had shifted my weight and balance and attitude in the proper way. It was the most wonderful feeling of achievement and liberation. A memorable moment in life. It was a bit like learning to ride a bicycle, but far more joyful and serene. The technique I acquired was not of course perfect, and has tended treacherously to abandon me at moments of difficulty or stress, especially when the way was narrow, but on the whole I began to feel that my skiing was getting better, and so it did. It never got to be any good on virgin snow though, which is really the thing to aim at. However, for enjoying all prepared runs it was perfectly satisfactory and pleasure giving, and occasionally highly gratifying.

Some resorts have remained little changed over 40 years, others showed regular accretions of lifts and links, flats and facilities and grew less and less like Alpine villages – while generally retaining a thin patina of pinewood – while trying to provide other things to do, lest overwhelmed by global warming. The most attractive places were generally Swiss, and one resort to which we have several times returned is Mürren. This is a small village in the Bernese Oberland, built on the edge of an alpine canyon, on the other side of which rise a great contiguous trio of mountains: the Eiger, the Mönch and the Jungfrau. It contains a good hotel, also called the Eiger, a few lesser places and many chalets, often old and picturesque. There were no motor cars and access was via a steep cog railway from a village in the valley below. Mürren has claims to be one the cradles of Alpine skiing, and certainly was one of the first places to which organised parties were taken, though in fact Davos was the first Swiss resort to be patronised by the English, initially for tobogganing, and then, with some help from Arthur Conan Doyle, for skiing.

Mürren was put on the map by Henry Lunn in the early part of the last century. His grandson, Peter Lunn, a former world champion skier and wartime spy who died in 2011 aged 97, lived in the village, and skied every day there was snow. He had skied for England from 1931 to 1937, leading the Winter Olympics team in 1936, was in intelligence from 1940, and a cold war spymaster thereafter. We had dinner with him once, and he talked of many things and people – especially Kini Maillart, a Swiss adventuress who travelled across China to India with Peter Fleming in 1935. (Both Maillart and Fleming wrote books about this: according to his they succeeded because he carried a .22 rifle, in hers it was because she spoke Chinese.)

Mürren retains some traces of ancient pagan tradition. The day before the annual Inferno race in January there is an evening procession around the village, with burning torches and cheerful bands, preceded by a cadre of marching village youths bearing huge cow bells which toll ominously as they step, as though foretelling doom for someone. Perhaps like the reception given to Carthaginian generals who, if they returned in failure, were led to the centre of the city to have their legs ceremonially broken. When the Murren procession reaches a spot on the upper side of the village, a huge bonfire is lit with a replica devil on top, which is slowly devoured, the flames licking up through lightly-falling snow. Close by, a 20-foot pyramid of ice is scaled by agile children, who slide down it in a way which would now be forbidden in England as far too risky.

The next day is the day of the Inferno race. Well over 1,800 people, at 10-second intervals, start close to the summit of the Schilthorn – weather permitting – at almost 10,00 feet. They race down past the village, and then descend by a twisting hairpin track to Lauterbrunnen, in the valley below. This is almost 15 kilometres. There is a stretch where the skiers have to race uphill, which adds both to effort and spectacle. Some of those who enter are serious competitors who wear stretchy catsuits, crouch professionally, put special wax on their skis and are most determined. Others are mere leisure skiers, ranging from the fast and competent to those rather less so. Through the introduction of a friend, John Steel, a planning Silk, pilot, neighbour and leading figure in the Kandahar club, I found myself entered for this race in 2005, decidedly unseeded, at number 1709.

It began from a tiny shed perched awkwardly on a steep slope, occupied by a starter in charge of the line of competitors, who edged cautiously sideways down the ice towards him. A bottle of schnapps hung from a string to give fortitude to the nervous. I tightened the chin strap of my rented helmet and pulled down my goggles. A tap on the shoulder and off I went, anxious not to fall at the first awkward bend, about 100 yards away and now cut up badly by the hundreds of previous contestants. I scrabbled sideways, made the corner, shot round a curve at the top of a high corrie, and embarked upon a long straight schüss. Here the idea was to bend down, bringing chest to knees, so as to minimise drag. This worked well for a short distance until pain in my thighs suggested a more upright posture, which I assumed with relief. At this point other competitors, still crouching, began to whizz past like human bullets, their hands clasped together as if in prayer before their faces and their sticks streamlined close against their sides.

I bent down again and found myself running neck and neck with a girl in a black outfit with a fur collar. I looked at her, but she did not reciprocate, her lips pursed in concentration as we approached the end of the straight stretch together. It was necessary to bear left, and I was on the inside of this turn, so had the putative advantage. But as I began to slow for the manoeuvre, she gained speed, passed me, and cut in sharply. In no time she was fifty yards ahead. She was now the only other skier I could see, and I clung to the receding view of her accelerating bottom as we neared the Kannonenrohr. This is a steep and somewhat formidable descending curve round a cleft in the mountain which leads down towards the village below. From it there was a fine view of the valley, and of cheering crowds. On its left was a reticulation of suspended nets, designed to catch anyone who lost control, and stop them flying over the rim and down a steep and rocky slope.

For some reason I felt that my performance at this point would be critical – perhaps the difference between coming 1789 and 1790. I planted my skis a little further apart and edged fiercely to get around the bend, then leaned sharply the other way to align myself with the short straight stretch before a very abrupt turn, where were gathered perhaps seventy enthusiastic watchers. Because I was going so comparatively slowly, there was now no other skier in sight as I raced bravely down towards the spectators, one of whom, Chloe Robson, I identified. She was smiling broadly and simulating enthusiasm by clapping her mittens.

My concentration momentarily impaired, I made rather a mess of the corner, but did not quite fall over, and ran on down a narrow, rutted path through a few trees. Emerging from these I saw the slope rising in front of me. Skiers were attempting to run, step or herringbone upwards. I had forgotten this feature of the course. It was much harder work to go up than to go down. But there was no anxiety save that of exhaustion, and over the next 200 yards or so I managed to overtake another skier. I believe this was the only person I passed in the whole race. The shouts and cheers were loud on this uphill stretch, and it was impossible to lag back given the encouraging attitude of the spectators. I reached the top completely exhausted, and began gratefully to slide slowly down the remainder of the course. The race was not over, but it was for me, for I cruised to the end without any attempt to crouch or accelerate beyond the speed naturally provided by gravity.

At the finish there was a splendid scene of jollity and enthusiasm. A Tyrolean band was thumping Alpine tunes out into the crisp and chilly air, flags and bunting streamed in the afternoon breeze, cow bells pealed, photographs were taken, and glühwein, schnapps and beer lubricated a large crowd of spectators and competitors who welcomed the late arrivals with ironic cheers. Announcements were broadcast from a battery of loudspeakers, prizes and badges were handed out, and from time to time a helicopter wheeled overhead, taking casualties off to hospital. I felt a bizarre sense of achievement, and wandered around reluctant to take off my competitor's numbered bib.

That evening, at the Eiger Hotel, the Kandahar club (an English skiing association which took its name from Lord Roberts of Kandahar, an early patron), had its dinner and prizegiving. Even the best of the English had not challenged the top Continental racers for the outright winner awards, but this mattered not at all, for there were club prizes for members in 27 categories – overall fastest, fastest woman, fastest man over 40, fastest over 50, and over 60, 'gentlemen' (apparently a distinct category, but maybe the over-seventies), fastest 'K Lady', fastest beginner, fastest junior member, most improved racer, most improved team, award for the most outstanding performance, and so on. I began to wonder whether I might not get a trophy for the slowest member aged between 58 and 59. The awards were announced by the Chairman and the cups handed out by Peter Lunn, whose status was that of a puckish winter god. And what cups they were: not tiny little plated trophies but huge, generous silver chalices and salvers, many engraved with the names of skiers dating back over 50 years. Each announcement was met by a table-thumping salvo of friendly shouts, applause, and ribald cheers. It was perfectly clear that though the best club member may not have finished in the top one hundred, beaten by dedicated continentals, that was not the point – here was the real heart and spirit of Alpine sport, at its amateur and inspiring best. Present too were one or two elderly Swiss celebrities who appeared to share this view.

John Steel is a considerable character, with a superabundance of self-confidence. One evening he suggested that we went out for a drink, so we walked to a stübli at the far end of the village. It was pretty full, and the chatter of conversation was loud. Looking across the room he noticed a French guide that he knew. The guide looked up, caught his eye and raised his glass in acknowledgment. John cried 'Pierre!' quite loudly, and the din lessened a fraction. Whereupon John began to sing the Marseillaise, very strongly, and in French. For a few precarious moments this was a solo, and then others – there seemed to be quite a few French – began to join in, and the room swelled with the stirring, savage anthem. At the pause which follows 'aux armes, citoyens' the guide's attractive dark-haired girlfriend stood up to her full height, reached above her head and struck a cow bell suspended from a beam at just the appropriate moment: 'Taaang...' The effect was magnificent, and for a moment one really felt that there was quite a lot to be said for the Gauls.

The verse finished. Then, incredibly, John embarked upon the second verse. He had the words for that too, though he was almost alone in this knowledge. Bravely he finished. There was a round of stunned applause. 'I think we had better leave now,' he said, and we retreated into the softly-falling snow.

A year or two later – through the good offices of Cleves Palmer, big cheese of the Kandahar and author of *Going Downhill Fast* – I entered the race again, this time with my elder son Roger, who is a good skier. Again we were late starters and had lunch watching the earlier competitors, many of whom inexplicably fell over at a particular point. I observed this and said how hopeless they were. Our time came at about 3 pm, on a shortened course, because conditions high up were unsatisfactory. I went first, shot down the initial slope, turned onto a descent towards trees, and then saw people waving me down from the side of the piste. I was having none of that, this was a race and I was not to be impeded. I accelerated. The next moment I was rolling over and over in broken snow. This was the point at which we had observed people falling. They stopped the race for a while, to repair the surface, causing Roger to wonder whether I had died or been carried wounded from the field. I took my time getting up, and then carried on. Soon I fell again through lack of concentration, and was aware of him skiing past me. I got to my feet and shot after him, cheered by my daughter from the crowd. I followed him down the succession of hairpin turns to Lauterbrunnen. I could not of course catch him, but was gratified to find him lying exhausted in a field beyond the finishing line. He had been trying harder than I had.

But attractive and entertaining though Mürren can be, the scope of its skiing is limited, and Carol and I went with various permutations of friends, or with our three children, to many other places, notably Zermatt, Lech, Méribel, Val D'Isère, Obergurgl, Klosters, Verbier, Selva and others besides.

Travel in Switzerland was and remains easiest, with railways of perfectionate reliability and helpful attitude. I once forgot a rucksack containing binoculars, a camera and some money on a Swiss train when changing to another line on the way to Klosters. I rang our hotel, which said all would be well, and that it would contact the railway lost property for me. Next morning I went down to the station, and as I entered the booking hall, a cheerful girl said in English 'You must be Judge Harris, come for your luggage'. There it was, unplundered, and brought to the village in which I was staying. In England it would either never have been seen again, or, if located, would be available only at some distant depot, upon proof of identity, payment of a charge, and between awkward visiting hours. No English hotel would think it part of its service to help restore property left on a train.

In Verbier (also in Switzerland) one of our children, then aged seven, lost his ski pass. The hotelier rang the lift owners and we were given a free replacement. Swiss villages generally still look like pretty Alpine places, although modern chalets have nuclear shelters in their basements.

But one year, on the slopes above St Moritz, I saw a less cosy example of the Swiss approach. It was mid-afternoon and a group of six of us, returning to the village, cruised around a gentle bend to see a substantial figure lying in the snow. One of our party, Kristina Bonde, was a Swedish doctor. We stopped, she went to the body – apparently an abnormally large, comatose, Japanese – and found that he was not breathing. Though a highly fastidious woman, she did not hesitate to give mouth-to-mouth resuscitation, and after a few moments he vomited green pasta explosively all over her white ski clothes, and seemed to gasp a little – as indeed did she. Under her direction we heaved him onto his side into a recovery position, and a few moments later were aware of the heavy faff, faff, faff of a descending helicopter, which landed close by in a cloud of stinging snow. Two paramedics jumped out, ran up, and examined the stricken figure. They connected him with leads to some sort of battery kit, and administered several shocks, which jolted his body noticeably. We stood back among the small crowd of skiers now watching. The crewmen continued with their electrical measures for a few minutes, but then detached the leads, packed up the equipment and put it back into the helicopter. One of the medics opened the door of the aircraft and climbed in. 'What about the man?' I asked. 'He is dead. He does not need the helicopter. He will be brought down by the ski patrol'. And off they flew, leaving the corpse by the side of the piste, marked by a red flag, waiting for a sledge. A steady flow of skiers descended past it, through the snowflakes, to their tea.

We witnessed a more attractive side of another national character in a mountain restaurant on a high ridge, not far from Obertauern, south of Salzburg. It was lunch time, the inside tables were all taken, the day was not sunny, and it was cold outside. We became aware of a helicopter landing nearby from which a man dressed in black got out, together with a tall woman, also largely in black, and the pilot. They hurried into the restaurant and asked the chief waiter, in Russian-accented English, for a table. He said they were full. The man in black opened his wallet, but the waiter shook his head and repeated that they did not have any inside space available. At this the Russian took out several notes and went to a nearby table, to offer the diners money to get up and go away. They shook their heads, and he tried several more, but with the same result, even, in one case, when they were on their coffee. The manager in charge of the restaurant remonstrated that it was not appropriate to try to bribe his customers to leave their tables. The Russian argued with his pilot. The pilot argued back. After about ten minutes the trio left, returned to their helicopter and swept away into the leaden sky. It was a good example of the futility of trying to suborn prosperous and contented people, and an expensive way not to have lunch.

Winter sports can also bring out the best in people. On one occasion a group of five or six of us climbed, with a guide, to a pass leading from one resort to another over unskied terrain. We carried so called 'fatboy' skis to help on untracked snow. They were heavy, not very efficacious and both ascent and descent took us a long time. Eventually we arrived in the village we were aiming for, where it was necessary to wait some time for an early evening bus. There was a modest inn with a bar and tables, but few customers. Beside ourselves there were two groups of fairly elderly ladies and a small gnome-like man in a corner playing an accordion in a gentle, reflective way.

One of us, Maurice Robson, liked dancing and parties very much. They were indeed his métier. He asked the musician to try something more energetic, and bought him a drink. Inspired by this, the gnome struck up some cheerful alpine tunes, and we got up self-consciously and danced a bit. Maurice, into the swing of things, then approached the older ladies, who were tapping their feet gently. One by one, he would halt, bow, snap his ski-booted heels together, and in some tangled mock German, invite them to dance. He was a very good dancer, light on his feet, even in ski boots, and jovial, although with some of his usual partners he was apt to try to bend them over unexpectedly (which he once did, with lasting consequences, to my wife's sister Wendy on a grand piano in Zermatt).

The ladies, flushed with the pleasure of this unexpected exercise, smiled and skipped and jumped and galloped with real enthusiasm. One or two people came in from the street and joined in. The owner brought out little glasses of Poire Williams. Maurice danced on with an energy he had not shown on skis. After a bit, feeling perhaps that he was running out of partners, he darted into the kitchen and emerged with two cheerful girls, who flung themselves with enthusiasm into his impromptu party. He urged a couple in from the bus stop. After about half an hour of this, he noticed another woman, sitting quietly on her own. She was perhaps 50, good looking in a strong kind of way, wore a dirndl, and was attractively well built without being fat. She had a most pleasant expression. Maurice invited her onto the floor, and away they went. She was quick, neat and fluent, and every time he tried a hold, turn, or bend of an unwanted nature, she would step delicately around him with a playful smile. He tried harder and harder to manoeuvre her, and she played him deftly. Eventually the accordionist, with a final metallic crescendo, ceased to play, and to a big cheer the two dancers came – he perspiring, she gently panting – to our table. A few minutes' conversation revealed that twenty years before she had been the All-American polka champion. Maurice had met his match. But he had provided splendid entertainment for many people whose evening would have been dull without him. He was a remarkable figure.

France provides many miles of well-connected skiing, but often at the expense of distinctly unattractive resorts, to which travel is difficult. The autoroutes leading to several of the resorts in the Western Alps are frequently more coagulated with traffic than those into London during rush hour, and there are now policemen to stop you turning off them onto mountain byroads. Some years ago David and Clare Astor invited us to stay in Méribel with them. The journey involved high detours up the sides of a valley from which we could look gratefully down through the descending dusk on thousands of stationary cars. The next day we set off to ski. Both they and we had engaged guides - theirs an elderly, monoglot, teak-skinned Frenchman, ours a curly-haired young sophisticate married to an English public-school girl. They took an instant dislike to each other, and deftly separated us at the first cable car stop.

It was on our return from this holiday that I was nearly arrested at Heathrow. While waiting for our luggage to appear I was approached by a girl in a BA type uniform, who said she was doing some market research and asked if I was happy with our 'flight experience'. We had been quite badly delayed at Geneva, without proper explanation, and so I said I was not happy and would like to participate in her survey. Hearing of my discontent she said she did not, after all, think she would ask me anything and began to walk away. Peeved at this, I walked with her, remonstrating. After a moment she shot through a nearby door, So I sat down. A few minutes later I looked up to see three men dressed in black and carrying stubby automatic rifles standing over me. 'You have been harassing the staff' said one of them. 'I must ask you to come with us.' I refused, and explained my irritation at what had happened. It took some time to satisfy these absurdly over the top security people, who, I suppose, had little to do and were in want of diversion. But it was a startling incident, which greatly amused David Astor who stood chuckling in the background awaiting my incarceration.

We went for several years in a group organised by Rodney and Gillie Mann to Klosters. Rodney had very fixed ideas about a good day's skiing. Each morning we got out at the top of the cable car and he led us round exactly the same repertoire of runs until about midday. Only then might there be some flexibility, depending upon the chosen location for lunch. Rodney was a keen horseman who enjoyed hunting and steeplechasing and he has the figure of a jockey. He skied in rather the same way as a jockey might ride; crouched forward, arms forward, and as quickly as possible. He would go faster and faster, with a look of complete concentration, until, in an explosion of snow, skis, hat, goggles and exclamation, he would have a pile-up. A rueful shake of his head, and his wife would enquire anxiously 'are you all right, Gunner?' He would nod in a concussed sort of way, put his skis back on, and set off again. Slowly at first, but soon back at maximum velocity. It was a brave and challenging technique. He also had a good eye for country; in a strange resort he would scorn to consult a map but glance at the slopes and hills and shout 'this way!' We went with them once to the Galapagos, where you cannot ski, but where Rodney, normally a perfectly friendly man, was not very keen on making friends with the Americans on the boat. I was not very keen on our English travel agent, who had charged us nearly double what the Americans were paying for their - better - cabins.

All three of our children took cheerfully to skiing, but not to classes. On one occasion at Les Arcs, Hugh, then six, had spent two hours dragooned in tedious, low-speed tutorial exercises. After lunch the family went to the top of a big wide bowl of snow, and I said 'let's go down this, making lots of turns'. We set off. Hugh did not turn. He set his skis and his gaze straight down the hill and went faster and faster. I raced alongside him and shouted 'turn, slow down!' He glanced contemptuously sideways for a moment, set his jaw like a cartoon character and carried straight on. He had had quite enough of going slowly. A year or two later Carol and I were startled to see him and his brother descend the very steep and intimidating Tortin run at Verbier behind their tall and bearded instructor.

Roger and his three daughters, currently eight to thirteen, now ski black runs, snaking downhill in formation most impressively. They once watched with interest and mild concern as a certain figure fell near the top of one of these runs and slid, quickly and helplessly downwards for about 400 yards. Finally it stopped, and lay still for a while. I do not reckon to fall over much, had not enjoyed this experience, and took a few moments to collect my thoughts. The episode confirmed their view that Granddad was not really much of a skier.

We have skied with quite a variety of people: Charles and Catherine Powell, he an extraordinary linguist who can dart between all leading European languages to great advantage; Miles and Mary Tuely, she an ex-instructor who taught her husband to ski in his middle age, and always keen to explore off the beaten track (where we do not always follow); Chloe Robson, a dressage enthusiast who is always much fitter than the rest of us, and who virtually taught herself to ski, starting in her late twenties; and Hugh and Nicky Sherbrook. Hugh, yet another qualified instructor and very elegant on skis, hates time 'wasted' at lunch and would watch our party embark on course after course with impatient scorn, for he had come to ski, not eat. Nicky, his wonderfully sociable wife, a small, tidy, rapid skier, was equally ready to stop for a drink or bomb on down a mountain.

In recent years many of our earlier companions have dropped out for one reason or another, but one couple has gone in the opposite direction. Jeremy Ackroyd was once a land agent in North Oxfordshire, where we met. A cheerful and enthusiastic man, of stalwart appearance with definite opinions on most subjects, he migrated his family via the East Midlands to Cumbria, where for many years he ran the Lowther Estate, near Penrith, and became a specialist in rights of way – in which he was a national expert – trees, and geology. His wife Livvy, besides being invariably fun, friendly and amusing, has a fine mind, which she can turn to anything, from Bridge to the social life of Shropshire, or Oxfordshire (with which she remains entirely au fait, though has not lived there for many years). This attractive and energetic couple wanted an interest to share, and after Jeremy's retirement they decided to take up skiing. They did this wholeheartedly, going for three weeks at a time to Obergurgl, a high resort near Innsbrück, where they had much tuition. Sometimes the difficulties in visibility which can occur on snow in awkward light seemed insurmountable. But they persevered, and after a year or two of this regime they invited us to join them. They got better and better, and Carol and I did not, until we coincided quite acceptably. The Ackroyds were at last ready to strike out to other resorts, to the Dolomites, to Arosa, to Lech, to Courchevel – the Alps were their oyster, and they drove from resort to resort in a large Audi without regard for snow and ice, regarding us Harrises as rather bland and weedy for travelling by plane and train. Jeremy it was who talked me into wearing a helmet (red, with a dark visor) which, while it makes me resemble a ladybird, does transform one's sense of comfort and security. And on a holiday with them I bought for the first time, aged 71, a new pair of skis. I hope to use them for the remainder of my life. Skiing is after all an easier way of negotiating mountain slopes than walking. The wonderful sensation of covering undulating and descending ground, in pristine mountains, with rhythmic turns at comfortable speed remains as captivating as it was when first achieved.

My grandfather's business

My parents married on 1st October 1940, between the battle of Britain
and the Blitz. My father's mother is to the left of the Groom, my mother's father
to the right of the Bride

F.C. Wesson. Ironmaster.

I have always liked cars, even at two and a half

With my sister

Wedding in Norfolk, 25th July 1970

My parents with our elder son

HARRIS X

CONSERVATIVE

9 High Street
Penistone
Sheffield S30 6BR

Dear Elector,

Britain is running at a loss: deeply in debt, with wealth and wage levels below those of similar European countries, and with prices rising fiercely. The position is grave for us all

Britain has to earn its living in a rough and competitive world. This just cannot be done by labouring on under even more state control, nor by one side of industry fighting the other. Together we must try to create more for all, not squabble over what little we have

Living standards can only rise if our commerce and industry make profits to pay for them. This is why now, above all, is no time for more nationalisation, which cost us and lost us a staggering sum last year. Enterprises must be encouraged, not crushed by state interference, high taxes or restrictive practices

Think carefully before you vote, for the parties are not the same. We need a government which will put people before the state, commonsense before prejudice, enterprise before envy and creation before division. A strong government, not some balancing act of a coalition, one which will rule according to the whole nation's needs, not just the demands of the strong

You want a real and hopeful future for yourself and your family. So vote Conservative. It's commonsense for the common good

Yours sincerely

Charles Harris

Published by Mrs B. Town, 9 High Street, Penistone, Sheffield S30 6BR
Printed by T. D. Hattersley, 67 High Lane, Haywood, Sheffield

VOTE for your FUTURE

CHARLES HARRIS

CONSERVATIVE

COMMONSENSE FOR THE COMMON GOOD — VOTE CONSERVATIVE

Charles and Carol Harris

Charles Harris is . . . .

29 works as a Barrister, and is married to a farmer's daughter

They have an 18 month old son

He enjoys outdoor life, mountaineering, carpentry and history

He has written on the law and on employee participation in industry, and has worked in forestry

Visiting a local colliery (Photograph C.P.A.)

THE CONSERVATIVES WILL :

- **ABOLISH RATES** over a five year period
- **ALLOW COUNCIL TENANTS** to buy their homes at two-thirds market price thereby also saving the taxpayer the cost of housing subsidies
- **REDUCE MORTGAGE RATES** to 9½% by by taxing building societies less
- **CARE FOR** the handicapped, the poor and the elderly

- **STOP INTERFERING WITH INDUSTRY** and let it get on with earning Britain a better living
- **ACT TO HALT RISING PRICES** with all round restraint on government taxation, and prices
- **ALLOW THE EUROPEAN COMMUNITY** to prove its worth as a strong and forward looking union bringing benefits to the individual and to the nation

- **GIVE FARMERS A CHANCE** to produce with stability and security with realistic prices for them as well as for the housewife
- **STRENGTHEN BRITAINS DEFENCE** and restore her international weight
- **LET PARENTS HAVE A SAY** in their children's education
- **RUN BRITAIN FAIRLY** in the interests of all sections of the community

THIS TIME BE POSITIVE — VOTE CONSERVATIVE

Election literature 1974. Insufficiently persuasive to overturn a large Labour majority, but enough to beat the Liberals

Aged forty

Portrait by Dick Smyley 1996

Inverbroom house party

Wife and dog near Cape Wrath

Hugh, Kate and Roger

In the presence of authority: my wife and a prime minister

Taking Silk - 1989

Maurice Robson with his stalker Willie Matheson

On the hill at Erchlas. George the stalker is on the left, looking cheerful

Shooting party. Robert Parsons, farm at Radford

Not quite last. The Inferno race

I have always like solitary walking, so
long as there is company at the end of it

Exhaustion: walking from Murren
to Kandersteg, standing above
Oeschinensee

Upper crust

Carol and Kate in Somerset   Oxford. Kate takes her MA

Some pedestrians. Maggie Chilton, on the right, once walked 26 miles
in one night - though not on holiday

Carol's parents in conversation

Looking out of Africa

Circuit Judge 1993

Summit party in Switzerland. Just under half the height of Everest, but less crowded

Oxford Judges in 2003, with the Lord Chief Justice.

Standing L to R: Ann Campbell, Anthony King, Michael Payne, Richard Matthews, Tom Corrie, Vivienne Gatter, Conrad Seagroat (normally in Hong Kong High Court). Sitting L to R : Julian Hall. Lord Woolf, the Author

The Oxford Combined Court. This is a conversion of a rather stylish Morris car
showroom. Neither courts nor car showrooms are built to this standard now

A minor ascendancy in Northampton. From the ground, Judges Morrell, the Author, Bray, Wide and Mitchell

27th January 2017, last day in court

From left to right - HHJ Clarke (my successor as DCJ), HHJ Lamb, HHJ Pringle QC, HHJ Vincent, The Author, Lord Judge, HHJ Ross, Mr Justice Spencer, HHJ Hughes

The extended family in France. All except the smallest climbed
some quite respectable mountains

Blithe Spirits. Two granddaughters.

All the grandchildren 2019

Westcott Barton Manor, home since 1975

Chapter 11

On the bench

On 21ˢᵗ May 1990, the year after I took Silk (and in which Germany was re-united, the channel tunnel completed and Mrs Thatcher resigned) I was appointed a Recorder – the title given to a barrister (or solicitor) who sits occasionally as a judge. I think that Roy McAulay had suggested my name to the Leader, and to the Presiding Judge, of the Midland Circuit. In that golden age no personal application, or indeed input, was needed. 30 years later, in 2017, over 2,000 people – including my elder son (successfully) – applied for 135 Recorder vacancies. A long and thorough, not to say exhaustive, national selection process (in which I played a small part) was carried out over many months by the Judicial Appointments Commission. Under the old system people chose those whose characteristics they knew to be suitable. Under the new, any personal knowledge of, or connection with, an applicant disqualifies a selector from considering them. Both approaches have some merit.

Since 1979 judicial training has been required for newly-appointed judges sitting in crime (from 1985 this also applied in civil). And so, on the 21st April 1987, after being made an Assistant Recorder (probation to see if you might become a Recorder) I had attended the first of many courses. After a while these came to be held for general convenience in central England, at Warwick University (misleadingly named, as it is much nearer Coventry), or at a rural conference centre near Northampton (where a number of extra-curricular inter-judicial relationships were struck up, though not by me). My first course was at Roehampton. It was presided over by Mr Justice Beldam, who was approachable, friendly and had a sense of humour. He was assisted by Mr Justice Ognall, a man of whom many were slightly frightened because of his somewhat testing interrogations of those attending. One student on that course, probably less nervous than most, was David Neuberger, beginning his bid for the judicial summit, achieved in 2012 when he became President of the Supreme Court.

We were lectured on topics like the preparation and conduct of a trial, and practical problems in sentencing. There were indeed many such practical problems; they were to get much worse, and have not yet been resolved. It might be thought that one of the reasons people are selected to be judges is that they are believed to have the judgment to decide what is an appropriate sentence to pass. However, the Government, and to an extent the senior judiciary, do not trust trial judges either to get it right, or to be consistent with each other. Periodically too the government seeks to alter sentencing practice, which is a matter for the judiciary within a framework established by the legislature. Often, when the prisons are full, the government will be keen on light sentences. Sometimes, when some particular crime is prevalent, it likes to signal concern by measures to increase sentences. There has been a constant flow of amendments to legislation and of judicial 'guidance', in an attempt to reduce, if not entirely to extinguish, the discretion of the judge who has actually tried the case. Obviously it is not desirable to have discrepant sentences imposed by different tribunals for offences which are or seem similar, though no two cases are ever quite alike – as I once endeavoured to explain during an interview on the Today programme. But it is quite another matter to have such a reticulation of statutory provisions and guidance from the Court of Appeal that judges find it hard to know exactly what they can or cannot do. That is what was happening.

As time went by the position grew so complicated that those responsible for judicial training engaged the services of a Cambridge academic, Professor Thomas, to give lectures to the judges, in which he attempted to explain to them the intricacy and contradictions of the statutory provisions they were supposed to apply. These talks he made highly amusing, but it was of course perfectly absurd that legislation imposed by the Government via Parliament was so complex that it could not be understood by the Judiciary, still less by the defendants who were to be sentenced. This was pointed out from time to time, but was ignored by those who drafted and enacted the legislation. A style of drafting was adopted which made it impossible to see what the law was without looking at previous provisions, themselves often far from pellucid. It was rarely thought appropriate to compose, in a self-contained manner, both comprehensive and comprehensible. Speakers on the topic used to vie with each other to produce the finest examples of the incomprehensible. Lawyers were entertained. Laymen would have been aghast, and rightly so.

Those responsible for the treacherous morass of sentencing law appear to have paid little attention to the practicalities either. Sentencing, broadly speaking, takes place in two situations: either after a contested trial when a defendant has been convicted by a jury, or on a day set aside for a succession of sentences upon those who have earlier pleaded or been found guilty. At the end of a trial the convicted person, and indeed the jury and the public, legitimately want to know as soon as possible what the sentence is going to be. But it is now very common for sentence to be adjourned, to obtain reports and worry out the complications, for delivery on another day, thus involving the expense of a further hearing.

In a morning of sentences (commonly a Friday) a judge might have a list of perhaps a dozen cases. It is essential to move through these with some expedition – though celerity was often hampered by the inability of the staff manning the cells to bring defendants into the dock promptly. (Occasionally the court waited longer for the prisoner to be produced than I took in sentencing him). If in each or several cases awkward questions arise about what can be done and how it can be achieved, the whole process becomes bogged down and needlessly prolonged. It also creates a very poor impression in the minds of spectators (let alone those convicted) if it appears that both judge and counsel have to struggle to work out what sentence the law allows to be passed. Ill-drafted sentencing provisions also inflict much extra unpaid work on the badly paid barristers, and on the Court of Appeal, which has to sort out the many mistakes which are inevitably made.

After my few days' training I was sent to Oxford to watch and sit with a Circuit Judge in action. This was Patrick Medd, a polished, careful and courteous tribunal. He had a precise mind, manifested by an interest in taxation, and an interesting history. Son of a solicitor, he had hoped to enter Parliament, and stood unsuccessfully at Swindon in 1955. Thereafter, having been seen and rejected by 29 constituencies, he decided to concentrate on a career at the Bar. During the war, as a young officer, he told me he was given the unusual task of driving several hundred mules from Somalia to Kenya, with the assistance of one NCO. These all arrived safely, only to die of some equine disease.

I learned a good deal from Patrick Medd, especially the value of calm and politeness in court whatever the provocation – which can sometimes be considerable. It is usually better to absorb or ignore a little invective with impervious dignity than pompously to set about punishing it. As homework he asked me to draft a form of general directions for jury trials. He corrected it slightly and I used this throughout my 24-year career on the bench, without further modification. This would have horrified those who periodically issue judges with loose-leaf tomes of guidance. This 'guidance' sometimes seemed aimed at making important changes in practice without any corresponding change in the law. Perhaps the most remarkable example of this is the burden of proof. In criminal cases the traditional test was to direct a jury that they had to be satisfied 'beyond reasonable doubt' before they could convict. This was well understood. It is a phrase approved by the House of Lords, and which Lord Scarman said in the Privy Council in 1979 was the 'time honoured formula'. It then began to be thought by some, it is not clear why, increasingly appropriate to use the word 'sure'. The Judicial Studies Board in its 'Bench Book' of specimen directions for Judges to give to a jury, issued in May 1999, said: 'How does the prosecution succeed in proving the defendant's guilt? The answer is – by making you sure of it. Nothing less than that will do'. There was no mention of 'beyond reasonable doubt'. In most minds, including mine, 'sure' carries a somewhat higher connotation of certainty than 'beyond reasonable doubt'; it implies a state of mind close to, if not indistinguishable from, certainty. Judges now are explicitly told to use the expression 'sure'. But there has been no modification in the law to bring about such an important change. The concept of reasonable doubt is readily understood, and largely common sense. I always used it, sometimes with a trace of emphasis on the 'reasonable', and never had a jury ask a question about what it meant. But being 'sure' is a good deal more difficult. What exactly does that mean? Judges sometimes get into difficulties when attempting to elaborate or clarify. If it means the same as beyond reasonable doubt, then why not stick to the latter? If its effect is indeed different, then a change in such a vital aspect of our criminal law should not be effected by specimen directions.

Armed with my brief training and modest experience in crime, I conducted my first criminal trial in Northampton. Not in the 17th century Sessions House – whose facade was described in an English Heritage report as 'wonderfully vigorous Restoration stuff'- for it had been closed in 1986, and has remained empty ever since, except when used as a film set. My debut was in a soulless converted Co-Op building near the Derngate Theatre. It involved one defendant charged on two counts and went smoothly to start with. Counsel were agreeable to each other, and to me, and my carefully-prepared summing up seemed satisfactory – indeed I felt it was a fine example of the art. I retired to await the verdict, which was not long in coming. I returned to court, feeling a little tense, though presumably less so than the accused. 'Will the foreman please stand,' said the Clerk. 'Mr Foreman, please answer yes or no. Have you reached a verdict upon which you are all agreed?' 'Yes.' 'Do you find the defendant guilty or not guilty on count one of the indictment?' 'Not guilty.' 'Not guilty. And is that the verdict of you all?' 'It is.' I did not hesitate: 'Let the prisoner be discharged' I said, incisively. 'But,' said the foreman, looking puzzled, 'we find him guilty on count two'. In my anxiety to seem brisk and efficient I had quite forgotten count two. Counsel for the defendant rose to suggest that the second verdict could not properly be taken, as the accused was no longer in the charge of the jury. There was probably something in this, so I asked Counsel for the Prosecution for his submission. He asked for a few moments to consider the position, which I was very ready to grant. I inquired of the defendant if he would be so good as to remain in court as a problem had arisen, which happily he agreed to do. After about 20 minutes the barristers returned to say that agreement had been reached that the conviction would not in the event be challenged, and would I please proceed to sentence, which, in the circumstances, it was submitted, might be a clement one.

For the remainder of the time that I was at the Bar I spent about three weeks a year trying small criminal cases, each time feeling a little more confident, but ever surer that crime was not what I wanted to do.

In 1989 I took Silk, as described elsewhere, and in 1993 I decided, for a number of reasons, to take an appointment as a Circuit Judge. Perhaps I did this too soon. Certainly I did not allow myself much time to develop a good practice as a Leader, though I had some worthwhile cases, including one in the House of Lords. Less importantly, I also enjoyed the clothes one wore as a Silk – a nicely cut soft shouldered tail coat of broadcloth, and an 18th century style waistcoat with many buttons and useful pockets.

But the situation in chambers was an unhappy one and I found it difficult to persuade myself to seek other chambers and in effect start my career afresh. The children were leaving school, so the cost of finding fees for education was greatly reduced, and the possibility of sitting at Oxford, a pleasant place and close to home, had arisen. I had been at the Bar for over 25 years, and felt like a change.

I attended for a short interview with an existing Circuit Judge and a civil servant. It was not testing. I was asked what I found most difficult about sitting judicially and replied that it was hard – though important - to remember the names of all the staff and ushers at any particular court. This was met with an understanding smile. Now, the selection process is elaborate and prolonged and involves amongst other things applicants filling in forms giving examples (largely incapable of verification) to demonstrate the various qualities supposedly required. It is by no means clear that current methods, though certainly open and fair, produce better appointments. Currently there is a shortage of good applicants for judicial positions, and the High Court is at the moment (mid 2019) well below complement, which is a grave situation. It is partly caused by low pay in comparison with the cream of the Bar, high taxation, and harsh pension arrangements introduced without sufficient thought. (Medical consultants are currently limiting their work explicitly because of complicated and punitive pension arrangements devised by the Treasury apparently without concern for the consequences).

However, in my time the process was neither demanding nor arduous. A letter dated September 1992 arrived from Robin Holmes, head of Judicial Appointments, telling me that he 'had it in mind' to recommend me to the Queen for appointment to the Circuit Bench. It was followed by another in February 1993 saying that the Queen's approval had now been received and 'the way is clear for you to be sworn in by the Lord Chancellor'.

Appointments are made by Letters Patent, in my case signed by the Queen on '9th February in the forty-second year of our Reign', and countersigned by the Lord Chancellor, Lord Mackay of Clashfern. The document was enclosed in an attractive small red leather valise, which matched the ones I was given upon taking Silk, and upon becoming a Recorder. I swore 'well and truly to serve our Sovereign Lady Queen Elizabeth the Second' and 'to do right to all manner of people after the laws and usages of this realm without fear or favour affection or ill will'. Appointment also involved an invitation to tea in the Lord Chancellor's fine quarters in the House of Lords. Lord Mackay is a Scotsman of particular charm: quiet, with a gentle expression and shrewd eyes. He was a much-respected lawyer, and one of Margaret Thatcher's most successful ministers. One of his particular skills was holding the ring between the five judges who normally constituted a bench in the House of Lords. These individuals were occasionally keener on arguing with, and making points against, their fellow judges than in engaging with counsel at the lectern. Lord Mackay was also good at making himself accessible. At a Commonwealth legal conference in Vancouver I saw him – a very busy man - lingering at breakfast in the dining room for well over an hour, so that people might bump into him informally.

As soon as I had been appointed I felt not at all triumphant or delighted, but rather experienced a strong sense of anxiety, remorse and regret. The life of a promising youngish QC which I had just relinquished seemed most enviable, that of a Circuit Judge limited, tedious and poorly remunerated. I went so far as to make inquiries of the Chairman of the Bar Council as to whether, as far as he was concerned, I might return to practice. He said yes, slightly to my surprise. (Judges are supposed never to do this, and upon appointment agree not to. It is however questionable whether this could be enforced if ever put to the test.) Not being too much of a pioneer, I stayed where I was, almost certainly the right decision.

I had discussions with the Midland Circuit Administrator in order to agree an itinerary, or 'sitting pattern'. This was very important. Many Circuit Judges are rather passive about this and find themselves sitting at just one court centre, sometimes large, inconvenient and dismal and, indeed doing just one kind of work, usually crime. Some become trapped in family work, a desperate fate because of the unhappy plight of many of the children whose situation they have to evaluate but often cannot effectively alleviate. I had done little crime at the Bar, and none for the last few years. While quite content to do some criminal work, I did not want to find myself doing very much. It was and is slow and repetitive. It also gradually came to involve a very large number of sexual abuse cases, which are unpleasant both for judges and jurors. These can currently make up more than half the work of a criminal judge. Nor did I wish to sit at only one court, for there is much more pleasure to be had from variety – different staff, different fellow judges, different journeys and different atmospheres. Living as I did in North Oxfordshire, I was well located for several places. After discussion it was agreed that I would sit at Birmingham, Warwick, Northampton and Oxford. Oxford would be my base. All these courts were at that time on the Midland (or, strictly, Midland and Oxford) Circuit, and were readily accessible by car, which was important. They varied considerably in character. I was very fortunate to be able to enjoy this pleasant and unusual balance, which I did for many years.

Birmingham, England's second city, I knew well having been at university there. It had suffered from substantial post-war rebuilding projects, which tore down sound Victorian streets and installed a high-level inner ring road – a sort of urban motorway – itself to be wastefully demolished only a generation later. Criminal trials had for many years been held in a complex red brick palace on Corporation Street. But there was now a large new construction, the Queen Elizabeth building, with pleasant courtrooms and good facilities. Its senior judge, known as the Recorder of Birmingham, was often promoted to the High Court bench.

At least a dozen judges sat there, and they gathered in the judicial dining room for acceptable lunches, useful for exchanging news and views about the work of the court, the state of the trials, and discussion of legal problems. An amusing, small, bearded man called Ian Black was one of them. He had a very sharp and capable mind, but did not wish to be imposed upon. He had various stratagems for avoiding long and tedious trials, involving careful, staggered, early holiday reservation and other precautions. At a time when lunchtime drinking was losing favour, he would always ensure that a bottle or two of red wine was open and circulating, one of which he would consume himself, and he was apt to tease the more serious judges. He had printed a set of what he called 'Black's twelve Golden Rules' for living comfortably with the

Establishment, to enable judges not to be prevailed upon to try cases they did not wish to try. These included 'Never tell them how long you will be summing up,' 'If you volunteer to help out for you will only get some awful shit from someone else,' 'Never sit early and never sit late,' 'Beware of all eager beavers,' 'Ushers frequently know more about what is going on than Listing does' and so on. When at the Bar, even when a successful Silk, he used to economise on hotels by driving to court in a motor caravan and sleeping in the car park. He liked these vehicles, and once toured the Rocky Mountains in a Winnebago. I asked how he found the traffic. He replied that for most of the day as he gently wound around the hills there was nothing at all going his way. Only when he pulled in for the evening did a huge and inexplicable cavalcade pass along the road he had been navigating.

I tried a substantial case in Birmingham involving large-scale importation of drugs from the Pakistan/Afghan border. The evidence involved clandestine activity in Peshawar and a nearby village called Darra which has a large local industry involving the bespoke manufacture of working replica weapons, some of good quality. Several of the witnesses called were of the John Buchan type, operating as secret agents complete with Pathan camouflage and Indian accents. One of the defendants was represented by a rather slippery London QC, who improperly sent me notes about how he would like me to sum up. He made a number of submissions about admissibility which I rejected, whereupon he would react with theatrically-simulated astonishment. His client was convicted, appealed, and lost his appeal. Some ten years later, in the autumn of 2004, I was written to, twice, by a Customs and Excise solicitor, asking for 'relevant material' about this trial. I replied asking what this query was all about, as it was unexplained and seemed most mysterious. I had no reply.

Peter Crawford QC was the senior judge in Birmingham at the time, a handsome, capable and outspoken man, of robust views and with little time for bureaucratic complexities. He had tried my last case as a barrister. One lunchtime in 1993 he was musing over a suitable person of legal significance to invite to visit the court. I suggested Michael Howard, then Home Secretary, whom I knew, originally through the Inner Temple and the Bow Group. Michael came to Birmingham, inspected the courts, held discussions with the local judiciary and administration, and addressed a packed courtroom. He was a persuasive speaker and impressed a number of those who did not care for his politics. He was not disconcerted when it was suggested that in only about 5% of cases did a crime end up with a conviction. (It appears that the position now. 25 years later, is significantly worse. Because the police investigate so few crimes and the Crown Prosecution Service proceeds with far fewer trials than it might, the criminal justice system is simply not an effective method of detection, punishment or deterrence. Burglars operate with virtual impunity. But, oddly, the police seem quite keen on spending time on so called 'hate crimes' where someone might be upset about disagreeable remarks).

Much of the civil work in Birmingham was transferred from the Victorian County Court, on the fringes of the old gunmakers' quarter, to a new Civil Trial Centre. But, unlike the Queen Elizabeth building, this was not new at all: it was a converted department store, inside which a number of courts and judicial chambers (rooms in which judges worked when they were not conducting trials) were inserted. The prime objective of the architects seemed to be to construct courts with as little natural daylight as possible, although the building's outer walls consisted largely of fenestration with interesting high-level city views. Some rooms were constructed with no windows at all. One such claustrophobic internal cell was shaped like a triangular slice of cheese. Some judges accepted this, but I did not, which led to a little passing friction, but a different room. The whole edifice was a maze of corridors and internal fire doors, confusingly different on each floor, which meant that getting in and out of the building could take a long time. Occasionally one was tantalisingly confronted with doors to the street, which were marked, as though they were sentient, by notices stating 'activated by security'. Sometimes, activated by frustration, I went through them to get to the outside world.

As time went by Birmingham became increasingly inaccessible. The

Aston Expressway, a dual carriageway leading to its centre, gradually became so coagulated that I took a different route from the south, which passed through areas such as Kings Heath and Moseley, 19th century suburbs with pleasant Victorian terraces. These had gradually become occupied by people of Indian or Pakistani extraction, whose marts and costumes gave an exotic veneer to this part of the city. Soon this approach too became so slow as to be unacceptable. When I began to sit in Birmingham it used to take just over an hour from home to court. When, after a few years, I stopped going there, the journey was closer to two. Besides what the radio likes to refer to as 'sheer volume of traffic', matters were being made much worse by modifications to the central roads, which narrowed the main routes and blocked all the short cuts (on one of which I once had quite a nasty collision, partly my fault). It was as though city planners wished to insulate the centre of Birmingham from access from the outside world, anyway by car. Their measures certainly insulated it from me.

Northampton must in the 18th and 19th centuries have been an attractive county town, with a handsome central square. The square still exists, but is now surrounded by coarse urban development in most directions. I called it on one occasion, in a document which came to public attention, 'largely ruined'; a phrase which was publicised in *The Times* and elsewhere, and with which there was general agreement. The court centre, built to replace the Sessions House and faced with very pale bricks, is no masterpiece. Not offensive as such buildings go, it is neither handsome nor elegant, and the courtrooms resemble large white shoe boxes with roof lights. When I began to sit there the senior Judge was Francis Allen, who only did crime, and did it at tremendous speed. To be fast is certainly much better than to be slow, assuming fair trials with proper outcomes. But velocity should not be overdone, and with him just occasionally it was. Francis was a friendly and helpful man who liked driving a small open sports car. One of his hobbies was long-distance walking, for which I believe he had great stamina.

I tried a case in Northampton arising from a riot at Whitemoor Prison. At one stage I was asked to order that a witness should give evidence in handcuffs. This is unusual, and only done when there is demonstrable danger. I refused the application, and was looking down at my notebook as he was brought into the witness box, quite close to the judge's bench. When I looked up, I saw what appeared to be a very large green lizard. Upon scrutiny it appeared that the man's entire neck and head – he had no hair – had been tattooed with green scales. I felt I might have been wrong about the handcuffs. Over the scales were wisps of tattooed ivy, which twined around a circlet of tattooed barbed wire. It was highly disconcerting, and very difficult to avoid staring. However, appearances, as they say, can be deceptive. Whatever his underlying psychiatric condition, he spoke in pleasantly modulated tones and was no fool. At one stage prosecuting counsel said to him 'Well, Mr So and So, how can you expect the jury to believe a word you say? You are a convicted criminal.' 'That' he replied, 'is a very silly observation, if I may say so. My conviction is for murder, and murder does not involve dishonesty.' Counsel was taken aback, and a loud rustle of amusement ran around the court.

At Northampton I had an early success in civil work. Employees – usually Scottish – of the nearby Corby steel factory had brought several hundred claims in which it was contended that they had been rendered deaf by reason of the noisy conditions in which they had worked. Many of these claims had been brought years after the men had retired, as a result of advertising by firms of solicitors, along the lines: 'Are you deaf? Did you work at Corby? You may be entitled to damages.' Not surprisingly many people thought it worth having a go. But there were questions of limitation, namely had the case been brought too late, too long after the plaintiff knew or should have known that he had been harmed by the conditions of work. There were also problems of causation, for older people often go deaf for reasons which have nothing to do with noise exposure at work. The volume of litigation threatened to swamp the Northampton County Court, and this being a major problem it was thought appropriate to hand it to a junior newcomer. Fortunately, I had some experience at the Bar of this kind of litigation, and I tried three claims as test cases. It was soon clear that all the plaintiffs, to the extent that they did have noise-induced hearing loss, had known perfectly well while they were at work that the noise was affecting their hearing. They had chosen to do nothing about it, in some instances for a decade or more. I found that they were not entitled to proceed, being out of time. You cannot put a cause of action on a shelf and leave it there, to take down and use much later when the mood takes you. The plaintiffs appealed, and I was upheld. The rest of the cases were then either discontinued or settled. This was regarded as a most satisfactory outcome by those running the court, and indeed by me.

In 2004 the government announced plans to allow 24-hour drinking. Since a high proportion of crimes of violence were committed by people who were drunk, and since many town centres were already rendered nocturnally disagreeable or frankly dangerous by so-called 'binge drinkers', this did not seem sensible. In January 2005, while sentencing three men from Kettering for assaults committed while inebriated and high on drugs, who had left their victim in a coma, I indicated that the proposals seemed a very bad idea. I called the convicted men 'urban savages', which was accurate. These observations caught the attention of the national press, and there were headlines and many prominent articles (one by our current prime minister), over several days, in papers ranging from *The Times* to the *Daily Mail*. The BBC also got in touch and I did several radio interviews, unusual for a judge. The government had been pointing out that so-called continental drinking hours might be thought a good thing. I observed that continental-style drinking required continental-style people, happy to sit civilised at tables chatting philosophically or romantically – not stand up holding bottles and shouting at each other while consuming, literally, a gallon or more of beer before roving off aggressively into the night. The coverage was extensive and very favourable. The government, for no apparent good reason, went ahead and abolished the restrictions on drinking hours. Public drunkenness and associated violence duly rose, as did pressure upon police forces and hospitals.

I liked working at Northampton. It was a pleasant brisk cross-country drive, the staff were friendly, in some cases very friendly, and the judges good company. One of these was Richard Bray: an able man, three months younger than me. He did not take Silk, and went on the bench in 1993. But what he really enjoyed were golf, tennis (both real and lawn) and cricket. He was keen to put in as much time at these pastimes as was possible. He sat largely in crime, and like Francis Allen, liked to get through his cases with maximum expedition. There were occasions when, having arrived at about 10.15 and sat at 10.30, he took a plea, sentenced, and was away again by 10.45. But this was rare; more usually it took him an hour. He did not discourage the press in his court, and refused any suggestion that he accept a 'ticket' (i.e. be given authority) to try sexual cases.

For most of the time that I sat there Northampton enjoyed proper catering (since abolished for economy reasons), and those lunching were often amused by Bray's unrestrained remarks about senior members of the judiciary and the administration. He enjoyed teasing Judge Peter Morrell (now ordained), whose anecdotes could be of some length, and another judge, Charles Wide, who was very punctilious in his case management and always regarded it as astonishing that I sat on the national Criminal Procedure Rules Committee. I had indeed been surprised to be appointed. (After he succeeded me in that position the Rules – until then commendably spare – began to expand exponentially). Wide, married to Ursula Buchan, a gardening expert and descendant and biographer of the author John Buchan, left Northampton to better himself in London, though he did not, I believe, get exactly the position he wanted. I enjoyed his company. Another regular was Ian Alexander QC, but we did not see much of him at lunches; he liked long frauds, sat unusual hours, and was often bravely recovering from injuries received while out hunting.

The dining room at Northampton has now been converted by the Court Service into a 'judicial kitchenette', complete with memorial plaque, and the male judges sit pathetically at its specially-commissioned round table, now next to a sink, with triangular cellophane packets of sandwiches. The female judges tend to bring more interesting and wholesome food, salads in translucent containers, and they sometimes use a plate. The cupboard-lift, in which proper cooked food used to arrive from the kitchens below, including at the appropriate time Christmas lunches, sits empty and unused.

The Bench and Bar in Northampton benefitted from a generous line of Sheriffs, who gave us all lunch once a year, often attended by a visiting High Court Judge. On one occasion this was James Hunt, a shrewd, amusing, robust and heavily-built man with a fine bass voice (he had prevented *Hello* magazine from publishing pictures of the Douglas/Zeta Jones wedding). He got up to thank our hosts as follows: 'The definition of hospitality is the art of making people feel at home – when you wish they were. It is time for us to go'. It was not just sheriffs who enlivened things. For many years the Lord Lieutenant of Northamptonshire was Lady Juliet Townsend, a wonderful bustling woman of energy, altruism, charm and common sense. Granddaughter of FE Smith, the famous advocate and Lord Chancellor, she had been a discreet Lady in Waiting to Princess Margaret, and was an author who reviewed for *The Spectator*. Whenever there was any excuse she would arrange splendid civic parades, with a band playing and ceremonial marching to the handsomely porticoed All Saints church in the centre of the square. There would be a stimulating service with resounding English hymns sung at excellent volume. She died, a young 73, in 2014. Her husband, equally estimable, runs the best bookshop for miles around, in Brackley.

Warwick was the most picturesque and atmospheric of the courts at which I sat. It was a fine eighteenth century building with two octagonal pillared courts, each with Corinthian columns supporting top lights with stucco embellishment. The jury box in the number one court was near to and level with the judge's canopied seat and small desk. Counsel, jury and witnesses were all close together, and defendants sat in a dock surrounded by metalwork, low down in the centre of the room. There was a high-level public gallery, occasionally filled with vocal supporters of the prisoners. Trials there were invested with a real sense of occasion and of history. Elsewhere and upstairs was a third courtroom, small and sunny, decorated with photographs of past High Sheriffs, and used mainly for civil work, though occasionally juries were empanelled, awkwardly, from the steep stone staircase for a minor criminal trial. On one occasion one of the potential jurors was a friend of mine, Miranda Seel, a slim and elegant woman who lived not far from home. On seeing her as I entered the hall at about 9.30, we exchanged a social kiss. News of this shot around the court staff – 'the judge is kissing a juror!' There was a great deal of ribaldry, and the clerk ensured that the lady in question was not empanelled in my court. My usher that day, a female black belt at judo, said that this was not to happen again.

The senior judge at Warwick when I began to sit there was Michael Harrison Hall, himself of some historical interest. A tall and stooping man, he had practised at the Birmingham Bar and lived conveniently at Barford, a small village about two miles away. He was dark, with a little of the appearance of Charles the Second. His eyes were hooded – he occasionally simulated sleep in court at moments of tedium – and his lips were full, accustomed to accommodating a wine glass. His mind was pretty sharp, his manner languid, and he did not waste words. Not ambitious, though an able, confident and an effective judge, he was no more industrious than he needed to be. At lunchtime it was customary to rise at 1pm and then go through to the drawing room of the adjacent judge's lodgings. There, beneath a number of modest historical portraits, was laid a circular mahogany table, with proper cutlery and glass. Harrison Hall would be standing with a sherry decanter poised, his own glass charged but barely begun, and would dispense amontillado or Tio Pepe to those joining him.

We were waited upon by an ex-steward from HMS *Ark Royal*, and generally had soup, roast meat and vegetables (though Harrison Hall ate no green vegetables at all) and then some kind of tart, cheese and biscuits and coffee. For this we paid a municipally-subsidised £5. To one of these lunches the journalist and TV presenter Anna Ford was brought as a guest by Bob Marshall Andrews QC, a Labour MP and an amusing speaker and occasional playwright, who was sitting at Warwick as a Recorder. I was late, not introduced, and took some time to recognise her. We had an interesting talk about what behaviour might justify throwing wine over politicians. These lunches lasted until the court service closed the courts at Warwick, although nobody actually wanted this closure except the police. The work was transferred to a characterless modern building (inappropriately incorporating a police station) in Leamington Spa. There, in a newly-designed and expensively-constructed courtroom, it was quickly discovered that the jury box had been placed in such a relationship to the judicial bench that the judge could not see two of the jurors, and vice versa. This was not a mistake made by 18th Century architects. The Duke of Edinburgh came to inspect these new premises, and asked one of the Judges what his role was. 'I am the Resident Judge' he replied proudly, meaning that he was the senior judge at that court. 'I see,' said the Duke, 'do you have a comfortable bedroom?'

After Michael Harrison Hall's retirement, things were not quite so happy, for there was tension between two of the other judges (who rather disliked each other) about the disposition of work and other matters. The new judge in charge became known as 'Two Gun', because he combined running Warwick with running Coventry. When I visited, although we got on well, there was often a tang of anxiety or discontent hanging in the air. Judge James Pyke was perhaps the most discontented, because he was, he often told me over breakfast at a nearby pub, regularly allocated work which he felt another judge should be doing. He would then regale me with accounts of the delightful concerts he planned to attend, or had attended, in New England, where he thought he might retire.

Oxford, where I had never appeared as an advocate, was the main reason I had joined the Circuit Bench in 1993, as I expected it to be both enjoyable and convenient. Both, in due course, proved to be true. It is one of England's most attractive cities (dire traffic arrangements apart) and 15 miles south of where I live. The court building is in a conversion of a handsome Morris car salesroom and garage. I embellished my room with animal prints and an original painting of a Lord Chancellor by Felix Topolski. Some judges made their chambers into a cosy combination of study (desk and files), kitchen (electric kettle, cupboards full of cups, saucers and biscuits, a mini fridge), and sitting room (two or three comfy arm chairs). The Oxford premises, which contain some good courtrooms (one of which, number six, I later helped to design) are in St Aldates, opposite the police station. Outside this the police regularly parked - on double white lines, and in a bus or cycle lane, for hours on end. After a year or two I reported this flagrant contempt for highway regulations by letter to the Chief Constable – one Peter Neyroud, who was academically qualified to an extent unusual for a policeman. Despite several reminders, he never replied. He came to lunch at court one day and told me that he never did reply to correspondence. This was a surprising thing to hear, especially from a man who has written several works on police ethics. However, the improper police parking did, largely, come to an end.

I had hopes of sitting mostly in civil work at Oxford and had so agreed with the circuit administrator in Birmingham. But when I first arrived I was told by Harold Wilson, then senior judge at Oxford, that 'there really is no civil'. Harold was an avuncular man. Aged 62, he had been in the RAF, had once worked as a schoolmaster, and had been in charge of courts in Coventry before coming to Oxford. He was of modest size, slightly rotund, very friendly, and a pleasant, skilful and popular tribunal who felt that all judges should do every kind of work and not specialise. He was determined and formidable in his dealings with the administration. He fostered esprit de corps by arranging small judicial dinners in a Siamese restaurant in Summertown.

When he said that there was no civil, he was not far wrong. There seemed to be three reasons for this. Solicitors need to get a good service from the courts they use, both during the procedural gestation of a case and when it comes to trial. Oxford had suffered for some time from a procedural judge who had been found awkward and difficult, but he had gone. The civil listing officer was not at all an easy woman to work with. But most importantly, the Judge who did try such civil as was litigated was remarkably slow. James Irvine was one of the most delightful people one could hope to meet. Always smartly turned out in black jacket and waistcoat and striped trousers (with double, forward facing pleats in classical style), he often wore a buttonhole, and always exuded a slightly elaborate but very distinct charm. When I first arrived at Oxford he greeted me with an enthusiasm that was most endearing. He was sociable, quick-witted and an attractive self-deprecating raconteur, who liked to ask guests to lunch at court.

He was quite a good lawyer, though too punctilious. But above all, he was exceedingly slow. Normally a judge would take notes as the evidence was given, jotting down an elision of such questions and answers as were relevant, distilling the material evidence, and recording at the rate of speech. James however, would say 'watch my pen'; halt the flow of testimony, and write down exact questions and answers in careful script. This process could take a very long time indeed. I was told by a number of solicitors that trials which might have been expected to take a day or two before a judge of ordinary expedition might take up to a week before Judge Irvine. His conclusions were rarely wrong, but legal time costs money, and parties want swift resolution. So though he was a popular man, he was not really very satisfactory for civil litigation. For reasons not explained to me he never did crime. Perhaps he was best suited to adoptions, where he radiated kindness to the children and their new parents and entertained them with displays of legal headgear.

Not only children were thus entertained. Quite often we had visits by substantial groups of foreign lawyers, whom we would receive in one of the larger courtrooms, providing a bench of two or three judges to talk about English law. James Irvine would go into court equipped with three wigs: a bar wig, which has tails, curls and a bow; a bench wig – short, dense and unembellished; and a full-bottomed wig, with descending banks of curls down to the shoulder (now entirely ceremonial). These he would model to the rows of earnest visitors and combine the displays with explanations of the various other articles of judicial attire – jabots, bands, robes, hoods, sashes, tippets – he was a virtuoso with the appropriate vocabulary. After about 15 minutes of this his audiences would be quite satisfied that they had an excellent understanding of the English legal system.

I twice gave talks to large parties of Chinese so-called judges. They could not understand how the government here ensured that the courts reached the decisions it wanted. I explained the concept of judicial independence. They had no concept of this whatsoever, and both accepted and expected that government should be able to influence and control the bench. Ideas of justice in large parts of the Far East are very unlike our own. In Japan almost every criminal conviction involves a confession by the Defendant, detained in discomfort for as long as it takes an admission to be forthcoming.

Two other judges were based at Oxford at that time. Richard May, later His Excellency Judge May, was a criminal specialist and enthusiast. He positively enjoyed criminal law, criminal procedure and criminal trials. He wrote about them. A swarthy man of grey complexion, he did have a sense of humour, but it needed to be unearthed. At one time interested in politics, he had stood against Margaret Thatcher at Finchley, and he was a friend of the then Labour Lord Chancellor, Derry Irvine. In 1997 Irvine persuaded him to become a judge at the International Criminal Tribunal for what had been Yugoslavia, in The Hague. I suspect that May came to regret this. He had a lonely and difficult time there, trying Slobodan Milosevic, a wily, brutal tyrant, in disagreeable and hotly-contested proceedings which lasted not weeks, nor months, but years. He had to do this in company with two other judges (not English) neither of whom had any practical knowledge of how to run a criminal trial. The whole burden fell upon him. He contracted a fatal brain tumour while still in this employment and died in July 2004, a few weeks after he was knighted.

Paul Clark was a different character altogether. He was almost professionally amiable; a member of the Garrick, and extremely friendly to everyone, especially to the dons of Oxford colleges, where he liked to be entertained. Born in 1940, though with dense black hair showing no trace of grey and an always-tanned complexion, he looked younger.

He had been keen to get onto the bench and was appointed at the early age of 45. Although he had been accomplished academically, he was not keen on civil trials which were at all complex and strove very hard to get the parties to settle. Sometimes he would come into my room and say: 'I don't think I am really cut out for this case Charles; would you like to have a go at it?' He once did this after the case had started.

Towards the end of his judicial career he had the misfortune to be knocked off his bicycle by a Mini and sustained a serious head injury. He returned to work, but was not quite as he had been. He retired early. He was to die of cancer in 2008, aged 68. A memorial service was held for him at New College, at which, unusually, an old friend read out an address which Paul had himself composed. It was very unlike the speech I had made at a dinner I had organised to celebrate his retirement. He had been married since 1997 to another Circuit Judge, Jackie Davies, a Yorkshire woman of some determination and pith, known professionally as a Sister of Small Mercy. She sat in Doncaster, not convenient for a conventional married life, and succeeded me in due course as President of the Council of Circuit Judges, an office Paul had himself held 13 years before. She too spoke eloquently at his memorial; a service at which there was no reference whatsoever to Paul's first wife, by whom he had three children.

It was as a colleague of these personalities that I began to sit at Oxford. An early and unusual case involved an appeal from magistrates in a matter concerning red deer. Anthony Barclay, a local landowner, bred these on his property south of Oxford, where periodically they were shot for sale as venison. This saved them the trauma of capture and transport to a slaughterhouse. The local authority one day sent a man to inspect this process, who reported seeing frightened deer running at the fencing. Barclay was prosecuted for causing suffering to the animals, and was convicted by the magistrates. On the appeal it rapidly became clear that the animals had been startled not by any activity of his, or of his rifleman, but by the unexpected appearance of the inspector, a man who admitted knowing nothing at all about deer, and who himself had caused them to panic. The appeal was allowed, and substantial costs were awarded, which the prosecution was most reluctant to pay. They had to be recalled to court on two occasions for the order to be enforced.

A sadder trial involved a double-decker bus which was driven so fast as it turned off the A40 dual carriageway that it rolled over, killing a number of passengers. The driver rather surprisingly denied doing anything inappropriate, but was convicted. One of those killed was an American girl called Misty Autumn Dubois, whose parents attended the trial, and the cadence of whose unusual name I shall always remember.

In May 1997 I sentenced an Oxford undergraduate to three years in a young offenders' institution for possessing more than £2000 worth of ecstasy, cocaine and cannabis for supply to other students. For some reason this made the front page of the *London Evening Standard*, and, less surprisingly, it caused quite a stir amongst the occupants of the Oxford colleges – one of whom was my younger son.

My early attempts to try civil work were obstructed by the then Listing Officer. Besides trying to control the allocation of rooms to particular judges, which was not her job, she had her own ideas about the importance of civil, rating it below both crime and family, and she also seemed to think that it was open to her to move judges from one town to another, without discussion or agreement. On one occasion, when I had been listed, unusually but appropriately, to try a substantial personal injury case at Oxford, she relisted it without explanation the evening before, in front of Judge Irvine, and sent a message that I was to go to Warwick. This was not behaviour to be tolerated and I complained to the Presiding Judge of the Circuit, the Circuit Administrator, and elsewhere. Soon afterwards she left, and matters improved considerably.

In 1996 I was authorised to try High Court cases, and did my first in Oxford, in March of that year. It lasted six days. It should be explained that a lot of High Court work, usually more difficult or valuable than that regularly done by Circuit Judges in the county courts, is not in fact listed before High Court judges. Because there are not enough

High Court judges, some Circuit Judges are used to do their work. They are not however paid High Court rates for doing so. To have this authorisation is a modest but agreeable accolade and enables the recipient to sit at the Royal Courts of Justice in the Strand, where he or she is treated as though a real High Court Judge (and addressed as My Lord, or Lady, rather than Your Honour). It is of course unfair to expect High Court work to be done at Circuit Judge rates. But considerations of fairness do not always rank high in the minds of those responsible for judicial employment, as was to become apparent.

It was in London that I was invited in 1998 to award £750,000 commission upon the purchase of the Ritz hotel for £75 million three years before. The claim was a determined speculative enterprise, the evidence was complicated and unconvincing. The plaintiff, camouflaged in opaque corporate wrappings (Agincourt Associates Ltd, a Liberian company belonging to a Channel Island Trust, established by a Greek), simply could not show that it had effected any relevant introduction or was the effective cause of the sale, which had proceeded after discussions between Sir Charles Powell, on the board of the vendor company, and one or both of the Barclay brothers.

In the same year I was not persuaded that a Barings Bank executive was entitled to an £800,000 bonus when his bank had lost £860 million as a result of Nicholas Leeson's unauthorised trading.

More difficult to resolve was a claim for the value of a remarkable 13 carat pink salt-water pearl, lost in 2008 by a London jeweller to which it had been entrusted. The owner sought $650,000, and his evidence disclosed that there were several international dealers, buying and selling at remarkable (though unpublicised) prices to secretive men of extreme wealth, often in the Persian Gulf. This persuaded me that the shop's 'market-price' valuation of $250,000 was considerably too low, and that the claim was justified.

In a case against Warwick University I tried as a High Court Judge in May 2002, I had to consider the position in a situation where a plaintiff who had sustained a very modest personal injury was suspected of exaggerating her disability. She had cut her hand, but was later contending that its use was seriously impaired, and she sought over £135,000 in damages. The defendant's insurers engaged an inquiry agent to visit her at home under the ruse of market research. The agent was able secretly to film her, revealing full function in her hand. The plaintiff's lawyers argued that this was 'illegally obtained evidence' and should not be admitted. It was, and doubtless still is, quite common for plaintiffs to exaggerate, or even to invent, disability in order to obtain substantial damages: in other words, fraudulently to seek to obtain money by deception (for which they are never prosecuted). What are defendants to do if they cannot protect themselves by some modest though improper subterfuge? I held that the trial would be unfair if their evidence could not be put before the judge. Seven months later the case went to the Court of Appeal, which found itself in some difficulty. It had to recognise the relevance and fairness of admitting the evidence, but it did not wish to encourage infringement of privacy. It held that it would be artificial and undesirable to exclude the evidence (so the appeal failed), but on the other hand it was wrong to obtain it, so it ordered the defendant, the winning party, to pay the costs. As Lord Woolf CJ said: 'We do not pretend that this is a perfect reconciliation of the conflicting public interests. It is not.'

Lord Woolf (Harry as he is known by Bar and Bench) is a friendly and approachable man who rose high in the judiciary. He visited us at Oxford on one occasion, took a close interest in all that was going on, and allowed himself to be photographed in court with the local judiciary, to the delight of the Oxford Times.

In the Spring of every year a new High Sheriff is sworn in at the Oxford Combined Court. The largest courtroom is packed with family and supporters, judges occupy the jury box and rows of former Sheriffs fill counsels' benches. These events are handled with formality – sometimes jovial formality – by a visiting High Court Judge (though I swore in one Sheriff, the estimable Lady McLintock). A lengthy antique oath is read with varying degrees of fluency from an unpunctuated text, and short speeches made. (One year an outgoing sheriff became rather carried away, and talked for rather too long. His wife was keen to follow too, but was deftly thwarted by His Honour Julian Hall). At the ceremony, each former sheriff and each current judge used to be called by name, rise, bow and sign a register. This was followed by a 'shield hanging' ceremony at which a little coat of arms would be dedicated to the wall of the hall outside. This all took quite a long time, so every few years the programme was modified a bit to shorten it: the public signing has now been omitted. These ceremonies provide a touch of history and pageantry, and an opportunity for the Lord Lieutenant, with impressive uniform and deft phrase, to remind the county of the quality and significance of the outgoing sheriff. The sheriffs themselves, if ex-soldiers (as many once were) wear dress uniform and proper swords; if civilian, then an expensive (thanks to tailors Ede and Ravenscroft) confection of velvet knee breeches, eighteenth century coat and jabot, and sometimes a dinky little weapon seeming more apt to bend than slay. Some lady sheriffs wear impressive dress-coats, and all sport confident hats jauntily embellished with plumes or aigrettes.

Sheriffs are usually altruistic people; dedicated, hard-working and charming. Catalysts and facilitators in the county, most foster a particular charity, visit establishments of a caring kind, encourage worthwhile organisations and give receptions, garden parties and dinners at which all sorts of people are invited to mix. It is interesting to note the changing character of the shrievalty. Between 1954 and 1960 there were seven ex-soldiers in succession. In 1984 Isabella Hutchinson was the first female sheriff – in a line which went back 783 years to 1201. The next, 13 years later. was Lady French, wife of a High Court Judge. As time goes by more and more have been female. In the decade from 2010 there will have been be six women. The lady sheriff for 2020 lives in the same romantically set house as Isabella Hutchinson did 46 years before. Many female sheriffs have special talents. Oxfordshire has had a fine singer; a biochemist, plant enthusiast, chatelaine and keen shot; a wine expert with astonishing stamina and outspoken enthusiasm; and a director of one of France's great companies. But the men can be pretty good too. Several have been people of remarkable acumen and charitable disposition. The Sheriffs of Oxfordshire have always been keen to associate with the Judges and hospitable to them, a debt which I sometimes feel has not invariably been satisfactorily repaid.

Chapter 12

Making a court flourish

A civil trial exists on several levels. The subject matter itself might be interesting – why did a car catch fire, was a woman being cheated by her son-in-law, was the horse dangerous, where did the world's most expensive pearls come from – and the personalities of the witnesses will vary infinitely, and can be very engaging. The advocates will have different techniques, strengths and weaknesses. There will be a sense that, after ages spent in preparation, now is the showdown. The state of the law may be clear, developing or uncertain. As the parties come in and settle themselves with their files, bundles and unnecessary plastic bottles of water, an atmosphere will emerge: often tense, sometimes relaxed or business-like, sometimes frankly antagonistic. There may be a chatter of spectators, there might be a press reporter, though latterly local papers could rarely be bothered to attend civil trials, and thereby missed a lot of interesting material. The usher will have been out among those attending and reporting things she thinks the Judge might like to know. Atmosphere in court is partly the consequence of the elements just mentioned, partly a matter of the architecture, type and age of the court (a Victorian library at the Royal Courts of Justice, full of wood and old leather, a clinical white space at Northampton) and partly the character of the Judge. Some are popular, some disliked, a few are feared, some admired, one or two not highly regarded. Occasionally, if the case is difficult, the advocates formidable or the subject matter delicate, the Judge himself might be nervous. But this happens less with experience.

It is of course satisfactory when judges are liked by litigants or counsel, though they should not try to make themselves popular by seeking obsequious laughter. But nor should they operate as silent sphinxes, concealing what they are thinking and instilling a sense of chill and anxiety. As well as being disconcerting for the parties and witnesses this type of judge is often unpopular at the Bar because they give no indication about how they perceive the evidence or the effect of the relevant law – which means that barristers have to try to deal with everything, when almost always the heart of a case is in a small compass.

The aim should be to conduct trials in a pleasant and efficient way, getting to the crux of the matter in hand without wasting time, but properly exploring what needs to be explored. This is easier done in civil than in crime, where judges try not to intervene much and where there is often pressure to introduce irrelevance, especially if it might assist a defendant.

Litigation is a serious matter for the parties, who will probably have invested a lot of money, time and hope in anxious contemplation of their day in court. They should never feel that the tribunal is hurried or flippant, though an occasional touch of humour can lighten proceedings and lubricate progress agreeably. It is helpful because the participants will relax a little, witnesses may speak more easily and the parties may co-operate more readily.

Both litigants and advocates will be reassured if at an early stage the judge can demonstrate a grasp of the issues, show that he or she has not made his mind up prematurely and is approaching the trial in a fair and disinterested manner. (Disinterested means impartial, and is not a synonym for 'uninterested' as many people seem to believe. It might also here be observed that an 'issue' does not mean a 'problem'; it means a question about which there is disagreement, which may require determination. And 'determination' does not mean strong adherence to a fixed intention, it means a finding or resolution).

In the 1960s and 70s it was normal for a judge to go into court having done little or no preparatory reading, and it was up to counsel to 'open' the case in detail, explain the factual background, the evidential disputes, and introduce the documents and the relevant law. This could take a long time and is no longer thought to be appropriate. Now, before a civil trial starts, the Judge is supposed to have found time to absorb the pleadings (documents from each side setting out their case), read the witness statements – which are now disclosed in advance – and looked at the so-called 'skeleton arguments'. These are, or should be, a succinct written summary of the background, the points at issue and the contentions to be made, both factual and legal. In a case with expert evidence the judge should also have looked at this and appreciated its tenor.

This approach has some obvious advantages. It can save time in court. But too much preparation in this context is not a good thing. It gives rise to a risk that the judges mind may be prematurely made up, based upon what has been read, rather than upon evaluation and appreciation of the actual live witnesses and the outcome of discussion (called argument) with counsel. If your mind is already made up, or even predisposed, it may be hard both to look upon a matter in a different way, and for those arguing the case to enjoy a fair run at their task. A further disadvantage of too much judicial preparation is that many cases settle just before they are due to begin – 'at the door of the court' – and when this happens judges may feel that time spent in prior work (generally their own time the night before) has been wasted.

There were of course areas of the law in which it was possible to be both knowledgeable and confident. But in others one might well be a great deal less expert, and, occasionally know nothing at all. (I never had an entirely sure instinct about the law of property, which often seemed to attract erudite counsel who were clever lawyers rather than good advocates). In such cases it was always a good idea to transmit some indication to the Bar. Not, ideally, by announcing 'this is law about which I am completely ignorant', because generally litigants seem to expect judges to be omniscient and might lose confidence, but to say, 'I believe this is an area with quite intricate legislation, and I would appreciate your submissions on the law at the outset'. This would let those conducting the case appreciate your state of mind, and they would then provide the necessary education. They would know where they were. The more confident the judge, the more readily does he or she admit to ignorance where it exists.

The essence of the judicial task in civil cases is to find the facts where these are not agreed (which is what a jury has to do in crime) and then apply the law to these facts. Sometimes the law itself may be unclear, and it is then necessary to decide what it is. The law is to be found in previous judicial decisions, statutes and regulations, but not textbooks. Textbooks are helpful guides but are not determinative. A look of tragic gloom can overcome an advocate who has been asked what the law is, reads a paragraph from a book, and is then asked 'do you have the authority for that proposition?'

Modern procedural rules envisage that evidence will generally be received by putting in a witness's written statement, and then for the witness to be cross-examined upon it. This might sound sensible, and sometimes is, but in cases where there is significant factual dispute this course has considerable disadvantages, and I often did not follow it. The statement will normally have been 'taken' and written up by a solicitor or other agent. The judge does not know what the witness would have said if asked to give evidence to the court in his or her own words. Very often a witness statement would be in language far removed from that which the witness would naturally use. 'Mr claimant,' said counsel, opening his cross examination, 'what did you mean by the word "exiguous" in the fourth paragraph of your statement?' Blank look. 'Well. I don't really know'. 'So you used a word whose meaning you did not understand. Why did you do that?' 'My solicitor drew up my statement.' 'Yes, but you read it and signed it as true. How could you do that without knowing what it meant?' This immediately puts a witness at a major disadvantage, which he or she would not have suffered if asked to give evidence live, and naturally casts doubt upon the reliability of the evidence produced in support of the case.

Weak points may be camouflaged by careful drafting of statements so that relevant material is absent. Listening to witnesses giving evidence, while noting their statements, it was often apparent that there was substantial discrepancy between the two. This in itself was revealing. Cross examination, a wonderful instrument for establishing the truth when well carried out, takes far longer if it first has to be established what witnesses would have said if left to themselves, before challenging and testing what that turns out to be.

There is a further advantage in requiring witnesses to tell their story to the court live (which in criminal cases is always done, unless there is no dispute). It is that they will first be questioned sympathetically and carefully by their own barristers, who will not be trying to trip them up or show them in a bad light. A witness can then gain some confidence in the witness box, which is an alarming and exposed place to find oneself. If the first questions put are awkward to deal with, as well they may be in cross examination, some will never do themselves justice.

Counsel sometimes find themselves in difficulty when asked a question from the bench about some detail or aspect of the litigation, or about some matter which could probably be resolved between themselves. Rather than provoke a spell of embarrassment in open court in front of their clients, it was often helpful to rise for five minutes so that they could have a word with each other. This occasionally produced unexpected settlements. If some pre-trial step or procedure (of which there are now lamentably many) had been omitted, it was generally useful to ask if it made any difference before engaging in analysis of why this was and who was at fault. Mostly it made none.

When I first began to sit as a judge I was startled by the modest quality of some of the barristers and solicitors who appeared before me. The task of an advocate is to present his or her client's case persuasively and accurately, to attack the opposing case effectively, and to inform – but never to mislead – the court. To do this requires detailed preparation and deft presentation, as well as quick thought, articulate language, technique with witnesses, and legal knowledge. Often some, or sometimes all, of these qualities were missing. In 1994 I wrote a series of articles, called 'The Art of the Advocate', for the *Solicitors Journal* in an attempt to be of assistance to those who needed it, and this material was also used in some lectures to Bar students at the Inner Temple. These were well received but, like occasional observations in court, could hardly be expected to have much widespread effect. Throughout 24 years on the bench I periodically encountered advocates who failed to do quite basic things. Some did not dress tidily and looked a mess, some did not prepare properly and did not know the detail of their cases, some could not elicit evidence or cross-examine effectively and with focus, and a few did not understand or accurately articulate the law. Sometimes all these faults were combined, occasionally compounded by lateness or an almost incomprehensible accent. But there were many advocates of style, skill and grace who expressed themselves attractively, cross-examined with charm and incision, were a pleasure to listen to and who guided the court though complexity and difficulty. When both sides were of the same high quality it was a delight to be the Judge, especially if the subject matter was intrinsically interesting. There could be few more agreeable ways usefully to spend a day.

What was less agreeable was to come in every morning at about eight o'clock and find my desk covered with sets of papers put there by the court staff after I had gone home leaving it clear the night before. There might be ten, fifteen, twenty bundles – some in long term confusion, with brittle, decayed elastic bands, pieces of tape and torn sheets of paper –concerning the gestation and progress of cases not yet ready for trial. Some would be straightforward and properly arranged, but others might be an infuriating tangle of correspondence, a muddle of court documents, a contradiction of previous orders, violently or sorrowfully expressed letters from litigants in person, cases sent from other courts and all manner of matters in which things had gone wrong or not happened at all. I much disliked this work, which came to me after 1998 when I was first appointed Judge in charge of civil (the so called Designated Civil Judge, or DCJ). I used to tackle it impatiently along the line of least resistance, disposing first of the papers which needed only a glance, and finally reaching those which really called for a furnace. Over time a certain instinct developed, and it might only be necessary to read the last few documents. In really messy cases it was often best to make an 'unless' order – unless you do so and so by such and such a time, the case will be struck out – or to call the parties in for a short hearing, where by question and answer it was generally possible to specify some sensible resolution.

It is commonly asserted by the ignorant or hostile that judges are out of touch, or lack contact with ordinary people. This is utterly wrong. Circuit Judges deal daily with the widest possible variety of individuals, from the most unfortunate or hopeless, who may have nowhere to live, no work, no money, and many associated problems, to the highly successful, who will have different things to worry about. Judges deal with human predators and human prey. They deal with the fit and the ill, those who have been let down by commercial organisations, those who have suffered physically or financially from negligence or breach of contract, or from the consequences of divorce, injury or death. I have had cases involving athletes and quadriplegics, jockeys and bookmakers, miners and scaffolders, policemen and crooks, workmen and tourists, property owners, drivers and passengers (in cars, buses, trains and planes), airlines, universities, horses and dogs, teachers and schoolchildren, local authorities, soldiers, businessmen, bankers, scholars, students, and even litigating barristers. A Circuit Judge trying civil cases sees perpetual permutations of the brilliant and the dim, the energetic and the lazy, the astute and the stupid, the malign and the angelic. They come from all classes, races, ages and religions, and many different nationalities. There is an ever-changing daily display of different people thinking and speaking in a variety of ways. Witnesses range from the illiterate to the world's leading experts. This abundant variety made for varied and agreeable work and was indeed a fertile process of continuing education. One was not out of touch.

Cases are usually listed for hearing many months in advance. Quite often there would be late applications for an adjournment, sometimes only days before trial. There was rarely a good reason for these, and I rarely granted them. If a substantial case was adjourned at short notice it would frequently mean that no other case could be found to replace it, and court time would be wasted. A late application often indicated a weak case, and if refused, a settlement might well follow. If a case did come out of the list at short notice, judicial annoyance would probably be expressed, but it was often in fact welcome because this meant that there was some time to work upon outstanding judgments. (An outstanding judgement in this context does not mean a very good one, it means one which has been 'reserved' – that is postponed for later delivery after work on its preparation.)

When it comes to final speeches in civil cases, some judges simply sit back and listen for as long as counsel want to go on, and do not intervene to focus upon what they think are the important aspects of the case. If the judge is sitting there writing, barristers might assume that he or she is noting what they say, though in fact she might be writing a judgment to the background music of their speech. I used to try to summarise in a few sentences what each side's case appeared to me to be. Counsel could then agree or seek to persuade me to the contrary.

It would then be time for judgment. It is a judge's duty to reach the necessary conclusions to decide a case. It is simply not permissible to say 'I cannot make up my mind', however tricky the problem or evenly balanced the evidence may be. (I once had to decide why an expensive Japanese car inexplicably burst into flames in a garage one winter's night; there were three rival possibilities, none at all likely). Judges need sufficient self-confidence to be decisive. Sometimes the party seeking to establish a case simply fails to provide sufficient evidence to enable the tribunal to be satisfied on what lawyers call the balance of probability, which is the test in civil litigation. In such a case, that party will lose. Sometimes, if the case was clear or simple, judgment could be delivered straight away, without pause for preparation. That is called an ex-tempore judgment. Judges in England (unlike most other jurisdictions) often do this, and it is a much quicker process than going away and writing it out, but it is wise to have decided before you start to deliver your ex-tempore judgment what the outcome is to be, and why. It is easy to embark upon findings and legal analysis without being sure where this will end, which is a recipe for rambling and confusion. I would generally adjourn for an hour or so in a case of modest difficulty, or for a week or two in a complex matter. When composing a judgment, it was always prudent to bear in mind how it would read if the case ever got to the Court of Appeal. If you thought it would seem satisfactory there, it probably was.

Courts rarely allocate time for writing judgments, which generally had to be researched and composed at home. This was, and is, another reason why Judges can feel themselves underpaid and under pressure.

Within a year or so of starting to hear civil cases at Oxford it was gratifying to gather that solicitors and barristers were beginning to say that the service which the court was able to provide was agreeable to them. The volume of work picked up. They appreciated, I think, a brisk, pleasant, common-sense approach. So did the staff responsible for listing, who found that their timetables were not coagulated by work which over-ran or was adjourned. Listing arrangements were in fact often less than satisfactory. In principle 'listing', that is deciding what cases would be listed before what judges, and for how long, is a judicial responsibility. It is for the judges to decide what they will hear and when. In practice day to day this would be quite unworkable, requiring continuous analysis of pressure of work, case progression, diaries and judicial availability. Courts therefore have Listing Officers whose full-time job it is to match the work with the available judiciary. Some judges seemed to accept that they had to do whatever the listing staff had given them, and might become seriously overloaded. It was most important not to fall into that trap. When anything went wrong, and cases were stood out at short notice, the court service would be quick to point out that listing is a judicial responsibility. It was sometimes important to remember that it certainly was and take matters into one's own hands, whatever the view of the staff.

The work of a listing officer is demanding and requires skill, tact, judgment and experience. It is something of an art. He, or more often she, has to know what a case involves, how reliable solicitors' time estimates are, whether or not a listed case is likely to settle before or at trial (most do) and to what extent to over-list to allow for this, the barristers involved and their availability, and the characteristics of the available judiciary: quick, slow, or – worst of all – liable to adjourn if at all possible.

The Court Service is very reluctant to accept that listing officers should be skilled specialists. I have sat regularly in about eight civil courts, and only in one has the same person been allowed to do the job long term. In Northampton, where I sat for over twenty years, the same excellent civil listing officer, Christine, was left in place throughout (in fact during this period she took time off to have several children with generous associated maternity leave, but commendably was left in post to resume her work when ready to do so). In Oxford, or Reading, it often seemed that no sooner had the listing officer begun to learn the work than she would be replaced.

When I began at Oxford there was a curious system whereby a man in Reading with a home-made computer system listed for both Reading and Oxford, with results which were unsatisfactory for both. I managed to get this altered, though there was a view that 'central listing' must be more efficient or 'better' than each court making its own arrangements. This was fallacious. A person listing for the place at which she worked was likely to take more care and pride than one listing for somewhere else, and would be much better placed to sort out any problems. There would also be less of a tendency to make litigants travel long distances, by for example transferring a case from Slough to Milton Keynes, which might mean a most awkward, expensive or impracticable journey at short notice. In two courts for which I had some responsibility towards the end of my career, Bedford and Luton, there was often no single person in charge; two or three were supposed to act interchangeably. There was no focus of responsibility. It was a predictable recipe for disaster, and there were disasters.

The extent to which trials run smoothly, and to which they are agreeable to preside over, depends of course very much upon the quality and personality of the advocates. However, a judge sometimes has to deal with people representing themselves – litigants in person. This is an increasingly common situation, because governments have reduced almost to extinction the availability of legal aid. And so, because people who need to litigate cannot themselves afford to pay for lawyers, they find themselves trying to conduct their own cases. It is generally most unsatisfactory. If you cannot afford to pay a doctor nobody expects you to treat yourself, and legal problems are often more important and more complicated than health problems. Why should you be expected to be able to advise and represent yourself in court?

Many difficulties arise. Litigants in person may not know whether the facts about which they complain give rise to a valid claim at all (what lawyers call a cause of action). They may not know how to commence litigation. This used to be simple but is now complicated by a plethora of rules. There are also many rules about how cases should proceed, what material should be disclosed to the other side, and how evidence should be acquired and presented. Expert evidence might be needed. It will be necessary to obtain leave for this. As and when a case comes to court it will require presentation; many litigants in person have no idea about how to go about this. 'All rise' will say the Clerk. The Judge will come in, bow to any advocates present, and sit down. Whereas a solicitor or a barrister would then stand up, introduce themselves and their opponent, and start to explain the case, a litigant in person will simply stare anxiously at you. 'Now,' I might say, 'I gather this is a boundary dispute. The owner of number 15 says that the owner of number 17 has taken some of her garden by moving the fence. Do we have a plan?' One of the parties might then proffer a large shopping bag full of unpaginated sheets of paper and photographs, unattached to each other, generally undated, but embellished with stick-on labels. 'It is all in here, sir'. 'I have not seen any of that,' says her opponent. The Judge's pleasant feeling of matutinal enthusiasm starts to ebb.

Should such a case finally get under way, and a witness give evidence, it is then time for cross examination. Litigants in person rarely know how to go about this. 'You have never admired my husband, have you?' was one opening question of utter irrelevance. It is commonly thought, and sometimes suggested, that the judge can 'do the cross examination'. But while a judge can and will certainly attempt clarification, he or she will be in no position properly to cross examine, for this requires prior detailed analysis of the available evidence, and preparation, in order to be able to deploy it to challenge, unravel and disprove what a witness has said. It is not an easy thing to do while maintaining both real and apparent impartiality. Cross examination is adversarial, and therein lies its purpose and value. But Judges are impartial.

There are other considerations too. There may be questions of law which a lay person is unable properly to research, understand or deploy. I tried one case in which an elderly farmer helped by his teenage granddaughter was sued by a tenacious accountant over complex rights of way. Neither side had any idea of the applicable law, and the Court of Appeal later concluded that I had not got it right. With advocates present this would not have happened. Judges cannot be expected themselves to know the intricacies of all relevant law. Lay litigants will not have the necessary authorities. Furthermore, many cases should be settled. This requires calm negotiation, which often proves impossible for individuals who have long been in fierce contention with each other. The consequence of government policy of forcing litigants to present their own cases by denying them legal aid has had various inevitable results. Trials take place when cases should have settled; trial preparation is inadequate and improper; trial conduct is defective, and the results often unsatisfactory and unfair. It puts upon a judge a burden which it is awkward and inappropriate: in effect, to extract and argue each side's case, often with their material in hopeless disarray, before deciding it in a disinterested manner. Besides producing a distinctly inferior form of justice, such cases take much longer than otherwise they would, thus negating the putative cost saving.

These practical problems, which seriously inhibit satisfactory trials, are but one aspect of the difficulties which commonly arise. Some litigants in person are of course admirably reasonable, but some are so convinced of the validity of their cause that they cannot accept failure. They will endeavour to bring hopeless appeals, and when these are dismissed become very angry. They sometimes start a campaign against the court staff, alleging deficiencies of one sort or another in dealing with their repeated applications. And sometimes, when all else has failed, they will try to bring an action against the Judge. (This cannot be done, and has been the law for about 400 years, as Lord Denning explained in a case called Sirros in 1975). A litigant in Bedford, a plumber, ran this course. He tried to sue the Judge who had the case before I did, then me, and then the Judge who had it after I did. He sent elaborate letters to the Queen and to the Lord Chancellor. These, drafted in formal and obsequious terms, he accompanied with cheques in their favour for modest sums, as compensation for the time he hoped they would spend in contemplation of the inadequacy of the judiciary.

Every so often a senior judicial figure would appear at the court centre at which one sat, to see how we were getting on and whether there were any particular difficulties, or, indeed, examples of good practice which might be of use elsewhere. These visitors might be the Presiding Judge of the Circuit (each circuit was invigilated by one or more Presiders – High Court Judges given the job of supervising what was going on, and fielding any difficulties); the Senior Presider (a Court of Appeal Judge to whom the Presiders answered and reported) the deputy Head of Civil Justice; the Master of the Rolls (the person in charge of civil justice), the Lord Chief Justice or even, occasionally, the Lord Chancellor. These notables – almost invariably friendly, highly talented and grossly overworked – would arrive in the morning, speak to the senior staff, inspect the court offices, and have interviews with the leading criminal and civil judge. There would then be lunch, at which all the judges would have an opportunity to make observations. I sometimes arranged for some local solicitors to come in for a discussion as well, so that the views and attitudes of the court users could be ascertained.

The staff, who were asked to prepare some figures and statistics, might be anxious on these occasions, and sometimes the judges were too. In February 2006 Lord Dyson, Deputy Head of Civil Justice (later a Justice of the Supreme Court and then Master of the Rolls from 2010 to 2016), came to Oxford on such a visit. We were all nervous, but he was very friendly. It turned out well, and was indeed personally surprisingly gratifying, for he reported: 'as was made clear to me from talking to the staff and the practitioners, he is very highly regarded. Everyone I spoke to had nothing but praise for him.' I could hardly believe this, and nor could others. Local barristers and solicitors 'were complimentary about the service provided by the court. Several said that the DCJ was better than many High Court Judges. This was in grave danger of going to my head. But the visit did confirm how it had been possible to transform Oxford from a place with virtually no civil work to a busy and popular centre for litigation. A great deal of the credit for this was due to exemplary and conscientious District Judges (who did the smaller and preparatory work): Richard Matthews, Vivienne Gatter, Brian Bowman (a very audible man, who walked across Ethiopia, and kept cases short by having a chilly room), Ann Campbell and Alan Jenkins, led by the outstanding, kind, witty and modestly multi-lingual Michael Payne; and to the court staff, especially an excellent manager called Sue Hearn who was indefatigable in searching for administrative improvement. But it could also, I felt, legitimately be taken as something of a vindication of the way in which I had tried to approach the work.

The Lord Chancellor from 2003-2007, Charles Falconer, paid us a visit in 2007. Then a contentious and chubby figure – he has since lost a lot of weight – he breezed about the court centre, making a good impression upon staff and judiciary alike. We gave him lunch. In those days the judicial dining room was tiny and cramped, so we expanded into the adjacent library. Pam, our capable cook (unjustly to be made redundant, when cooking for judges was abolished very soon after a large dining room had just been built for us at considerable expense) excelled herself, and a jovial, useful and enjoyable time was had by about ten judges, the Lord Chancellor and his civil servant minder. There had been mixed views about Charlie, as he was known, regarded sometimes as a stooge of Tony Blair. But a few minutes in his company revealed (as they say, 'with respect') a sharp mind, quick uptake, social deftness and a pleasant and amusing manner. As he left, he said 'Is there anything I can do for you?' I did not think quickly enough to reply. A little later I came to know his wife, Marianna Hildyard QC, who became a Circuit Judge and sat at Luton, where she coped with energy and humour with a difficult court. (For several years she commuted from the drawing rooms of Westminster with a former Lord Mayor of London to their joint but unprepossessing place of work.)

One morning in June 1995, quite out of the blue, a letter arrived telling me that I had been appointed to the Parole Board. This existed then as now to advise the Home Secretary on the release on licence of both determinate and life sentence prisoners, and on the recall to prison of anyone released on licence who misbehaved during the licence period. The essence of the parole system is that convicted prisoners would not serve their full sentences if they could be released early without risk to the public. Parole is popular with those running overcrowded prisons, because it removes prisoners, and with the government, because supervising convicts on licence (done to a pretty limited extent) is much cheaper than keeping them in prison. Parole can be very unpopular with the general public, however, who feel that prisoners are not serving the sentences imposed upon them by the judges, and also feel, often with justification, that released prisoners will constitute a risk and a danger by re-offending, which often they do: 112 homicides in 2016/17.

Lord Belstead was the Chairman when I joined. He was Lord Lieutenant of Suffolk, a former Minister and Leader of the House of Lords. There were about 90 members, a mixture of judges, psychiatrists, probation officers and a number of JPs and other people with relevant experience. We operated in groups of three, each with a judicial chairman, sometimes dealing with applications on paper at the Millbank HQ, and sometimes visiting prisons, where we met the applicants face to face. We tried to reach unanimous decisions and usually, with a bit of give and take and deference to the views of others, it was not difficult to do so. Occasionally however a panel member – there was one in particular - might decide that her view was implacable, and her mind not to be changed. This could be quite time consuming. The courtesies of discussion could become ice sharp.

Visiting prisons was often dispiriting, involving much waiting, many searches and accompanied walks through endless locked doors, each noisily opened and shut by warders carrying big Victorian bunches of keys. At Bristol it was discovered that I had a tiny penknife attached to my car key ring. This caused absurd consternation (though in some prisons Stanley knives were available to prisoner hobbyists). At the hearing the prisoner would be produced to hear what was being said, and was sometimes represented. Often a prisoner would seem reasonable and harmless. One, at Long Lartin, a prison near Evesham which I liked to go to as it involved a pleasant run over the Cotswolds, seemed to me to be so polite and agreeable that when the panel fell to discussion after he had left the room I said that I would not mind giving him a job as a gardener. The psychiatrist on my right drew in his breath: 'I do not think I have ever seen a more dangerous man,' he said carefully. This was disconcerting, and illustrated the wisdom of the panel's composition. The prisoner remained inside.

Periodically the Board members were given the benefit of talks by experts of one sort or another. On one occasion (under a new Chairman, Baroness Prashar, a lady very different from her predecessor, and who has occupied a remarkable host of official positions of one sort or another) an academic woman was invited to speak to us about what she called the over-representation of black people in prison. By this she meant that the percentage of black prisoners in the prison population considerably exceeded the percentage of black people in the population of the nation as a whole. From this premise she inferred that the police were wrongly arresting too many black people, the Crown Prosecution service was wrongly prosecuting too many, juries were wrongly convicting too many, and judges were improperly imprisoning too many. It did not seem to occur to her – or if it did, she did not articulate it – that there might be another explanation consistent with her data. Her audience, including I am ashamed to say me, sat mute, rendered inarticulate by a powerful atmosphere of political correctness.

From a prisoner's point of view parole requirements were often unsatisfactory because he (most prisoners are men) was expected to show remorse, which normally involved an admission of guilt. There were probably a few prisoners who were wrongly convicted, and if they adhered to their innocence they found it very hard to get parole. Sexual offenders also often found it difficult to bring themselves to admit guilt. Furthermore, prisoners needed to show some merit by completing courses in prison, for example on 'anger management'. Many prisoners were in places where insufficient courses were available, and were themselves frequently moved from prison to prison which might badly disrupt remedial work. A number of those released on parole did in fact re-offend and were recalled. By 2001 around 46% of prisoners were being released on parole.

It was quite interesting work, made more agreeable by some of the Parole Board staff. There seemed to be a lot of Indian ladies there who were cheerful, intelligent and fun. One told me that I reminded her of her father, which was a bit disconcerting, especially since I was about 52 and she around 40. The staff liked attending visits to prisons not too close to London, because if there was two days' work they could stay overnight at a hotel local to the prison. Usk, in Wales, which looked like a toytown prison with little crenellations, was a pleasant place for an overnight stay. But I always tried quite hard to deal with cases with expedition, and usually there was no second day. This used to cause a little glumness and some mock-hostile banter, but it never affected the basic charm of personnel denied their night away.

My time with the Parole Board came to a rather precipitate end. I was booked and had prepared for a prison visit, but I was rung at the last minute the evening before and told that this had been cancelled as I had reached the end of my five-year appointment. That was that. It seemed an odd way to behave.

From time to time, at Oxford and elsewhere, there were requests to sit on the Bench by people who were considering being Recorders, or were otherwise interested in a legal career. Some were young barristers wanting to be Marshals – a vestigial form of the position described in an earlier chapter. Normally all went well. I would do my best to explain what was going on, and the visitor would sit demure and deferential at my side, though perhaps sometimes surprised at one thing or another. Once however, I had with me the vivacious, attractive and self-confident daughter of a friend. While listening to cross examination, she took to writing, and ostentatiously passing to me, little notes, with an air of manifest exasperation and surprise. 'How can she ask that?' 'That is nonsense, it contradicts what he said before.' 'This person is obviously lying.' This of course raised eyebrows in court. We had to rise for a few minutes for a brief discussion. She decided in the end not to come to the Bar, though not before she had spent a couple of weeks with a notably articulate High Court Judge, who irritated her more than I did.

Andrew Burrows sat with me for some days before he became a Recorder in 2000. He is one of England's top academic lawyers, currently Professor of the Law of England at All Souls, and from June 2020 will be a Justice of the Supreme Court. Lean, cheerful and friendly, he has an intellect which is probably about double mine, and his powers of legal analysis and recollection are formidable. His presence was a test of a different kind. I conducted some modest piece of litigation rather self-consciously, thinking not only what I was about to say in my judgment to resolve the dispute in question but how to formulate and articulate something which would not appear jejune to such a fine mind. He was very tolerant, invited me to speak at St Hugh's (my daughter's college, of which he was a Fellow), and has on subsequent occasions been most encouraging over one or two judgments I have delivered which achieved a little prominence; decisions where I had providentially reached by some sort of instinct what he had concluded by deep learning.

In 2008 I was asked to organise the annual conference for the Designated Civil Judges, and various senior members of the judiciary. I invited Andrew Burrows to speak, which he did with great insight and fluency (and scarcely a note). When he finished, he invited questions. Nobody in the audience of about fifty felt sufficiently self-confident to engage with him save Martin Moore-Bick, an especially erudite member of the Court of Appeal. The audience listened in rapt admiration as the two fine brains engaged with each other, locking their intellectual antlers with considerable relish. That evening the after-dinner speech was given by Lord Justice Scott Baker, a Court of Appeal judge who had recently, as coroner, conducted the inquest upon the deaths in Paris of Diana Princess of Wales and her paramour Dodi Al Fayed. He gave us a gripping account of the personalities concerned, and the many difficulties of managing such a sensitive hearing, involving some remarkable allegations by Al Fayed's Harrods-owning father. Michael Mansfield, who took Silk at the same time as I did, and went on to achieve a remarkable reputation as a formidable and awkward left-wing advocate in difficult cases of major interest, was, said Scott Baker, impeccable. Whereas one or two others were quite difficult.

Once or twice I debated with myself whether to apply to become a High Court Judge. I would not have got there from the Bar, even had I prolonged my time as a Silk. Though I had had some successes, my practice and earnings were unlikely to have been of a quality to have made a strong case. However, within a few years on the bench quite a number of my more significant judicial decisions had not been appealed, and many of those which were had been upheld, sometimes in terms which were quite gratifying. This would have been a realistic springboard. I could certainly have presented myself legitimately as a judge with sufficient grasp of the law to justify appointment.

There was in particular a window of opportunity after the credit hire cases (explained elsewhere) reinforced by a decision upon commercial agency which went to the House of Lords. However, though I could, I think, have done the civil work pretty well, ordinary High Court Judges were (and are) expected to do a substantial amount of heavy crime at first instance, and also to sit in the Court of Criminal Appeal. One of them, Mr Justice Tugendhat, wrote a paper explaining that, for a typical QB judge, up to three quarters of the work might be crime, which many found frustrating. And most High Court Judges spend about half their time in London and the other half going around the country on circuit, sitting anywhere from Manchester to Newcastle, Leeds to Bodmin. They rarely sleep at home, unless home is in London, which in my case it was not. This peripatetic existence, living out of a suitcase in lodgings in large cities, would not have been enjoyable.

Furthermore, although I felt I could manage the work, it might have been a substantial effort to do so. I had seen a number of people whose abilities I thought I knew, and did not believe to exceed my own, appointed to the High Court bench, for whom the regime was clearly a struggle. And a relentless one. Several had strained every sinew to get there for years, often by giving time and effort to judicial training of one sort or another, and by sitting on committees and volunteering in many directions. Their efforts were rewarded by appointment, but thereafter the pressure of the cases they had continuously to try, compounded by paperwork they were expected to deal with, and the way of life they had to embrace, meant that their lives became very stressful indeed.

On the other hand, as a Civil Circuit Judge in charge at my own courts and occasionally sitting in the High Court, exercising control over the work I did, under no particular pressure and living agreeably at home, my judicial life was not at all unpleasant – indeed it was often extremely enjoyable. I tried quite a number of interesting and difficult cases, and often worked hard in the evenings and at weekends, but it was not stressful or relentless. I could not be told to go to Preston or Liverpool, or embark upon the grind of disagreeable criminal trials which might last for weeks. I did not have to save up numerous complex reserved judgments to work upon during the summer vacation (just as well, as Circuit Judges do not get a summer vacation). The pay differential was and remains fairly modest – while Circuit Judges are not highly paid for what they do, High Court Judges are very seriously underpaid, which is one reason why there is now such difficulty in getting top-quality applicants. (A modest attempt has recently been made to alleviate this). So, although there still remains some cachet as a High Court Judge, and it comes with a knighthood, I never applied. I have no idea if I would have succeeded. Quite probably I would not. But part of me regrets that, unambitiously, I did not try. I remained instead in what was a pretty satisfactory situation. Indeed it has been suggested to me that to be the Civil Judge in Oxford was, looked at in the round, perhaps one of the most agreeable judicial positions of all. But it would never satisfy the seriously ambitious.

But the work was not always free of frustration. I decided a case in 2011 called Sayce v TNT. It concerned the proper way of calculating damages when a person had had her property (in this case a car) damaged, and unreasonably turned down the offer of a free replacement. Common sense would indicate that there was no loss to be compensated for. The law is supposed to reflect common sense. The plaintiff in question chose to rent a replacement vehicle and sought to recover the £3,446 this cost her from the defendant, who had offered her a free car, which had she accepted would have cost her nothing.

The issue was of some major significance. There were two cases decided in the House of Lords and several previous decisions of the Court of Appeal which made it quite clear that where such an offer was unreasonably turned down a plaintiff would have no claim. There was another, more recent, observation of the Court of Appeal, in a case called Copley, which was not essential to its decision, was difficult to understand and inconsistent with the House of Lords authority, to the effect that 'if a claimant does unreasonably reject or ignore a defendant's offer of a replacement car the claimant is entitled to recover at least the costs which the defendant can show he would reasonably have incurred. He does not forfeit his damages claim altogether'. I asked counsel at the trial to deal with the question of whether or not the later case was correct. They both refused to engage and simply said that I was bound by it. I held that the law was as stated in the House of Lords. When my judgment (which had been greeted with widespread enthusiasm among solicitors, the bar and in the county courts) reached the Court of Appeal, that tribunal, while making clear that it accepted the logic of my legal conclusions, held that it was procedurally improper to have found as I did when counsel had not argued the point, and because I was bound to follow the decision in Copley. And so I was wrong. This was, I felt, not satisfactory. If Copley was inconsistent with the House of Lords decisions then it had been wrongly decided, and the doctrine of precedent (following decisions of a superior court) should not be found to mean that I was bound by it when the reasoning was not part of, or necessary to, the decision – in lawyer's language when it was obiter dicta, not the ratio decidendi of the judgment. The Court of Appeal actually said it did 'not think that [the material part of the judgment in Copley] forms part of the ratio decidendi and therefore it was not binding on the judge [me], but... he ought to have followed and applied it nonetheless'. The Court of Appeal did not allow a further appeal to the Supreme Court, although 'it would be beneficial for these questions to be considered at the highest level as soon as a suitable opportunity arises'. I still feel quite rueful about that case.

Chapter 13

Sporting life

Sport means different things to different people: ascending a frozen waterfall with ice axes and crampons, perspiring round a squash court, or watching fat men throw darts. There is no doubt that many people feel 'sport' in some guise is quite important, whether they themselves actually do anything active or not. It is a tribal substitute for those who follow football, providing a focus and sense of loyalty otherwise absent from their lives. The energetic feel that sport provides a way of getting fit or healthy, although it seems very clear that the more running you do the more likely it is that you will be troubled by problems in your knees, hips, ankles or feet. The more rugger you play the more likely you are to be crippled in middle age, and golf is bad for your back.

I got limited pleasure from team games, save occasionally soccer and sometimes hockey, perhaps because I never played a starring role in any team to which I belonged – unlike my elder son who once scored the winning goal in his school house-match final and regularly played for his school first eleven. There was excitement to be had from hockey, with its running and flicking, and stirring moments at short corners.

There is also something to be said for mixed-doubles tennis, when played in sunshine with amusing people on summer afternoons. Being fairly agile and quick, I could generally get to a ball, but lacking skill or instruction I rarely had any suitable stroke to get it back. This was not a recipe for contentment.

From my mid-twenties, I have done a little shooting – often as a guest – though sometimes too little to be very proficient. I did not always understand why I was invited. On a good day I may be adequate, but only rarely have there been star moments when one only had to look at a bird to kill it. In about 40 years I can only remember being congratulated a few times, twice for fluke high single shots. But once – just once – I was told by an enthusiastic and discriminating host that I had 'shot like a god' at one of his partridge drives, and indeed I had. How and why I do not know.

I have belonged to four shoots. One, long ago, at Fawsley in Northamptonshire where we wandered hopefully around the ruins of a fine old house, now restored as an expensive hotel; one at Kiddington, a substantial shoot based upon a gracious classical park; and two at Rollright. The first of these latter was run by David Seel, a considerate host and skilful exploiter of no great extent of land; the second by John Steel, who bravely took over when David decided to give up. Bravely, because some rented land which had furnished two or three good drives was no longer available. Both their wives produce outstanding traditional lunches and radiate a glamorous welcome – no small achievement when entertaining the same people on a regular basis. Robert Parsons at Radford and Peter Browne at Glympton were also both remarkably hospitable in inviting me to many delightful days, as did John Alston in Norfolk. Carol's father was always most generous, several times with grouse invitations to a moor in Derbyshire; a place where an earlier tenant had died in his butt and been brought down on a donkey – normally used to carry ammunition – while the day continued, that being assumed to be 'what he would have wanted'

Some people, quite understandably, do not think much of using live creatures reared as targets, and it is hard to explain the satisfying exhilaration of connecting with a fast-moving bird which cartwheels in the sky, then dives, dead, to the frosty ground. Pheasants fly at up to 50 mph, partridges rather less. Grouse – very quick and at very low level – are the hardest of all. Successful shooting involves swift reaction, co-ordination and a certain determination. It is quite a public activity. The other guns and the beaters will notice how you are doing. 'Hard luck' they will say, 'the wind was tricky,' or 'the flight line was deceptive'.

One of the oddest things about shooting is how little time in a day is actually spent doing it. If the bag is, say, 200 birds, equally divided – which never happens – between eight guns, that is 25 birds each. Each engagement, from first catching site of the bird to pulling the trigger, might last up to five seconds, often less. Five times 25 is 125 seconds, or just over two minutes. You will probably miss more than you hit, so, say, six minutes of shooting, to include unsuccessful shots. A day's shooting typically starts with the guns arriving at 9 am, sometimes after a significant journey. There will probably be two drives before elevenses, two more drives before lunch, and one or two after lunch. People normally leave soon after 4 pm. Without travelling time, that is seven hours. The cost of a day's shooting (at pheasants or partridge –grouse are far, far more expensive) is commonly estimated at £45 per bird. Do I get £45 worth of pleasure every time I shoot a bird? Even allowing for agreeable social intercourse, to which much importance is legitimately attached, shooting is a curious pastime. You would not for example be content with a day's skiing in which you only skied for six minutes.

Shooting is not, however, cruel. The birds die more expeditiously than most humans, who often spend years decaying in pain and humiliation, and their deaths are far more agreeable than those of a chicken, sheep, pig or cow, especially if those are unlucky enough to be finished off in a halal slaughterhouse.

Stranger, to me, is salmon fishing. I tried for several years but have never caught a salmon. I am sure that to play and land one is most exciting, especially with a large strong fish. However, such fishing, unless you are lucky enough to be a guest, involves renting a stretch of river at considerable cost, and frequently days and sometimes weeks will go by without a single salmon being caught. Fishermen, or women – women are often more successful than men, perhaps because they take the advice of a ghillie more readily – will explain that the water is too high, or too low, the light too bright, or perhaps too overcast, the rain too relentless, or insufficient. Should you be lucky enough to land a fish you are generally required to take the hook out of its mouth and put it back into the water. This strikes me as a curious form of entertainment. Added to this there appears to be every reason to suppose that it must be very painful for the fish to be dragged about by a hook in its mouth. Nobody would dream of catching birds or rabbits with hooks, and fish have highly-developed nervous systems. As far as I know it has never been demonstrated that they do not feel pain. Fishermen quickly shy off this subject, talking about 'cold-blooded' animals.

Some argue that fish pull hard against the hook and will often take a fly or bait again a short time after being hooked, so they cannot find the experience too disagreeable. But the former may simply be a panic reaction, the latter an indication of lack of intelligence.

There is however one traditional sporting activity which has given me very great pleasure. Deerstalking in the Highlands can be incomparably stimulating, exciting and gratifying, combining as it does the atavistic hunting instinct, in mankind since the dawn of time, with wild and beautiful landscapes and considerable physical effort. Some see stalking as a stealthy walk in a wild place, with fine air and stirring views. Others are naturalists, enjoying the chance to observe at close range the private lives of red deer: large, shy, handsome creatures. Many people enjoy the satisfying pieces of equipment. A rifle, for example, is a most agreeable item: handsome (unless burdened with silencer and bipod), sturdy, precise, lethal, pleasantly balanced, sometimes of beautiful workmanship, perhaps of some maturity and full of associations. Good binoculars too can give immense pleasure, not only because they are capable of carrying the eye and the mind across a distant moor to immediate and secret closeness, but also for their quality and feel.

Some get pleasure from pitting their bodies against the hill, the elements and the distance. For them the more ground covered the better the day, and Scotland becomes a large outdoor gymnasium. On the whole one does not go to the hill to talk, but there is much pleasure in the company of the stalker or the pony man who may have decades of observation, experience and anecdote to pass on while waiting with you, chilly in a sodden hag or rocky cleft, or warm under blue and heather-scented skies.

And there are those, and I am one, who enjoy the ritually structured progress of the day. A comfortable not too early start away from the lodge, full of breakfast and the encouragement of those whose turn it is not. A Land Rover ride to the starting point, where the stalker may cautiously disclose his contingent plans. Perhaps a short voyage up a loch, into the heart of the hills, bronze water slapping and creaming around the flanks of the boat.

And then comes the climbing, a mountaineer's approach march, when muscles warm and minds anticipate and the world begins to fall away beneath your feet. This leads to purposeful but leisurely reconnaissance, picking out the russet deer amidst the wilderness by eye, binocular or telescope. The stalk itself can be of infinite length and variety: waiting, crawling, retreating, running, listening, panting – and always being aware of the wind. This stage can take minutes, or it can take hours. And then the shot, towards which the day has been building, the culmination of a kind of steady mental tumescence. It should be a moment of calm and confidence: a good view, a modest range, a comfortable position, trust in your weapon and ammunition. But often there will be handicaps: rain, sleet, mist, obscured sights, cramp, damp or cold. It is difficult to shoot well if breathing heavily, harder still if shivering. You need to slip into a moment of deep concentration, when all else is forgotten. After the shot, a moment of satisfaction, and sometimes too a pang of sadness, for a fine animal has just leapt the last great burn of life, on his way, one hopes, to graze and rut and canter in the endless sunshine of some cervine Elysium. Respect is due to his spirit.

Then you may sit for a spell beside the stag looking out over vistas of heather and water, scree and stone, towards some distant island, loch or hill. But the day is not finished yet. The deer goes onto the back of a sturdy pony, and you follow along stony paths, hooves on rock the only sounds as sunset eases into dusk, the antlers swaying to the pony's gait. This is the apotheosis of the returning hunter, as, snug in tweed and wool, damp from the day but warm from the march, muddied with peat and speckled with blood, he strides happily homeward.

I shot my first stags in 1981, at Inverbroom, then the property of Maurice Robson, a characterful neighbour of ours in North Oxfordshire, and his two sisters. It was in fact his sister Christina (tall, dark, Russian speaking and artistic) who first invited us to join a party there. The lodge is set in a valley south of Loch Broom, not far from Ullapool, in 19,000 acres, and it was to be the source and scene of many years of pleasure. Maurice was at that time an accountant, the son of Laurence Robson, founder of the well-known city firm of Robson Rhodes. He had quite a shrewd and well-filled mind, but his enthusiasm in life was not accountancy. He liked to hunt, to shoot, to stalk and to fish. He liked to make funny speeches. He enjoyed living on the Oxfordshire estate, Kiddington, which he had inherited from his father (who had bought it in 1954) and visiting the family's two Scottish estates. These his father had also acquired: Erchless Castle, on the Beauly river, not far from Inverness – given to Maurice on his 19th birthday – and Inverbroom. With occasional exceptions, we stalked at Inverbroom until 2003, when sadly it was sold.

The annual pattern did not alter much. Guests could never be certain that they would be invited. Most sporting hosts like to make their arrangements many months in advance. Maurice, generous but impromptu, normally made his at just a few weeks, or even days, notice. The prime time for red deer stalking is the first two weeks of October, which commonly coincides with the rut, when the stags are out on the hill roaring like vegetarian lions. Often invitations did not arrive until mid-September: it was a recurrent annual anxiety.

There were various regulars. One was Sebastian Thewes, a rumpled Scottish antiques expert whose lined face resembled that of a Frenchman fond of absinthe, and his wife, a cheery well-connected person and a most competent cook. Sinclair and Christina Bonde, a Swedish couple, lived partly in Fife and partly in Sweden. Sinclair was quite a forceful character. Fond of moose hunting in his native land, and a fast skier, he had various enterprises based upon Charlton, his Scottish house. For some time he nurtured the hope that he might be able to acquire the title Earl of Caithness, a quest which he thought he might finance by the sale of a venerable golf club which had surfaced in one of his attics. A strongly-built man a little over six feet, handsome, despite receding hair, he was a good companion on the hill. We had many agreeable days stalking together. His wife, small and blonde, was a doctor, who had great difficulty gaining permission to practise in Britain. She was a charming but fastidious person – she did not care to share his bathwater.

Another regular couple was Hugh and Margie Brett, who lived at the time in Oxford. He was a solicitor and an expert in intellectual property, indeed a professor, but not a man to burden his conversation with intellectual material. Dark-haired, considerate and easy-going, he did not stalk, but did fish, and did so with patience, putting in many crepuscular hours and often coming back successful. Margie, a woman of great determination and enthusiasm, fished well too, and was not the type to give up. She once lost a dog in Cornwall, and for days threw herself into its recovery, travelling great distances, talking to everyone and following any slender lead. Eventually a seer divined that the dog was alive, and it was duly found marooned on a rock between sea and cliff. She was good at coping with Maurice.

For Maurice, as the years went by, did need coping with. He had, perhaps, left marriage a little late, waiting until 1985, when he was 41. He married Chloe Edwards, then 29, who had more Scottish ancestry than he did, and had come to Oxfordshire from Suffolk with a dressage horse or two. She was a striking woman, with black hair, a strong and attractive build, a fluent turn of phrase and a considerable sense of humour, which, as time went by, she needed. She was not very keen on going to Inverbroom, did not enjoy stalking, and did not fish. Though she catered for the shoots at the Kiddington estate, she tried to forbid the duck drives which often concluded a day. She had thought of Maurice as an unusual man with a kind and entertaining personality, with whom she would be happy. But it was soon clear that theirs might not be a marriage of great contentment. They went to East Africa on honeymoon and came back to Kiddington, whence, she thought, Maurice went up to London in order to return to work. After a day or two she rang his office, and asked to speak to him. 'Mr Robson is still on honeymoon'. He had secretly gone fishing in the West Country.

Carol and I saw a lot of them both as neighbours in Oxfordshire. We went to Scotland each year, and they sometimes came skiing with us in return. There was a time when at dinner parties in Scotland, in the Alps or at home, he would rise, go 'chink, chink', upon a glass and make a very funny speech, without apparent preparation. These entertaining extempore performances became rarer, and might deteriorate into bellowing. It was then that he needed sympathetic attention. Margie Brett was good at this, so was Carol, and so was a local magistrate and neighbour, Von Parsons (who when first she came to Inverbroom was quite inebriated with the spirit of the place and treated Willie Matheson, the stalker, with something like reverence). Maurice increasingly embarrassed and infuriated his wife. They eventually parted, divorcing in a sea of expensive acrimony.

But there were many years in which, before this happened, we enjoyed wonderful holidays. I went out often with Willie, an active, ginger-bearded man of middle size and (since his beard was pointed) rather Elizabethan appearance. He was loyal, skilled and patient. Sometimes he found himself asked to take out a party of up to seven people – once including an American photographer – an absurd number with which to close upon deer. His technique was to lead an hour or two of spectacular walking, and then ask all save the person going to take the shot to 'bide a while' in a hollow or peat hag, while he and the 'Rifle' conducted their approach. The wait might extend to several hours, which frequently deterred those subjected to it from coming out again. He was a man of great guile. He rarely had a day without success, and habitually got to within about 75 yards of his quarry. I have found with later experience with other stalkers that they may well be content to get to 200 yards, unless encouraged to do better. While this is a range at which it is often perfectly possible to shoot a stag, it is to put more emphasis upon the shot and less upon the stalk, which is not the object of the exercise. Willie was also remarkable in that often, when an approach seemed hopeless, he would say 'we'll bide a while', and a few minutes later, the deer would do exactly as he had hoped, and wander closer.

In 1989 I purchased my own rifle, a Parker-Hale.270 with an attractive stock, of which I became extremely fond. It has a good telescope sight, but no silencer (which I think ruins both looks and balance). One day in October of that year I was told that I could go out on my own to stalk a stag – a considerable accolade. The 'beat' was a substantial area of undulating terrain between the lodge and the main road to Dundonnell and Gruinard. I knew this ground and set off at about 10.30 to climb to where I had it in mind to begin. I saw few deer as I moved cautiously from ridge to ridge, handicapped by a little mist. Frequently I paused to spy with the utmost care, but could not find a suitable stag, or sometimes any stag at all.

I moved steadily into the wind, but the available ground was shrinking appreciably. I had eaten my 'piece' – a squashed roll containing some meat – at about 3pm. At four I ate my only other food, a Mars Bar, and began to contemplate failure. I turned uphill to my left where some rocky outcrops hid a number of small pools or lochans and noticed a few hinds near my path, but they were scattered and seemed without male company. I moved gently past them.

It was about 5 pm when I heard a roar. A stag's roar is a stirring thing. It pulses over the hill, powerful, pagan and challenging. It lingers on the ear and culminates in a series of heavy grunts. This one was repeated, and sounded fairly near. It came from the far side of a rocky bluff, a convex hillock about thirty feet high and fifty yards across, with boulders strewn about it. I took my rifle from its cover, loaded with the utmost caution, and crawled onto the hillock. Soon I could see, about 140 yards away, the stag standing with a group of seven hinds, tossing his head and stretching his dark, heavily-maned neck. I was downwind of him, but his gaze was in my general direction.

Lying as low as I could, and moving one limb at a time, I eased forward from one small boulder to another, keeping the stones between me and the stag and stopping completely whenever he seemed to be looking directly at me. I took about half an hour to cover some 30 yards. Willie would have been proud of this rate of progress. I was now within a satisfactory range, and eased the rifle forwards. Taking care to cradle the barrel clear of the rocky surface with my left hand, and pressing the stock firmly into my shoulder, I brought the sights up to the appropriate spot, and squeezed the trigger. The stag leapt forward about twenty yards, stood, and then collapsed. The hinds wandered off. I had done it.

I now had to try to retrieve the dead deer. I gralloched it, which means cutting an incision between the ribcage and the hind legs and pulling out the stomach and other contents of the body. When you have cold hands this is pleasantly warm work. But then, without help, I had to try to drag the animal, which weighed about 15 stone, towards the lodge. I had some rope to put around the antlers, but as I only weighed about 11 stone, the task was one of fearful difficulty. It exemplified the expression 'dead weight'.

For about one and a half hours I tugged and pulled, until, though I could see the lights of the lodge in the valley below, about a mile away, it had become quite clear that I could not hope to get it there. Besides which it was becoming dark. I then found myself doing a curious thing. With a suitable blade of my Swiss army knife, I cut off the head and neck of the beast, which took a surprisingly long time, and then set off with the trophy back to the assembled party, waiting for their dinner. Everyone was rather startled. I was beyond exhaustion, but utterly happy. Never have ten minutes in a huge Victorian bath, the room caliginous with steam, the tub opaque with hot brown water, felt so close to paradise. Then down to dinner, to rally weariness by courses into satiation. That night I slept like the happiest bear in hibernation.

Dinners at Inverbroom could be remarkable affairs, often amusing but not to everyone's taste. Frequently they did not start until well after 9 pm, though the cook (if there was one) would have been ready by eight. If the wives were catering, then there would be strongly articulated annoyance. Neither category of cook much enjoyed the host's insistence that when there were lobsters, there had to be a live lobster race across the kitchen floor. Some of these animals, up to a foot long, were – quite legitimately – determined and fierce. As dinner progressed there would be cries to the 'Rifle' of the day to make a speech, the idea being to give an amusing account of the day's stalk. This was all right if you were used to it, but demanding if you were not, and all remarks were greeted with heckles and cheers, or boos and cries of simulated incredulity. One new arrival, a rather awkward personality, had too much to drink by way of preparation and produced a map to show where he had been. He delineated, with no regard for scale, a spy on the flank of Ben More (a mountain 20 miles to the north), a stalk around Lairg (30 miles to the east) and a shot taken on the beach of the Summer Isles. He did not come again. It was generally best to rely on self-deprecatory hyperbole, associated with some mild fantasy, preferably with an erotic twist, aimed at our host, who in the early days had a proactive way with the wives, all of whom specialised in deflecting his advances – some involving a degree of physical contact which would not now be acceptable in Hollywood – with perfect charm and mildly lacerating observations, to which he was entirely impervious.

This pattern continued for many years, with some variations in cast. One year Chalky White came up; an experienced businessman and horseman, with a comfortable air of wisdom and a sense of humour. This was tested upon arrival, because our host had double booked, and there were tenants in the lodge. Our party had to decamp to a small farmhouse, with no heating which he or I could activate. In due course, Chloe arrived to turn it on.

After the stalking became unavailable at Inverbroom, we enjoyed a number of seasons at Erchless castle, a harled country house with turrets, close to where the rivers Farrer and Glass combine to form the Beauly. This was less wild and beautiful than the west coast, though the accommodation was better. Here too was a shrewd stalker, with a dry sense of humour, called George. A tall, long-legged, rangy man with dark hair and weather-beaten, pliable features, he had lost a tooth playing shinty (a rough Scottish form of hockey) and often seemed a little glum and pessimistic. He too normally achieved success for his Rifles, though it often involved an achingly long preparatory grind by Land Rover over an ill-maintained track to the north-west of the estate.

His main complaint involved dealing with foreign customers, who were ill-disposed to accept his instruction about which stag to shoot. When an Englishman goes stalking the object of the exercise is to have an interesting stalk, and the stag that is shot is commonly a poor specimen, or past its prime. This improves the quality of the herd, fulfils the role of the absent predator and means the deer do not starve or freeze to death. But for many Continental stalkers the object is to bag a good 'head', that is one with a large set of antlers, preferably a Royal (which has 12 points). It can be appreciated that these objectives can conflict. If you go out with a professional stalker then, unless you are his direct employer, you are expected to defer to his judgment and instruction. Some of George's customers were not always keen to do this, and occasionally shot a better stag than they had been told to. George found this beyond infuriating.

Prowling in woods above Erchless one afternoon, I heard sounds of a disturbance through the trees. I crept quickly towards the noise, and came to the edge of a small clearing within which two stags were starting to spar. Of roughly equal size, they circled and feinted, stamping aside the brush, totally engaged with each other. I slipped unnoticed to within about 15 yards and stood behind a pine. As though obeying a command, each withdrew a few feet, gave a heavy chivalric prance and leapt at each other, head on. Their antlers clashed, jarred and meshed. The two stags put their heads down, their muzzles within inches of the grass, and strained and pushed and heaved in elemental adversity.

Their hooves scrabbled for purchase, the muscles in their shoulders, flanks and thighs coiled with effort, as silently and desperately, they strove against each other. Back and forth they manoeuvred, panting, with flecks of foam at their mouths, neither prepared to yield-or both perhaps in fear to disengage. Their safety entirely depended upon the resistance of their antlers to facture, and their footholds in the battered turf. Neither seemed obviously the stronger, but after perhaps two or three minutes the deer to my right shook his head with desperate vigour, his antlers unlocked, and before his opponent could lunge to spear him he twisted away and fled between the trees toward the open hill. The victor stood, trembling with unreleased tension for some time, before pulling himself together with a shrug and stepping off in another direction.

We have stalked elsewhere. Once at Dunan, between Loch Rannoch and Corrour, a very attractive spot, surprisingly remote, which belongs to Hamish McCorquodale. That week was notable for the nocturnal retrieve of a capsized Argocat. A party came off the hill to report the incident, and Charles McBean and I went out as dusk fell in another one, to see what had happened. We got the stranded machine out of a burn but the young chap who had been driving it had lost all confidence, McBean (who, as a Brigadier, had been accustomed to dealing with young men) drove one machine cautiously in front, firmly instructing and encouraging the nervous youth to follow in his tracks, which after some hesitation, he did. It was a long, tricky, dark descent, and both drivers performed admirably. We got to dinner about 10pm.

One year I rented Rhidorroch, an old Victorian lodge just north of Ullapool, virtually unchanged for over 80 years. The house sits on a small plateau looking south over its loch, in a most handsome situation. Beyond the water are woods occupied by sika – smaller, wily, distant cousins of red deer, who whistle rather than roar, and crouch and hide if suspicious, rather than run away. They have a sharp, elemental cast of feature, like something from the edge of an Arcadian painting in which satyrs and dryads might dwell. I only stalked a sika once, and he took refuge in a shallow glen of hollows, with a tumbling stream. He dodged in and out along the steep banks of this burn, often pausing to see what the stalker and I would do. He would move very fast, then pause in cover. Eventually he emerged for a second to get his bearings, and that was long enough for a successful shot. It was most exciting.

One of the many good things about Rhidorroch was the cook, Kirsty, a daughter of Mrs McKay Scobie, the owner. She produced remarkably delicious Highland food, in particular roast sika, which I found it almost literally impossible to stop eating. She now runs a fish restaurant in Ullapool. Our party there included Mark Charnock, a retired gynaecologist, active, fit and a most erudite conversationalist, but prone to see danger to his ankles if rushing too briskly over the hill; Guy Hungerford, by now a retired barrister, vigorous and invariably amusing, but keen not to test his constitution to breaking point; and Hugh Brett, who took Guy, Mark and the enthusiastic wives off to play golf at the Ullapool links, where a fine time was had by all.

Carol and I have also had generous invitations from Andrew and Rowena Feilden, to the Ardverikie estate on Loch Laggan. Here – though they do not themselves occupy it, preferring a comfortable smaller lodge the other side of the water – there is a fine example of inventive Victorian Gothic architecture, with asymmetrical and fantastical towers, slightly reminiscent of the castles seen in Bavaria. It was a place visited by Queen Victoria in 1847, decorated by Landseer, burned down in 1873, and rebuilt again thereafter. The house has more recently been used for the television series *Monarch of the Glen*, and the Netflix production of *The Queen*.

We have been there for hind stalking, which takes place after the stag season closes in October. The weather in November can be bleak, cold and challenging, but the Feildens' hospitality is correspondingly warm, and there have been wonderful outings, in snow and wind, in attempts to close with groups of hinds, which are far warier than a stag with his mind upon promiscuous mating. At Ardverikie you are not required to make a speech at dinner, merely to engage agreeably with a friendly cast of entertaining and informative guests drawn from the local great, good or amusing. (Local, in Scotland, means within about an hour and a half of fast motoring. Sadly, motoring in Scotland is less quick than it was as the police seem to regard going not much over a low limit, on an empty road, as a serious offence).

Andrew, a former soldier and High Sheriff of Oxfordshire, slight, elegant, sharp-witted and articulate, is rightly proud of the considerable hydroelectric capacity on the estate. Huge pipes are buried beneath the heather, channels of diverted water foam about the glens and mighty turbine halls are dug, like large fortifications, into the wild and chilly hillside. All this he will proudly and knowledgeably display. He also took us one day to watch some tree felling. No question of axes or chainsaws, but a tracked machine driven by an operator who sits comfortably in his cab, controlling a long and powerful articulated hydraulic arm, equipped with a metal claw and a cutter blade. The machine crawls tank-like into the woodland and the great arm extends to seize a fifty-foot tree. A few seconds of power to the cutter, and then the whole tree is lifted bodily from the ground, turned horizontally, trimmed, cut to length, and stacked in a pile for later extraction. The capability of such machinery is almost sinister.

Rowena Feilden is an astute and excellent hostess, with a repertoire of entertaining anecdotes, and remarkable connections. She also keeps her lodge warm and comfortable – not, as some do, bracing.

I have also tried stalking in the Lake District, where there are red deer. But there is little sense of remoteness and seclusion, and it is a rare moment when one does not catch sight of the M6, or some minor industrial enterprise. It is no substitute for Scotland. Indeed, one local estate owner (whose wife is a world authority on marmalade) has inhibited stalking activity because people out walking in the hills complain if they see evidence that a stag has been shot. These people's fondness for animals means that they prefer deer to die of cold or starvation rather than by a kindly, painless, unexpected bullet.

Things are healthier in the far north, where we have visited the Reay estate as guests of Amanda and Oliver Langdale. This is grand scale territory, with huge bleak hills of exposed grey rock, and mountains called Arkle and Foinaven. The land on which Oliver stalks and Amanda fishes belongs to the Duke of Westminster, who has an impressive team of stalkers, equipped both with up to date cross country vehicles and traditional ponies. The views are mighty, and the air is that breathed by Vikings. But there is one drawback: midges. In an English summer these are of little account: you might notice a few hovering in a sunbeam, you might brush some from your brow. But on the River Laxford they are serious predators. Amanda, who has been going to that estate, of which she is deeply fond, for over thirty years, had warned me to bring prophylactic substances (she did not use those precise words). She herself has a one-piece net garment, perhaps potentially erotic, which she could put on under her outer clothes, covering all from head to toe. In this she went fishing. She lent me a headnet, the sort of thing in which one might attend to bees.

The Langdales have been kind enough to have us up there twice, and I have been out on several beats with four different stalkers, and had some tremendous days, though curiously, no stags. Two days were with Oliver, who is perhaps Oxfordshire's greatest sportsman. A well-built, well-dressed, ruddy-faced man of rather over six feet (a land-based version of Captain Aubrey) he has hunted with the Heythrop for longer than the 44 years we have been in the county, and was field master for a time. This involved being out three days a week. He combined this demanding activity with being a senior partner at Savills estate agency, running a farm and various business enterprises too. With exquisite manners, he speaks quietly but with considerable sagacity. He and Amanda, a striking and quietly intellectual person, form a wonderful combination of energetic civilisation. On the hill with Oliver, or in conversation with Amanda, there is no flagging. Sadly, I have never fired a shot at Reay, but I have enjoyed its grand, eroded hills. The lack of a trophy, while depressing for the stalker, becomes of vanishing importance for the Rifle as he gets older.

Chapter 14

DCJ: some small authority

Before 1998 the parties to a legal dispute had been free, more or less, to proceed as quickly or slowly as they liked. Proceedings might be started and then left for months or years without being brought to court. When the delay grew very long a defendant might apply to 'strike out' the claim for 'want of prosecution'. If successful, the plaintiff's claim would be extinguished. In 1998 major reforms were introduced. It was thought desirable to put the court in charge of the progress of cases, and to make court orders stating what was to be done, by whom and when. Each side would have to do as it was told by a judge, with penalties, often by way of costs orders, for failure to comply. A new and very elaborate set of rules was drafted (not the simple ones envisaged) to facilitate judicial control and to direct litigants to follow a prescribed course.

At that time there was considerable optimism that litigation would become simpler and cheaper as well as quicker. This was the triple objective. To work this new regime a cadre of Circuit Judges who were experienced in civil work was established. Nobody could think of a suitable title for these specialists, so they were called, unimaginatively, Designated Civil Judges, or DCJs. Thirty were appointed to cover the country, which was divided into 'groups'. Many of these groups were in fact large cities such as Birmingham, Manchester or Bristol, but others consisted of counties and county towns. I was put in charge of the Northampton group, which also included Peterborough, and Oxford: a considerable territory, from the Fens to the Thames.

We DCJs attended for an inaugural meeting at the Judicial Studies Board conference centre at Millbank Tower on 18 September 1998. A new dawn was heralded. It would have been sensible for one of us to have been elected as a Chairman or President, and to have established ourselves as an organised body, perhaps the Association of Civil Judges, so that we could (and it might have been hoped, would) be consulted about the reform, management and improvement of civil litigation. But judges are not enthusiastic organisers, are independently minded, and no doubt each felt an egalitarian diffidence about assuming the limelight of leadership. So this did not come about. We remained as individuals, at the receiving end of whatever measures others – in the senior judiciary, the court service or on the rules committee – saw fit to impose. What is more, there was limited security of tenure. We were initially appointed for four years, a period which might, we were told, be extended for another four.

We were issued with a remarkably extensive list of job responsibilities, and these were from time to time modified by further additions. The list over time included responsibility for the allocation of all judicial work and for the 'just and efficient despatch of the business of the courts', for the overseeing of the deployment of judges in the group, ensuring that matters of importance were heard by a specific judge, maintaining regular contact with all the other judges, providing 'pastoral care and support' for permanent judges, including matters relating to their health, well-being and career, reviewing information relating to the business of the courts, preparing annual reports, ensuring so far as possible that all contested cases were brought to trial with a minimum of delay, liaison with the Department of Constitutional Affairs, the Court Service and other government agencies, attending 'symposia' and conferences, setting policies with court and diary managers, and discussing with the presiding judges sitting plans and deployment, so as to ensure an adequate complement of appropriate judges at courts within the group. All these duties to be combined with full-time sitting, and no extra pay. In January 2002 the then Senior Presiding Judge wrote to the Lord Chancellor: 'Administrative burdens seem to grow like pondweed in a warm summer.'

Although there were frequent suggestions that secretarial services would be provided, none materialised in Oxford. I did the job because I enjoyed civil litigation. Some DCJs worked remarkable hours, and worried a lot, in an effort to do everything they had been told to. They spent time drafting and circulating (the court service people called this 'cascading') guidance, instructions and suggestions to the judges in their groups. This was not always well received, for judges relish their independence and like to be left alone to get on with things. I took the view that if a court seemed to be working well there was no need for assiduous invigilation. A good judge neither requires nor appreciates constant supervision. I said that in any case of difficulty or uncertainty the matter should be referred to me.

Some DCJs also spent a lot of time trying to affect the workings of the court staff. This was not always welcome either. Furthermore, although these varied responsibilities were allocated with enthusiasm, DCJs had virtually no power, apart from that of personality, with which to exercise them. Judges had, of course, no authority whatsoever over what was spent on the 'just and efficient despatch of court business' (which sums the government severely reduced), nor in the choice or number of judges with whom we worked.

The civil judicial manpower in a group consisted of a number of District Judges (who supervised the progress of cases and tried the less expensive claims) and a much smaller number, perhaps only one or two, Circuit Judges. In my initial group, for example, there were about 17 DJs. Their quality varied from outstanding to quite good. Although I was 'in charge' of them I had no power to influence their appointment, or to get rid of them. Since the performance of a group, in terms of providing fair trials briskly, which is what matters, depended to an overwhelming extent upon the quality of the available judges, this was a major disadvantage. It was compounded by the fact that whenever a District Judge was promoted, retired, transferred or died it was generally not possible to obtain an immediate replacement. It was indeed impossible to establish who exactly was responsible for providing the replacement. Inquiries were deflected deftly around the Presiding Judges, the Department of Constitutional Affairs and the court service. Often inquiries led to the telephone of one seemingly powerful female official, who, over the years has operated in a number of significant capacities. (High Court judges have often been in some awe of her, and one told me that she had the memory of an elephant). Although I tried pretty hard, I was never allowed to locate the precise source of authority for fresh appointments to vacant positions. One might have thought that if a busy full-time judge ceased to sit another would clearly be needed forthwith. But no; the Court Service would embark upon a prolonged examination, over many months, of whether there was 'a business case' for a replacement. The DCJ could have explained whether one was necessary, and why, in five minutes.

In the 18 years during which I was a DCJ I was never formally asked when or whether a replacement judge was needed, or who such a replacement should be. On one occasion, in July 2004, an excellent District Judge, Ann Campbell, was promoted to the Circuit Bench. She represented 25% of the District Judiciary in Oxford. Months went by, but no replacement arrived. After fruitless 'liaison,' I identified a suitable person, a DJ who was working in Birmingham but lived near Banbury and wanted a transfer. Every difficulty was put in our way. There was a suggestion that he might be allowed to come in June 2005. At the end of 2004 I mentioned this in exasperation to the then President of the Family Division, Dame Elizabeth Butler-Sloss, a decisive and practical woman. I do not know to whom she spoke, or in what terms, but within days the transfer was agreed, and Alan Jenkins arrived shortly after. He turned out to be an expert glider pilot and classic car enthusiast as well as a robust judge.

In May 2005 I received a letter from the Department of Constitutional Affairs, Judicial Competitions (Courts) Division, saying that the department had been 'working for some time on ways in which the appointments process can be improved'. I was given the encouraging news that there had been an 'introduction of generic competences in place of criteria', and that 'the Judicial Appointments Programme Office liaises with Regional Directors to establish the Circuit needs'. But all that was necessary was to have a reserve list of approved candidates from whom a suitable replacement could be drawn when required.

At the end of 1989, the DCJs set about instituting the new civil regime. We held meetings with local solicitors and with the various local Bars. We went for courses of judicial training (which seemed largely to consist of suggestions about how to punish solicitors who did not comply with the new rules). We talked and listened to local judges and to court staff. This was not difficult if you were in charge of a city centre group, say Birmingham, for then all your judges were in one building and most of them came to lunch in the same dining room. But if your group was spread over several towns and counties as was mine, it was much harder to keep abreast of what they were thinking and doing. And, of course, there were different sets of court staff in different courts to contend with, not one. In Northampton, the new civil listing officer, a capable and very pleasant young woman called Christine Goodey, addressed a large meeting about the administrative arrangements. She was nervous but performed very well. She was to remain in post for over 18 years. Her speech was a rather better than one I heard delivered by the man who had been made DCJ for a neighbouring group at about that time. For nearly an hour he simply read out extracts from the new rules, punctuating these quotations by the repeated observation 'so that is how we will have to proceed'. Not all lawyers are engaging speakers, and this one always upset the staff on the rare occasions when he visited Oxford.

As I have said, my initial group involved Northampton, Peterborough and Oxford. Very shortly after it was set up and while I was busy trying to establish some esprit de corps throughout its extensive territory, the government decided that it wished to alter the long-established Circuits into which the country was divided for the purposes of the administration of justice, and to transfer Oxfordshire (and Hampshire) to the already very large SE Circuit. Nearly all barristers belong to a Circuit, of which there are six: the Northern, North Eastern, Midland and Oxford, Wales and Chester, South Eastern, and Western. High Court Judges visited these circuits to try the most important cases. It worked perfectly satisfactorily, and people were fond of their circuits.

The Senior Presiding Judge (Lord Justice Judge) pointed out to the Lord Chancellor in June 1999 that there was no evidence at all that the existing arrangements were not working well, that there was no reason to believe that the changes suggested would improve anything, and that they would positively damage civil and family justice (which did not appear to have been considered at all). The Presiding Judges on the SE Circuit stated that any increase in its size would be 'wholly unwelcome'. But no notice was taken of these clear, explicit and authoritative representations, which were simply ignored. The Circuits did not match the EU Regions, and probably for this unsatisfactory reason it was decided to take Oxford from the Midland and attach it to the already enormous (and notoriously difficult to run) South Eastern Circuit. Some attempt was made to oppose this, but it was weakly done and over-ridden. Not so on the Western. It was desired to take Winchester into the SE as well. But that Circuit put up a fight, led by Mrs Justice Heather Hallet, and supported by senior figures such as Lord Woolf. They indicated that whatever the government decided they would simply continue for judicial purposes to operate the Western Circuit as it traditionally had been. They won. But Oxford lost and ceased to be on the same circuit as Northampton and Peterborough.

So, no sooner had my group been established than it was torn up. Northampton was joined with Leicester, and Oxford with the Thames Valley, involving Milton Keynes, Reading, Slough and even metropolitan

Uxbridge, to the east of the M25. For a while I was anxious that I would be without any position, but was in the event offered a choice, and chose Oxford/Thames valley. It was in fact a bizarre group: listing was 'centralised' in Reading, I was based at Oxford, and the Group Manager had his headquarters in Luton, which was not even geographically within the area. This manager also dealt with a Surrey group in which the judge sat mostly at Epsom.

It was agreed that I could also continue to sit at Birmingham, Warwick and Northampton on the Midland Circuit. This aspect at least was very satisfactory for me, as most judges sit on only one circuit. I was sitting, I believe uniquely, on two circuits and in three Groups, which gave agreeable variety.

Quite soon the DCJs became aware that we were not all equal. In several of the big cities the DCJs were promoted to the rank of Senior Circuit Judge (a rank above Circuit Judge but below High Court Judge). This had two effects: they had security of tenure, able to remain in that post until retirement if they wanted to; and they were paid about 7% more, which in due course would also mean a better pension. It was entirely appropriate for people taking on and discharging extra responsibilities to be promoted and paid in this way. But only some were. Those of us who were not based in a single big city were not made Senior Circuit Judges.

After a while I looked into this. It seemed that it had been thought that in the large cities the DCJs should be promoted because there they sat alongside various categories of specialised judge, such as Chancery or Commercial Judges, who were SCJs, and where the top criminal judge would also be an SCJ. So it was only seemly that the civil judge should also be one. But this entirely ignored the question whether the city DCJs had any more arduous work to do than those in charge of several counties. They did not. In those days the court service produced useful accessible figures for cases 'dealt with' in every court. (By the time I retired in 2017 these had been hidden and were difficult to find). I studied these figures. It was clear that my group (and one or two others) were getting through as much or more work than some of the city groups where the judges had been promoted. The Oxford group in 2003/4 dealt with a total of 2,459 civil cases, whereas Birmingham did 1,710, Leeds 1,924 and Bristol 2,022. And the non-city jobs were also harder than the city ones because of the geographical spread, the difficulty of supervision and communication and the multiplicity of court staff. There was another point, which was that the specialist judges in the big cities in fact did a lot of the more arcane civil work which, for example in Oxford, I had to field myself. It was a clear injustice.

I raised this at a conference in May 2004. The Deputy Chief of Civil Litigation said that anyone in my position could make a case to him for SCJ status. I responded to that invitation, producing figures which clearly demonstrated the point being made. He then suggested that I should see what the circuit Presiding Judge had to say. Two successive Presiding Judges supported my application. For the year 2004-5 the figures were even more eloquent: Oxford 2,690, Leeds 2,130, Liverpool 1,895, Bristol 1,821 and Birmingham 1,489. But nothing was done about this, and it did rankle.

In July 2006 the President of the Queen's Bench Division re-appointed me as DCJ and I tried again, writing in June 2007 to the new Senior Presiding Judge. At that time, the figures which I showed him revealed that two large 'multi-county' Groups – Oxford/Thames Valley and Hampshire/Wiltshire/Dorset – were dealing with considerably more civil work than at least five SCJ posts. For example, Oxford was dealing with 2,548 civil cases whereas Birmingham was coping with only 1,762. Sympathy was expressed and it was indicated that the matter should be dealt with. But there were no doubt other and larger concerns, and again nothing was done. It was, I felt, a marked unfairness. A civil servant was eventually asked to investigate and a chart of various considerations was drawn up. Oxford was found, for reasons I was unable to follow, not to qualify. In the event I did not become a Senior Circuit Judge until 2014, ten years after I first raised the question, when the Group was extended from three counties to five and was serving some four million people. I had to make a fresh job application and be interviewed for suitability.

It is perhaps not always realised that if a Circuit Judge is not to be a complete pawn, to be used as the administration or the presiding senior judiciary see fit, it is as well for him or her to be alert to potential developments, and to keep open lines of communication with those in authority. For many years judges had understood that their sitting pattern, negotiated upon appointment, was not something which could be changed without their agreement. That is to say that they should not be required to sit somewhere they did not want to sit. This might obviously become inconvenient to an administration which wished to allocate work to a particular court centre, or perhaps to close an existing court, or to modify existing judicial dispositions. There was thus what lawyers call 'tension', or what others might call potential conflict. The presiding judiciary began from time to time issue circulars, asserting or emphasising that they did have the right to move judges about. They also sought to an increasing degree to control when judges might take their holidays. (Circuit Judges have an obligation to sit for 210 days a year, giving them about six weeks' holiday. The court service was keen always to refer to this, inaccurately, as 'leave'. Leave of course is a military expression indicative of a situation in which you are bound to be on duty unless given leave, that is permission, not to be. District judges had to sit for slightly more days).

It is obviously undesirable that several, or potentially all, the judges at any particular court might take their holidays simultaneously. But historically that had never seemed to happen; certainly it never did anywhere that I sat. And when a judge is not available to sit, then a deputy should be provided. This might either be a Recorder (a barrister or solicitor who sits as a part-time judge, or in the case of District Judges, a deputy District Judge – almost always a solicitor). There would not normally be much difficulty in rostering such substitutes, but they would have to be paid. Because governments have been fiercely reducing the sums available for the administration of justice in England (quite unlike their provision for health or foreign aid), this would involve a mild extra strain upon the budget. And so the DCJs were asked from time to time to control the holiday arrangements of the judges in their group. 'My' DCJs, who liaised sensibly with each other and were generally very conscientious would have been cross if I told them when they could go on holiday.

Some DCJs seemed to like to concentrate upon administration and case management, and would spend a lot of their time doing this rather than sitting in court. These judges, I thought, were perhaps wrongly prioritising and were not trying as many cases as they might have done. I felt that the main job of a DCJ should be to try the more substantial and difficult cases, not allocate them to other people. Perhaps rashly in this connection, I put myself in the way of some very major litigation. It was known as Credit Hire, not an immediately compulsive title, but a wave of legal disputes of some national significance.

The underlying situation was this. If a motorist had a collision which put his or her car out of action, another would be needed while the damaged vehicle was repaired or replaced. This would cost money which the victim of the collision might not have, or reasonably wish to spend. If he did spend it he would be out of pocket until the negligent driver paid up, which he might never do unless and until he was sued and found liable. Various companies ('credit hire' companies) devised arrangements whereby drivers might come to them and be provided free of charge with replacement car while theirs were repaired, and the credit hire company would seek recovery of the motorists' losses - and the cost of the provided car - on their behalf, ultimately by litigation, from the responsible driver or his insurer. Although the basic idea was simple and not objectionable, it raised a wide variety of legal questions, some of them of a fundamental and important nature. There were incestuous and very un-transparent contractual relationships, and circular payments, within and between the credit hire companies, the repairing companies and the actual providers of the cars. There were difficulties about the intricacies of consumer credit legislation, and whether or not such agreements were exempt. There were contentions that credit hire agreements were a 'sham.' Often a suspiciously long time was taken to repair the cars, thus prolonging the periods of hire for which compensation would be claimed. The longer the period of replacement car hire, the greater the cost. There were questions about how damages should be calculated. Many of the hiring rates were far above those readily available in the market. The car hirers were frequently unaware of the nature of the contracts they had entered into. These schemes became extremely popular and started to cost providers of car insurance (and ultimately their customers) a great deal of money. The insurers joined battle with the credit hire companies, and there were, nationally, many thousands of cases.

This became a major concern; the system was becoming coagulated and there was a danger that different judges might take different views about essentially the same facts. At a DCJ conference I found myself offering to try some test cases, which could be taken to the Court of Appeal, which could then give definitive rulings. There was a curious reluctance on the part of litigants actually to fight such cases, possibly fearing the outcomes. Many, after being listed, settled. But in due course I did try some, which duly appealed, only to settle before the hearing in the Court of Appeal. I persevered, and in 2001 five of these cases were gathered together and argued by leading counsel over a number of days. I reserved judgment and took the papers home to work on. There was a lot of work involved, and at least 14 separate issues. I spent many days composing the judgment in my study. Mostly over weekends, from about 9 am to lunch time, and then again from about 9 pm to midnight, and in the evenings during the week. Between about 2 and 4 pm, for some reason, possibly atavistic, I do not think with the same clarity or energy.

Parts of this exercise I greatly enjoyed, especially analysing the speeches in the Court of Appeal and House of Lords decisions. If I read several of these, and then came back to them 24 hours later and read them again, I felt I had a pretty clear idea of what the law really was. Appellate judges deal with the same thing in different ways and analyse the same problem from different viewpoints. These were pleasant fields in which to linger. But trying to make sense of some of the statutory provisions in the Consumer Credit legislation was something I did with less relish and confidence. The authors of the complex thickets of that legislation did not express themselves with the precision and style of the higher judiciary. I was acutely conscious that what I wrote would be subject to severe scrutiny by the losing side upon appeal, and of course by the Court of Appeal itself. I gave judgment on 14th September 2001 and awaited the outcome of the appeal anxiously, for I would look pretty stupid if my conclusions were found to be wrong.

The appeal was heard over four days in March 2002 (and reported as Burdis v Livsey [2002] 3WLR 762). I was greatly relieved to be upheld on 12 of the 14 points in issue, including all the important ones, and Aldous LJ generously concluded 'We should like to pay tribute to Judge Harris QC for the quick and efficient way in which he dealt with these cases and for producing a most comprehensive and readable judgment'. This was a great relief, and months of trepidation gave way to modest euphoria.

Thereafter I came to be regarded as something of an authority on claims of this kind, which did not tamely go away, but permutated in various directions over subsequent years. One of these was a case called Lagden v O'Connor [2003] 3WLR 1571 which went to the House of Lords. This involved a point about what lawyers call 'impecuniosity', a word used to apply to the position of a plaintiff without any money who cannot afford to do what he might otherwise do to limit his loss. Here too I was gratified to be upheld, and a long-established earlier authority was departed from.

It is very satisfactory to emerge from a tedious day in court to read a judgment from a higher court in which one's efforts have been vindicated or appreciated. Some judges shy away a little, where they can, from analysis of the law and prefer where possible to base their decisions on findings of fact. There are certainly some areas of the law which one might be keen to avoid, notable examples being that applicable to the provision of housing by local authorities, and various aspects of discrimination. (The former in particular, though of great practical importance, is a pretty complex mess, quite incomprehensible to those in need of housing, to whom it applies, and uphill work for lawyers).

I enjoyed analysing the law applicable to interesting or unusual situations, not overburdened by statutory complexity but with some tapestry of previous authority, or perhaps no previous authority at all. I enjoyed, for example, deciding whether it was open to an auctioneer at a sale advertised as without reserve to refuse to sell to the highest bidder. I found that it was not, and was upheld in the Court of Appeal (Barry v Davies [2000] 1WLR 1962). Then there was the case of the Northampton shoe manufacturer who wished to terminate the services of a selling agent. There are regulations of European genesis incorporated into English law about entitlement to compensation in these circumstances, but unhappily these regulations do not state how such compensation is to be calculated. The manufacturer wished to pay what was due, and the agent to receive that to which he was entitled. Their respective solicitors could not agree what this was. They came to the Oxford County Court in 2005. I decided that it should be based on the market value of the agency (which was very modest). There was an appeal to the Court of Appeal, which came to the same conclusion. There was a further appeal to the House of Lords, which also came to the same conclusion. I was pleased that Lord Hoffman (Lenny to his friends) said that my judgment was 'a model of clarity and common sense' (Lonsdale v Howard & Hallam [2007] I WLR 2055, 2064). This case was naturally satisfying personally, but is a fine illustration of the mess our legislation can leave people in. It is beyond ridiculous that the law was so badly drafted that it required no fewer than nine judges to decide upon the small sum that the agent was entitled to.

Another interesting case involved the question whether students who had paid to attend a course in historical vehicle restoration were entitled to damages when the instruction turned out, as it did, to be very poor, there was a lack of practical work and indeed of old cars to work on. I found that they were, in a decision which has relevance to schools or universities which might fail to deliver satisfactory education. Sadly, the defendant college felt unable to afford to appeal.

One of the pleasures of being a civil judge deciding questions of both fact and law is that virtually every case ends as you think it should (though a few decisions might be reversed by the Court of Appeal later). This is satisfying, and quite unlike being at the Bar, where some you win and some you lose, and also unlike crime, where juries do not always return the verdicts which the judge feels are appropriate. It is also agreeable to be able to redress wrongs and injustices which may have been inflicted; sometimes in modest ways, as where predatory parking control companies prey upon unwary motorists, sometimes in more serious situations, such as when dangerous horses were sold to inexperienced riders, with mendacious but sedative assertions about their gentle nature. For some reason there was a steady flow of these at Oxford, but none in Northampton or Warwick.

Chapter 15

A powerless President

In 2002 I became the representative of the Thames Valley area on the Council of Her Majesty's Circuit Judges. This is in effect the judges' trade union. A circular had indicated that the existing incumbent was retiring and asked if anyone would step forward. I thought it might be interesting. There was a slight hitch, as I was a member of two circuits, but John Samuels QC , who had led me some years earlier in a case about rally driving, persuaded the Council that this did not matter.

This body, headed by an annually-changing President, represented the Circuit Judges of England and Wales, in particular in their intercourse with the Lord Chancellor's department, and then with the Ministry of Justice – after the Office of Lord Chancellor in its traditional form was abolished (with no judicial consultation whatsoever) by Prime Minister Blair in 2005. In 2002 the Council was largely run by its Secretary, Shaun Lyons, who had been Chief Naval Judge Advocate before he had become a Circuit Judge in 1992. Lyons exhibited astonishing energy in the width and depth of his contact both with the administration and with the higher judiciary. He assimilated, discussed, drafted and negotiated over a wide spectrum, and informed and strongly guided a number of Presidents. Indeed, several simply sat mute at his side during meetings, while he ran the proceedings. When I first joined the Council it seemed that he spoke for perhaps 80% of the time, which was very impressive. We felt that nobody could do it better. Others agreed. Honours are given to Circuit Judges with astonishing parsimony, but he was made a CBE in 2004.

There were sub committees: Civil, Criminal and Family. I joined the former, and initially we did very little. The sub-committee chairman, Crawford Lindsay QC, relaxed, amiable and astute under a wild thatch of grey hair, never found much that he felt we needed to comment on. The Council met and chatted convivially in the Benchers' quarters in Middle Temple, looking out over its lawns, and ate a good lunch. After a year or two it came to the conclusion that a revised constitution was called for, which I was for some reason asked to draft. This provided as its mission statement:

The Objects of the Council of Her Majesty's Circuit Judges are as follows:

(a) To promote, protect and further the interests of justice and of freedom under the law.

(b) To foster and preserve the independence of the Judiciary, and in particular that of the Circuit Judges of England and Wales.

(c) To promote, protect and further the interests of such Circuit Judges, and to represent them as may be appropriate.

(d) To make such representations to government or elsewhere on matters relevant to the law, and to judges, as may be thought appropriate.

It was duly adopted.

In 2009 I had the honour and good fortune to be made a Bencher of the Inner Temple (the Benchers are its governing body), largely due to the good offices of Anthony May, then President of the Queen's Bench

Division, and very distinguished academically. He had sat in the Court of Appeal since 1997, in a career which was a telling contrast to my own. Called to the Bar in the same year as me, 1967, he was a QC ten years before I was, and became a Bencher 24 year earlier than I did.

In due course, in 2010, I found myself, on the Buggin's turn principle, and because one or two ahead of me had dropped out, elected as President of the Council of Circuit Judges. I felt that to be President of the largest body of judges in the country, some 700 strong, who tried almost all of the more valuable and significant civil work, and the serious crime, not to mention most divorce and many children's cases, should be a worthwhile thing. After all, the foundation and structure of England is its civil law. It was also a time when judicial morale was low and falling. (It has since fallen a lot further). The government had imposed upon us what was in real terms a substantial pay cut over several years, and a plethora of ill-considered and ill-drafted legislation.

At the outset of my term I drafted a background paper for circulation to all judges. This set out the position as I saw it:

'For some years now I have felt that we have been working in a deteriorating environment. National morality seems to be in decay, robust common sense is in retreat. The administration of our legal system is impoverished, and the country is in fathomless debt. But laws are still being created at a remarkable rate, rather beyond the ability of citizen or lawyer to assimilate. *The Spectator* estimates that some 35,000 new laws have been introduced in the last 12 years. Sweet and Maxwell, perhaps a better-known source of legal information, indicate that the last three prime ministers have introduced an average of over 2,629 laws per year. Over the last eight years there have been, annually, over 8000 statutory instruments and 40 to 70 Acts of Parliament. Much is enacted with modest legislative scrutiny. Curiously, despite this acute distension of the statute book, only 35% of the Law Commission's proposals between 2001 and 2005 have been implemented, compared with 70% before 1990.

The Ministry of Justice, created in May 2007 with a staff of 77,000, now employs some 95,000 people and costs £10 billion a year.

'Civil law is the foundation, structure and safeguard of a free, prosperous and advanced society. English Common Law has long been, and remains, a fine and flexible instrument. But law must be accessible. Over a decade ago civil procedure was thought expensive, slow and cumbersome. Lord Woolf called for simplification. Reforms were implemented. But instead of simplicity and cheapness, we have complexity and expense. The White Book is now 50% larger than it was before the reforms. The provisions dealing with costs covered just 74 pages in1997. By 2009 they covered 316, including 37 pages of guidance. Civil Procedure News has remarked on 'what a dog's breakfast the rules and practice directions and related sources [protocols and guides] have become'. The Court of Appeal has referred to a 'cumbrous and confusing three-tier hierarchy of rules and guidance'. The cost of civil litigation has become so excessive that there have been a series of inquiries into what might be done about it. Jackson LJ's preliminary report was over 1000 pages long and his final report half as much again.

'Statutes are often complex or obscure, requiring litigation to establish what their provisions mean. This is not good quality law. Statutes should be drafted, so far as possible, to be understandable to those to whom they apply. The Victorians understood this (e.g. the Sale of Goods Act). We seem to have forgotten the art and value of simplicity. Consumer credit is an area especially replete with caliginous legislation, yet it governs common everyday transactions by ordinary people and so needs to be clear, simple and readily understood. Data protection is impenetrably complex, and, as a recent Chairman of the Bar has said, is often used as a bogus excuse for withholding information which the public has every right to know.

'Civil litigants are expected to pay fees calculated to meet the cost of the provision of court facilities. It might be thought that this provision would be a very early charge upon the public purse in an advanced nation governed by the rule of law. Legal aid and the NHS were introduced at virtually the same time, to provide for different, but equally important, needs.

'The British Crime Survey suggests that some 10.7 million crimes were committed in 2008-9. Less than half of these (4.7 million) were recorded by the police. Of this 4.7 million, some seem not to be investigated at all. The overall clear-up rate for the proportion of offences which is investigated does not generally exceed 25%. Many suspects are simply warned or cautioned. In 2008 more than 38,000 people were cautioned for assaults, sometimes serious ones. (This clement approach is not, however, applied to motorists, who have usually not hurt anyone at all but are proceeded against with comprehensive and profitable efficiency). Some years ago *The Economist* reported that for every hundred criminal offences committed, only three or four people were convicted and punished. I have sought an up-to-date figure from the Home Office, but it has not been forthcoming. It is unlikely to be very different. The sad truth is that a very high proportion of criminal activity goes unpunished. Only about 15% of burglaries result in a conviction. But even with this very modest rate of detection and conviction, there is inadequate prison space, insufficient remedial training, and considerable pressure for premature release. The Parole Board has been unable to keep pace with the work it is required to do.

'*The Times* has reported that CPS lawyers are receiving bonuses linked to their success in confiscating criminal assets. If there is a financial stake in obtaining convictions, this is hard to reconcile with the fundamental principle that prosecutions should be conducted in an entirely disinterested manner. The independent Bar, one of the few remaining bulwarks of our liberty (such as it is), is under sustained pressure to reduce already very low publicly-funded fee levels. Criminal Practice and Procedure has become a growth industry. Judicial discretion in sentencing is steadily being eroded. Sentencing provisions are so complex that a well-known academic has made a career out of explaining them to judges. This should not be necessary.

'Law cannot be divorced from the society it applies to. In October 2009 almost one million young people between the ages of 16 and 24 were not being educated, trained or employed. It is clear that many children emerge from school effectively unable to read, write, calculate – or in many cases, speak – accurately, coherently or intelligently, let alone with any understanding of the history and nature of the country they inhabit, or any tools to make their way in it. It is hard for them to be model citizens.

'Drink in 21st century Britain is a vast leisure industry. Alcohol (unlike, say, fireworks, which hurt very few people but also give pleasure) is readily and very cheaply available 24 hours a day. As judges know, most crimes of violence are committed by people who have been drinking. Crimes of violence constitute about 20% of all offending.

'The family justice system is close to crisis. The 250 judges working in this area are some of the most altruistic and conscientious of all, and are probably under the greatest strain. Local authorities struggle to meet their responsibilities to children. The budget of the Legal Services Commission appears to be inadequate to fund competent representation for children and families, and there is an acute shortage of solicitors prepared to act on the terms which are available. Many parties come to court unrepresented. CAFCASS, the service whose task it is to represent children, is routinely failing to do so, or failing to do so timeously. Family courts have been under sustained criticism (only partly alleviated) for secrecy and putative bias against fathers.

'This then is the background against which we are working in 2010. It is not entirely encouraging. We shall do our best. The task of putting it all right is of course largely out of our hands, but I do not believe that we serve anyone's interests by always sitting mute about serious problems affecting the law, problems with which we daily contend. I would be interested to know whether members feel that the Committee should continue as a largely reactive and pastoral body, as it has been, or that it might occasionally take an initiative and express some opinions on matters relevant to justice and the law...'

Before I circulated this document, it came to the attention of the then Secretary of the Council, a judge who did not want to risk upsetting or irritating any influential people in government or the senior judiciary in any way at all. She, or some other member of the committee, reported me to the Senior Presiding Judge, a charming and capable man whom I had known at the Bar. He telephoned me to say that I should not circulate my paper as it was 'political', and the press might get hold of it. It was not suggested that any of it was untrue or not fair comment. In deference to his strongly-put request, and to his position of authority, I did not distribute it.

I regret that. It contained, it seemed to me, an accurate analysis. The

matters referred to were, to quote our constitution, 'representations...
on matters relevant to the law'. They deserved articulation, and if the
press had drawn them to the attention of the wider public, where was
the harm in that? There is indeed a good deal to be said for updating it,
for the position is no better nine years on.

One might now comment upon the expensive obsession of Wiltshire
Police with investigating ill-founded allegations of historical sexual
impropriety against a Prime Minister who died in 2005. Police publicly
searched the property of an elderly Field Marshall of impeccable
reputation, apparently after misleading the magistrate to whom they
applied for a warrant. Nobody has yet been held responsible for this. It
seems clear too that the police have deliberately and repeatedly withheld
exculpatory evidence from those charged with criminal offences, a state
of affairs which could hardly be more serious. Should judges, outside
the context of particular cases, not be permitted to comment, on the
grounds that it is 'political'? Might it not be remarked that none of
these reticent policemen has been prosecuted for attempting to pervert
the course of justice – a charge regularly brought against motorists for
giving misleading information about who might have been driving a car
above a speed limit.

The police are not disposed to prosecute those responsible for
shoplifting if the value is under £200. The desperate vulnerability of
small shopkeepers is obvious. Even burglary – which is one of the
nastiest offences, because many victims never feel safe in their violated
homes again – has been downgraded by many forces. The vast majority
of burglaries (apparently well over 90%) are never solved, and very
large numbers are not even investigated. While reported crime has been
rising substantially, the number of prosecutions brought has fallen by
40 -45% over the last eight years. The whole edifice of criminal justice
is in grave danger. There have been large reductions in pay for barristers
practising in crime: legal aid fees are now 40% lower in real terms than
in 2007. Many barristers earn less than tube train drivers and would
leave the Bar if they could.

At the start of my period of office it seemed as though I might be able to communicate with the world to some useful extent. Frances Gibb was kind enough to give me a substantial *Times* interview (for which a photographer spent an hour taking pictures) and she published an article I had written on the harm done to civil procedure. I spoke once or twice on the radio. But it soon turned out, to my innocent surprise, that the Office of President of the Council of her Majesty's Circuit Judges had virtually no significance at all. I wrote to the new Lord Chancellor, Kenneth Clark (himself a barrister), saying that I would appreciate a meeting. He did not bother to reply. The committee did not seem to find this either surprising or exceptionable.

In March 2010 we held a meeting at the Travellers Club to discuss the roles of both President and Council. I suggested that we might perhaps be a little proactive now and then, instead of simply responding to consultation exercises – responses to which little heed seemed to be paid in any event. 'No,' said the committee, 'We do not want any public comment or any pro-activity. Better to keep our heads below the parapet and keep our powder dry, lest we antagonise the government and they retaliate by reducing our pension entitlements'. (This, despite the council's self-imposed restraint, is exactly what happened anyway). The committee was not very keen on my occasional radio contributions either. It was never made clear when, if ever, the Committee might be disposed to look above its crenellations and use some of its dry powder. If it ever has, I have not noticed. There seemed to me then, and there still seems now, little point in a representative body concerned with the Rule of Law, the very heart of our national interest, being inconspicuous, invisible and inaudible.

On the lighter side, I thought, in the spring of my presidential year, that there might be a Palace garden party invitation for the leader of England's Circuit Judges to look forward to. Sadly, there was not even that, so diminished was our status. I did however organise a summer dinner at the Ashmolean Museum in Oxford, held in the sculpture gallery under the shapely marble thighs of antiquity. This was considered a great success.

The President is made a member ex-officio of the Judges' Council, which is a forum in which the senior judiciary discuss developments and difficulties at a high level. Being present only for a year, and only as a Circuit Judge, one was destined to be either a mouse or a meteorite. While I did make a few remarks, mostly I sat listening in awe, like Jim Hawkins in the apple barrel. At the end of my term I was thanked for 'characteristically robust contributions', but they were very few.

In October 2010 I was asked to sit on a committee on 'Qualities and abilities for the judiciary – a consideration of competence frameworks', ably chaired by a senior female civil servant, which was asked to draw up a list of the 'core qualities' judges needed. This was, we were told, to aid work on judicial appointments. There were four judges and ten civil servants on the committee. When this task was announced, the judges asked for a little time for consideration. We each jotted down notes for about twenty minutes, and then conferred with each other. Our lists of qualities and priorities were very similar. After another ten minutes we produced an agreed document on less than one page of A4. It was explicit and concise. The chairman thanked us and said that she would 'take this away'. We assumed the work was done. About six weeks later, the committee met again, and the chairman said that a paper had now been produced on core judicial qualities for further discussion. The paper turned out to be a booklet several pages long. We judges searched in vain for our page of agreed qualities, and did not find it. Everything we said had been either eviscerated or expanded and qualified into something unrecognisable, and had been clothed in a moist layer of political correctness. It indicated, for example, that 'valuing diversity' was a core quality. We had not mentioned this vague but fashionable expression, and when I pointed out that what judges most valued were honesty and accuracy, I was told that such a formulation would not prove 'acceptable'. I then began to analyse some of the rest of the new document, asking when and how its terms had been so dramatically, and unhappily, altered. After a few minutes it became apparent that several of the civil servants on the committee had been fully engaged, for several weeks, in the re-drafting of what the judges had agreed were the necessary 'core' qualities. They were looking rather unhappy, and I felt that normal politeness required me to rein in our criticisms. This was a remarkable example of pointless work being done at considerable time and cost to replace a sensible succinct formulation with material which was less a precise tool than some sort of contribution to an anodyne and voguish creed. If this is a habitual practice in the Civil Service, the sooner it is swept away the better.

I also spent considerable time that year with Judge Neil Bidder QC, in the preparation and delivery of the judges' submission to the Senior Salary Review Body which the Council made in November 2010. It was as depressing for us to prepare, as no doubt it was for the SSRB to consider, submissions upon an important subject when there was no practical possibility of any favourable recommendations the board might make being acted upon, because the Government had imposed a pay freeze. We pointed out that national average earnings had increased between 2003 and 2009 by 6% more than Circuit Judges' pay, that judges had no means of earning extra income, that they got no benefits in kind, no performance bonuses, health insurance or housing allowances. There were no perquisites of office at all. Nor, unlike MPs, could we vote ourselves a pay increase. We observed that in 1986 77% of the most serious criminal cases were tried by High Court judges, whereas by 2009 Circuit Judges were trying 75.4%. A complete reversal, but the government had not seen fit to pay CJs even the rates HCJs were enjoying 25 years earlier. A High Court judge in 2003 was paid £147,000, but a Circuit Judge doing the same work seven years later was paid £128,000. Almost all the civil work which used to be the diet of the High Court is now tried by circuit judges, who get no extra remuneration for it. Even when they sit, as many do, as High Court judges for weeks at a time, they have no extra pay. If they are unhappy, judges cannot resign to return to the Bar.

We also pointed out to the Board that while the complexity of the law had increased, the morale of those administering it had steadily fallen. A survey had shown that only 7% of judges felt they had sufficient time in an ordinary working day to do the necessary reading, writing and preparation. Even in 2010 it was becoming difficult to recruit, especially High Court judges. It has got much worse since.

These submissions were received with great courtesy by the

Chairman, Sir Peter North, a former Vice Chancellor of Oxford University, and his committee members, and our party was subjected only to an agreeable level of cross examination. As expected, no benefit came from our submissions or the Review Body's recommendations.

None had come in another direction either. In 2009 a grave problem had been exercising those responsible for the civil law, namely the explosion in costs, and their increasing complexity, despite earlier attempts at reform. An increasingly large section of the community simply could not afford to litigate One of the cleverest of the senior judiciary, Lord Justice Jackson, had been asked to report on this, and, working with remarkable speed had produced, in May 2009 a two-volume 663-page preliminary report, inviting comment. I drafted some replies on behalf of the council, on two aspects: how should people be expected to finance litigation, and to what extent should judges (as opposed to the parties) be expected to 'manage' costs? Lord Jackson, maintaining his astonishing work rate, produced a 557-page final report in December 2009. In it he quoted what I had said:

'By far the most attractive of the various possibilities dealt with in the report is before the event legal insurance of one sort or another. Equipped with this, an individual or small company could go through life confident that should there be a need to bring or defend proceedings it will be possible to do so. We... note that it is widespread already in litigation connected with motoring, and is also provided for in some contexts in many household insurance policies. It is already common in Europe, and it has the great benefit of simplicity. Another form of before the event insurance is membership of trades unions, now in decline, which traditionally funded their members' personal injury litigation against employers (and met defendants' costs orders if they lost) ... we very strongly favour before the event insurance. It could readily be encouraged by making the premiums tax deductible expenditure. As there is a large potential market, and purchasers would be insuring only against the possibility, not the actuality, of litigation, it might reasonably be thought that the premiums in a competitive insurance market would be low.'

Apart from indicating that insurers did not advocate it – without any analysis of why not – and observing that existing BTE insurance will 'adapt its products', Lord Jackson simply concluded that he did not make 'any specific recommendations'. This was a great pity, and a missed opportunity to provide in a cheap and simple way the wherewithal for ordinary people to go to court should they need to do so.

Sadly, he was not with us on costs management either. He wrote 'The most elegant and forceful attack upon the whole concept of costs management was delivered by Her Majesty's Council of Circuit Judges', and quoted the submission I had written:

'We view with trepidation and antipathy yet another area of out-of-court invigilation which it might be suggested the judiciary should take on. Consideration of parties' budgets would be a very significant and difficult exercise. It would also be very time consuming. If a judge is worrying his way through two rival litigation budgets, assuming he has somehow acquired the expertise to do so, he will not be trying cases. Judicial productivity would be likely to fall as fast as morale if we are required to do this work. It is work at which (whatever training may be provided) a judge is likely to be far less competent than the solicitors whose budgets are being managed. If the budget management was badly done it could cripple the proper preparation of a case. It would be likely to result in much ancillary litigation. We are not in favour of moving down this road, however beguilingly professors may argue for a quasi-business approach to litigation 'projects'. The best way to minimise cost is for skilled people to work briskly and economically because they want to, not because somebody is trying to control them'.

However, Lord Jackson did think it a good idea, and said that judges could acquire the necessary skill. This, in the event, they have tried to do. I never found costs management to be a very satisfactory exercise, though by the time I retired I was, I suppose, one of the most experienced civil judges in the country. These were further examples of the lack of significance attached to anything said by the Council of Her Majesty's Circuit Judges.

There remained the annual dinner to preside over. This was held in the New Hall at Lincoln's Inn: new in the sense that it had been opened by Queen Victoria in 1845, two months before the outbreak of the first Sikh War. It is a mighty and atmospheric building, designed by Philip Hardwick, an architect best known for railway stations and the Euston Arch. There was a gratifyingly distinguished guest list, headed by the indefatigable Lord Chief Justice, Igor Judge.

In my speech, which, curiously I found I was not very nervous about, I asked this audience rhetorically whether the Circuit Judges' Council should be as muted as it was:

'All public life contains politics of one sort or another. There is a misty borderland where discussion of the law blends into politics. Should we retreat from this march, or advance into it in the interests of quality and clarity? Is it too political to observe that most of our crime is caused not by sentencing policy but by drugs or alcohol, and that people behave as they do because they have been badly brought up and ill-educated, not because of insufficient community remedial work? May we not mention that if not taught their history, people do not know where they are? Is it wrong to point out the absence of discernible public morality? Which of our great institutions now think or move along clear, robust, independent and sensible lines? The Church does not fight the good fight, the Civil Service is diluted with political amalgam, our medical consultants are ruled by administrators, broadcasters are trepid in the toils of political correctness, the police behave with bizarre unpredictability. Who is left? The judges are left, the Bar is still left... some soldiers, some writers, a few MPs, and many ordinary people of common sense. I hope it is enough'.

This went down pretty well, but was not much of a legacy for a year in office. I handed over to my successor, Jackie Davis, a tough and practical Yorkshire woman. I do not think she had any more success than I did. Since then I have seen or heard virtually nothing from or about the Circuit Judges Council. It exists, but says nothing in public.

Both before and after I was President, I was sometimes asked to give interviews. These were usually on the radio, and I would conduct them over the telephone. I did several for the Today programme. Speaking in this way it was easy, and indeed sensible, to jot down for possible use a few phrases or useful figures. It was not the same on television. In August 2011 there was extensive rioting in London after the police had found it necessary to shoot a criminal called Mark Duggan. Hundreds took to the streets allegedly in protest, but actually to mount looting attacks upon shops and other property. Premises were set on fire, and disturbances spread to other cities. There were over 3,000 arrests, and there was some variety in the often quite severe sentences which judges passed. I spoke about this on the radio. ITV approached me for a TV interview, to which I agreed. A van bristling with ariels and full of communication equipment arrived at home. A mini studio was set up in the dining room. I was told that only my head and shoulders would be televised, so anything on the table would be invisible. Thus emboldened I made the great mistake of glancing down occasionally at some notes. When I saw a copy of the filmed interview afterwards I realised that lowering one's eyes in this way gave the impression either of looking distinctly shifty, or of going to sleep like a narcoleptic. My message, that no two cases are the same and each judge was properly exercising his own discretion, was not obscured, but it could have been more professionally delivered.

Chapter 16

Flights of fancy

I have always wanted to fly. As I small child I looked up enviously whenever there was a droning sound overhead, and at night I found myself piloting in my dreams whatever aeroplane had featured that week in *The Eagle*, an intelligent comic produced between 1950 and 1969 which carried cutaway drawings of machines such as the Hawker Hunter, the Canberra and the Shackleton. Every year my father used to take me to a Battle of Britain memorial display at a local airfield, generally Cosford. On one occasion, after much pestering, he allowed me, and my friend, Richard Barr, a short flight in a De Havilland Rapide, a small, elegant, 1930s twin engine passenger biplane. (Barr thinks he did not, and that we did this clandestinely). It revved up, taxied unevenly across the grass, and paused. Its engines roared and we raced off down the runway, springing quickly into the air. As we climbed it banked and turned so that there was a fine view of where we had just been, marooned on the earth. You could see into the cockpit too. I found this first flight a grand experience.

Foolishly, for reasons I cannot recollect, I failed to join the Birmingham University Air Squadron, with which I could have learned to fly in a Chipmunk, quite a powerful RAF trainer. I did however manage a parachute descent, also with Barr, when we were about 19. This involved going to an old wartime airfield called Halfpenny Green, where we and several others spent an hour jumping off a stepladder and rolling over on a piece of coconut matting in order to simulate landing. We were told that we had a reserve chute should the main one fail, but that there would be little time to deploy it.

Having completed our comprehensive training, we donned crash helmets and sturdy boots and clambered into an old high-winged light plane called an Auster. This took off briskly and climbed to some 2,000 ft. I was then told to get out of the doorway of the plane (the actual door had been left behind) and grasp the strut which braced the wing. This I did, and it was not too hard to hold on as the pilot had throttled back to about 90mph. I then let go. For a few moments – until the static line jerked the chute out of its rucksack on my back – the sky span about most disconcertingly. There was a mild jerk, and I was conscious of floating gently in the air, at some height, silently and most pleasurably.

Soon however it became clear that I was approaching the ground rather fast. I rotated the parachute as I had been instructed by pulling on the lines, so that I hit the ground going backwards, and then rolled over in the approved fashion. There was a loud crunch in the vicinity of my head. My helmet had broken. It had not done that on the coconut mat. It broke because I had managed to land on the tarmac runway. No sooner had I appreciated this than I was aware that the aircraft out of which I had just jumped was about to do the same. The pilot, I later learned, thought it fun to see if he could get down to the ground quicker than the parachutist, and often did. But he had not expected me to appear in front of him on his landing approach. However he was sufficiently alert to push the throttle forward, pull the stick back, and vault the plane over me to go round again while I disentangled from the billowing and uncooperative folds of my parachute.

I was much luckier that afternoon than was an adventurous female member of my Chambers, Tania Pond, in February 1989. She was quite an experienced sky diver and had, by her mid-twenties, done several dozen jumps. On her final jump there was a terrible misjudgement of some sort and she descended into contact with the propeller of the aircraft she had jumped out of, just as it was touching down. I imagine she felt nothing.

When conditions are good in the mountains above Tignes in the French Alps you can pay a modest sum to be tied alongside a shaggy haired Frenchman suspended below the wing of a hang glider. The two of you then ski off the edge of a cliff, and an after a sinking moment of uncertainty, stabilise reassuringly to descend gently and silently towards a frozen lake. This was pleasant until at a very low level the pilot swung the machine sharply through 180 degrees and, by pushing on a bar he was holding, spilt the air from beneath the wing. I expected at least a broken leg, but gratifyingly we crumpled gently into soft snow a few yards from a photographer associate of his.

My next flying experience was when Carol bought me as an imaginative birthday present an hour in a motor-glider. This machine, from Eastern Europe, was called a Grob, an ugly name for an agreeable device. It could take off under its own power without need of a tow and climb without the assistance of thermals. The engine was then turned off and the pilot and instructor could move silently about the sky, gliding in a fulfilling fashion. Should air conditions not favour the flight plan, there was no need to get stranded. It was always possible to restart the engine and fly home, or to some convenient safe landing place.

It is surprising that this sport is not more popular. It is of course less 'pure' than gliding in an aircraft with no engine, and much less testing of skill, but the removal of complete reliance upon air and wind does have something to be said for it. After all, there are very few substantial sailing boats which are not equipped with engines, which are used freely and without shame whenever it is necessary to get into or out of a harbour, pick up a mooring, or get out of difficulty caused by wind or tide. A motor glider can be viewed as the aeronautical equivalent of a small yacht.

An altogether simpler and older form of flight, pioneered by the Montgolfier brothers in 1783, is ballooning. Here there is virtually no control of direction, and the basket containing pilot and passengers is wholly at the disposition of the prevailing wind. In 1990 Richard Barr invited us to join him and his ballooning partner and co-owner Richard Holmes (manufacturer of high-quality teddy bears) in an event organised by the Ballooning Club of India. Teams from nine countries were invited to a 'Mela', which turned out to be a kind of rally in which hot air balloons were flown from a number of historic cities in Southern India, including Madras, Madurai, Mysore and Bangalore. The flights were interspersed with some strenuous travel and a few restorative stops in the Dravidian provinces of Tamil Nadu, Kerala and Carnatica.

Balloons, which had never been seen in that part of the world before, need to be flown in tranquil air with gentle winds. This meant gathering before dawn in municipal parks, parade grounds or stadiums, gaudy with bunting and enlivened by martial music, played with Gilbertian brio and swagger by groups such as the Trivandrum Pipers or the Bangalore Police Band. A local notable would speak to the crowd, and the Club President, an erstwhile MP and enthusiastic balloonist, one P V Gupta, would then announce a 'task' for the participants. Then, as the bands marched and countermarched, the teams would simultaneously inflate their balloons. The flames from the burners roared fiercely into billowing folds of multi-coloured rip-stop fabric, which would tower 80 or 90 ft into the morning sky.

Inflation was hot and exciting work, needing one person to control the burner, which lay upon its side within the tilted basket, two to hold open the aperture at the lower end of the balloon, and at least one more to control the top of the balloon via a rope. The canopy would slowly fill and become vertical, the basket would stand upright and then had to be held on the ground by a combination of people, weights or ropes. When all were more or less ready, and the balloons were billowing impatiently with buoyancy and tricky to control, there was a fanfare or whistle, and the balloons would rise, in theatrical proximity, to great cheers.

There were some accomplished pilots among us: Ivan Trifonov, the first man to fly from Spain to Africa (where Algeria forced him to ditch in the sea); 75-year-old Erling Sem-Jacobson from Norway (whose age was greater than that of his three young crew members combined); long range gas-balloonist Joe Starkbaum, eccentric Lancastrian Fred Fielder, and Barr and Holmes, who had crossed the North Sea to Denmark in an epic pioneering flight. Their balloon was one of the largest in the world at some 300,000 cubic feet and was capable of carrying 17 people, which made us a target for journalists and freeloaders.

The balloons ascended quickly, majestically accelerating over festive crowds and floating over baked rooftops packed with waving people. We passed over the coagulations of Indian traffic and then floated away over open country. Elysian views of paddy fields, palms and mediaeval settlements of mud and thatch lay below. Sometimes, as at Madurai, great statue-clad gopurams belonging to huge temples towered through the morning mist. Not infrequently life on the ground beneath would be disturbed, and on one occasion two water buffalo, startled by the sudden roar of the burner above them, galloped off at considerable speed through fences and foliage, pulling their plough behind them and pursued by their understandably irate and desperate owner.

Landings could be difficult. It was desirable to avoid water, trees, buildings, fences and standing crops, and essential to miss the ubiquitous low-level power lines. We needed to end up close enough to a road for the rather ineffective two-wheel-drive Mahindra 'jeeps', supplied by the organisers for retrieval, to be able to meet us. When a landing was made the balloons were instantly surrounded by scores of cheerful, ragged children. Their reserved and colourfully-dressed mothers would appear soon after and finger the balloon fabric pensively, as if considering its potential for a thousand saris.

In Madras we took off with some trepidation because the wind forecast was uncertain. No sooner were we up than it began to blow us towards the beach and the ocean beyond. It was essential to land, but, suspended as we were over that city's equivalent of Park Lane, it was not clear where. Barr spotted a yard in front of what looked like a factory and, with deft expulsions of hot air, lined up for what his passengers began to feel might be a tricky manoeuvre. We were not wrong, for the huge basket caught upon the ridge of the factory roof, and then tilted gently one way and another according to the movements of the passengers. Nobody could get out, because if they did the balloon would take off again. If the air in the canopy cooled too much we would all fall 30ft to the ground. Our position was delicate, but all behaved impeccably, trying not to sound concerned and making helpful suggestions to the perspiring pilot.

An Indian appeared below. We expected severe castigation. He cupped his hands: 'Would you like tea, or would you prefer a soft drink?' We tried to explain our predicament. He said he could get a ladder; we said that would not help. 'You will be off again shortly then?' he inquired. Amusing though this all was, the underlying position was not good. Some of the ridge capping began to crack and groan under the weight resting upon it.

We were saved by the arrival of the Norwegians. Sem-Jacobson had sensibly not taken off, but saw that we had, and that we seemed in potential trouble. He had followed us across the city, not without difficulty (though Indians generally accommodate forceful driving with surprising grace) and he now appeared in the yard below and shouted to us to throw down a rope. This we did and he and his team pulled us down into the yard against the remaining buoyancy of the balloon. This experience badly dented my wife's enthusiasm for further flights.

En route to the west coast we paused at Thekkady in the Periyar wildlife park, where a small group set off into some light jungle with a guide who was about 5ft tall (worryingly equipped with an umbrella, not a rifle) in search of elephants or, it was mendaciously suggested, tiger. Wildlife soon found us, but only in the form of leeches. Reactions to these from the different nationalities were interesting. The Spanish jumped about theatrically. The Germans and Austrians meticulously burnt off the predators with cigarettes. The French applied salt, which for some reason they carried, no doubt in anticipation of a delicious snack, Americans beat at them noisily, and the English simply pretended that the leeches did not exist – they did not hurt and mostly got into places where you did not see them. After a bit I noticed blood squirting out of the lace holes of one of my boots, which was quite disconcerting, and one woman detected a fat, sated leech very close to her perineum, which was rather more so.

We spent a few days at Ootacamund, once a famous hill station, 7,000 feet up in the Nilgiri Hills. Founded by the Collector of Coimbatore in 1819, it became the summer headquarters of the government of Madras. It was reached after hours of climbing in an elderly bus with no effective ventilation, through plantations of tea, rubber and eucalyptus. The journey was constantly illuminated by Arcadian vistas of alpine gorges and sub-tropical waterfalls.

Upon arrival at the town it became quickly apparent that the organisers had failed to agree mutually satisfactory terms with the management of our designated hotel, and resolution of this problem, if possible at all, looked likely to take a long time. I had a guidebook and knew of the Savoy hotel, a little higher up. Within a few minutes of my telephone call two white Ambassadors (Indian Morris Oxfords) appeared and bore the English away. To breakfast in the dappled shade on a trim lawn before one's personal bungalow at the Savoy hotel, reading the *Times of India* and watching the mist rising from the wooded slopes, was to feel a little of the joy of those present at its founding.

A short walk led soldier, explorer and expeditionist Charles Weston Baker and me to the door of the Ooty Club. Despite what I felt was our prestigious appearance and impeccable approach – complete with visiting card – the Secretary, clad in 20oz green tweed, denied any reciprocal hospitality arrangements with the Carlton or Cavalry Clubs, though he would have been pleased to admit members of the Royal Thames, which we were not. However, he finally surrendered to the suggestion that Queen's Counsel who had travelled 7,000 miles to get there might be allowed a short visit. Thus we saw where snooker was invented and where sepia photographs of the Masters of the Ootcatamund Hunt shared wall space with the masks of their quarry, the jackal. The head of a jackal is somehow more sinister than the mask of a fox.

Poor ballooning weather meant that there was time to visit Amber Vilas, the Maharaja's palace in Mysore. It is a vastly theatrical early C20 construction in an Edwardian Indo-Saracenic style, designed by an imaginative Englishman called Irwin. A mixture of stained-glass conservatory, amphitheatre, treasure house, and audience chamber, it was all on a fantastic scale. It had silver thrones, palanquins, doors and divans, and a mural several minutes' walk long, depicting life and times a hundred years before.

The safari ended in Bangalore, where only one man flew. It was the last flight for his well-used balloon and he hoped to find a suitable grave for it against some Asian palm. In this he failed, landing perfectly. We then set off, by no very direct route, to Bombay. Some of this was by train, in a reserved carriage. This was fine while the rest of the train had available accommodation, less so when it was full except for our lightly-occupied car. Not surprisingly perhaps, the passengers who were thick upon the platforms strove to get in. They shook the train. Mr Gupta cowered in his compartment and would not come out to speak to any of the railway staff. Weston Baker, with his military experience, held the doors closed. Thus we got through two stations, leaving with people clinging to the bars which protected the windows.

After a while, as evening was setting in, the station master at another stop produced police. Gupta capitulated, and we took perhaps a hundred travellers into our private coach. They were, on the whole, either shy or charming, and established little family camps upon the bunks and seats, some offering us small items of anonymous spicy-smelling food. We proffered chocolate.

And so we came to Bombay. Our next flight was with British Airways, who took us over Afghanistan, down into which it was agreeable to stare and to speculate upon what might be going on in the dangerous dun-coloured hilly wilderness below.

In my forties I became aware of microlights, which were tiny flying devices of two sorts. One resembled a kind of tricycle motor scooter hung beneath a large kite wing, with a little propeller at the back; the other was a very small and flimsy version of a conventional light plane, with a minute engine and propeller at the front. I tried out both sorts, and they were transient fun for pottering about locally and looking into the gardens of one's friends. But these machines, though cheap, were very slow, often very cold and had only modest range.

I was 56 before I decided to take lessons in a conventional light plane, which I did at Enstone Airfield, in North Oxfordshire, where there were two rival flying clubs, one each side of the mile-long WW2 runway. I chose the one which had an attractive modern, low-winged aircraft called a Katana, and an excellent flying instructor of very great experience called Roy Hill, then 62. A modest man, he had thousands of hours of flying recorded in his log book.

It was rapidly clear that controlling the plane was only one of a number of techniques to be mastered.

Taking off was easy: line up on the runway with brakes on, open the throttle, pause, then release the brakes and rush forward, gently pull back the stick and you are vaulting agreeably towards heaven. Steering with stick and throttle, and occasionally the rudder pedals, soon came naturally. The plane was easy and responsive to fly: you incline the control column very slightly in the direction in which you wish to turn, and turn it does. If you wish to climb you give a little throttle and pull back on the stick. To dive, you ease the throttle, and, for quicker results, push forward. Keeping in level flight requires some concentration, and a horizon point to align with, though there is an instrument to show what is happening, and an altimeter to indicate height – there is of course an important distinction between height above sea level and height above ground level.

Landing was the trickiest thing to master: it is essential not to go so slowly that you stall (which may lead to falling out of the sky at an awkward angle with fatal results), and you must align yourself properly with the runway, which will sometimes involve some angling or crabbing to cope with side wind. (On grass airfields it used to be possible to look at a windsock and take off and land directly into the wind, which is ideal, but now most airfields have hard runways on various fixed alignments usually roughly NE to SW.) As you approach the ground you need to be aware of your precise height because when you close the throttle the aircraft will sink quite briskly. Ideally it does so from a couple of feet, producing a most satisfying and scarcely perceptible bump. If you get this wrong and shut off power when you are, say eight feet above the runway, you will thump down horribly, and may jump up again. This feels bad, looks worse and can damage the plane. Judging height accurately on landing requires some experience and, oddly, the technique is to concentrate well ahead, not to look sharply down from the side of the cockpit.

Visibility out of the cockpit is important, and varies remarkably from plane to plane. Unlike a car, the instrument panel of many aircraft is set so high, or is so deep, that forward visibility is considerably restricted. Older aircraft, like the Spitfire or Hurricane, sit on the ground with a huge engine at a sharp uphill angle in front of you: no direct forward vision exists when taxiing or commencing take off. A few planes have been designed without a forward view at all, most notably the Spirit of St Louis in which Charles Lindbergh made the first solo crossing of the Atlantic in 1927 (this, it should be noted, especially by Americans, was not the first Atlantic crossing, which had been achieved eight years earlier in 1919 by Englishmen Alcock and Brown, in a Vickers Vimy with an open cockpit. It took them just under 16 hours at a speed of about 115 mph. They were both knighted and shared a prize of £10,000.)

After a few lessons I began to master landing. We practised at Wellesbourne near Stratford on Avon. The idea was to take off, jink round Charlcote House, complete a circuit of the airfield at slowly diminishing height, make a final turn above a tree topped knoll and then descend smoothly onto the runway. One day, after we did this three times without incident, Roy told me to taxi off the runway, and he jumped out. I was alone in the aircraft, to take off, circle and land on my own. This was a memorable moment. I lined up, opened the throttle, and vaulted into the air. All went gratifyingly well – indeed on touching down I felt so confident that I accelerated away, took off again and repeated the experience. I had now flown solo, a most satisfactory feeling and the fulfilment of a childhood ambition. I did some longer flights, once lingering over Banbury watching the queues of cars trying to get onto the M40, and once to mid Wales.

However, there is a lot more to flying than controlling the aircraft. Considerably more complicated is navigation, involving charts and bearings – though this is now largely superfluous in that everyone uses satnav, it is still expected and required that a pilot can get about with a map and compass. It was while looking at a map for such an exercise that I first noticed that the acuity of my eyesight, up to then perfect, needed a trace of enhancement for small print. But strangely I found the hardest thing to learn was radio communication with the ground. Most small airfields, and all larger ones, have a control 'tower' of some kind (Enstone has a tall shack) to order the take-off, landing and transit of traffic. The idea is that when you are some miles away an incoming pilot will radio to ground control, saying something like 'This is Golf Bravo Alpha Mike Tango, a Katana, flying at 2,500ft and 120 knots, currently 10 miles south of Wellesborne, request permission to land'. The controller, assuming that you have selected the correct frequency, then comes back, repeating your registration, telling you at what height to approach the circuit, what runway to land on, and any other requirement or information, such as how many other planes there are wanting to do the same thing. You then have to repeat the message, to ensure that there are no misunderstandings. Also, you will not be told, 'OK, land on the runway with a pond at the end', it will be something like 'Golf Bravo Alpha Mike Tango cleared to land on runway 225'. This number indicates the compass point towards which you are to land, thus 225 means that you are to approach from the NE and land on a runway in a south westerly direction. Although by then I had been a barrister for 25 years and a judge for seven, and so could be considered articulate, I found repeating everything with complete accuracy to be quite difficult, and tended to try to anticipate what the controller would say by jotting down a draft response on a notepad on my knee.

At some airfields you had to be good at changing radio frequency. For example, at Staverton, while you were flying over the government communications centre between Cheltenham and Gloucester you had to be on one wavelength as you flew towards the airfield, then change to another for the immediate approach and circuit, and yet another for parking after you had landed. The plane I was in required much knob twiddling. As well as flying, navigation and radio communication it was also necessary to learn about the weather (meteorology) and air law. None of this was very difficult, but it all had to be kept in mind. Roy told me that women were often much better than men at doing several things at the same time.

After a month or two I had accumulated about 35 hours of flying time – 45 were needed before you can become a qualified pilot – and came in one morning for another lesson. Roy was not there, and I asked why not. 'Well,' said the man who owned the flying club, who had a very familiar manner but with whom I never felt wholly at ease, 'he has gone and will not be coming back'. It turned out that the two had had some kind of row, and Roy was not prepared to stay.

'What about my lessons?' I asked.

'Ah, we have a new instructor – meet Tim. He will take over'. A youth stepped forward. He was I think 22, and looked about 16. Tim had only recently acquired his own licence, had about 100 hours of experience, and wanted to be an airline pilot. Roy had many thousands of hours. I was not happy with this change. Furthermore, it had occurred to me that I could not afford to buy a respectable aircraft when qualified, and I did not care much for the sort of sharing arrangements which some people had. There was invariably conflict about who might fly when, and whether some defect had manifested itself with a particular pilot or not. Light planes need a good deal of maintenance and inspection, and renting a plane was prohibitively expensive, especially when poor weather might strand you away from your home airfield for hours or days.

I had one adventure in mind, which was to fly right around the coast of Britain, which would have been a satisfying and in parts spectacular expedition. But beyond that it was not clear what I would do. Private pilots are fond of flying to Le Touquet for lunch, but that sort of trip is a pretty limited attraction especially since you can't drink if returning the same day. Using a plane to go to the Alps might have been fun, but mountains require specialist qualification, and you need an expensive aircraft like a Pilatus with substantial range and speed to make such journeys a viable alternative to Easyjet from Birmingham to Zurich. So I decided that the departure of my instructor meant that I should cease to fly. I never did get a licence. One of my children said he did not think I had the confidence to sit the exam. Since this was multiple choice box ticking, I think he was a little astringent.

I did have one more excursion in a single engine plane though. Pleased with the outcome of the 2015 general election, I booked a flight in a Spitfire which had been converted to a two-seater, and took off from Goodwood on 30th September. This should have been, and in some ways was, a good experience, though ludicrously expensive. The roar of the V12 Merlin engine with over 1000 horse power, take off from Lord March's estate, a flight out over the English Channel, circling round the Isle of Wight, diving down to inspect a square rigger full of cheering sailors, and speeding back and forth along the south coast were fine sensations. After a while the pilot said 'You have control', and there I was flying a Spitfire. I did this with some circumspection, but it curved and dived with wonderful alacrity and the views over its elliptical wings were splendid and evocative. But there was one major drawback – carefully not revealed on booking: there was no forward visibility from the rear cockpit, so I did not see the view enjoyed by the fighter pilots of 1940.

Every so often my pilot said 'shall we do some aerobatics?,' resumed control, and swept up towards heaven, turning upside down, rolling, swooping and slicing through the late summer air. This will have looked inspirational to spectators, but it had an adverse effect on my stomach and it was necessary to concentrate hard to avoid being sick. I steered us back via Chichester, and the pilot (who normally flew airliners) made an impeccable landing. I had forgotten my log book, for which a flight in a Spitfire would have made an admirable final entry.

Chapter 17

The calamity of complexity

Civil law is fundamental to English society. It is its foundation and structure. It provides remedies where someone suffers physical or financial harm when obligations have not been complied with. It deals with contracts (legally enforceable agreements), and torts (breach of a duty not to cause harm), it governs commercial activity, professional advice and much else besides. It is the means whereby citizens protect themselves against each other and the state. The Common Law – that is judge-made law – developed over the years in gentle increments by judicial decisions, is one of the great gifts of England to Western civilisation. But in order for people to enjoy the benefits of our civil law, three things are necessary: that the law is clear, that there is easy access to the remedies which the law has to offer, and that the cost of going to law is not prohibitive. These features are absent in England now.

First, clarity. In 1980, a Mr Fothergill landed at Luton Airport and found that his luggage had been damaged after he had checked it in. A shirt, sandals and cardigan worth £16.50 were missing. He sought compensation. Simple, one might think. But so complex was the applicable law, governed by something called the Warsaw Convention, incorporated into English law by statute, that his case went all the way from the High Court to the House of Lords. There Lord Diplock remarked 'Elementary justice... demands that the rules by which the citizen is to be bound should be readily ascertainable'. They were not. In the end the plaintiff lost because he had not submitted a complaint within seven days. Or take Mr Lonsdale, who worked as an agent, selling shoes to retail shops for a Northampton manufacturer which closed down in 2003 due to rising costs and a falling market. Mr Lonsdale's agency was properly terminated with due notice, but his solicitors knew about some legislation called the Commercial Agents (Council Directive) Regulations, which provided for an entitlement to 'indemnity or compensation' upon the termination of an agency contract. The question was, how much? The solicitors on both sides were quite unable to agree because the Regulation (which came from Europe and had been incorporated into English law with various complex sub paragraphs) simply did not say. Eventually the case came to the Oxford County Court. Counsel quaintly argued for a 'French approach', or a 'German approach'. After two days in court, and much work out of it, I gave judgment for £5,000. Mr Lonsdale, advised by his lawyers, thought this far too little, and appealed to the Court of Appeal. Three Lord Justices listened to extended argument, and in due course a 19-page judgment was delivered, dismissing the appeal. Still Mr Lonsdale's lawyers felt they were right, and appealed to the House of Lords. There, another five judges, the most senior in the land, considered the matter for another two days. They too dismissed the appeal. Thus, in order to find out what the law required, the matter had been considered by two solicitors, two barristers and no fewer than nine judges, all because Parliament failed to pass legislation which was clear and explicit. Members of Parliament, whose job it is to scrutinise legislation quite simply do not do it properly. About this they do not appear ashamed.

This failure is evident in many other areas, particularly in housing (where one question, as Lord Bingham pointed out in a book he wrote in 2010, 'had been addressed in fifteen separate reasoned judgements running to more than 500 paragraphs and more than 180 pages of printed law report. Even after this immense outpouring of effort it may be doubted whether the relevant law is entirely clear'...). Consumer credit law is just as difficult. These are areas of life of enormous importance to ordinary people, who are quite unable to understand the legal positions they find themselves in. Indeed even 'the courts are in many cases unable to discover what the law is' (Lord Justice Toulson in a case called Chambers in 2008). Governments have known this for many years, but do nothing about it. In 2009 the Lord Chief Justice and the Senior Head of Tribunals indicated that the Data Protection legislation was 'virtually impenetrable'. It is scandalous that Parliament passes such legislation.

And so ordinary people are often unable to discover the law. Some people are less ordinary, and also find problems. A few, born with conventional masculine bodies, like to behave and dress like women. Some believe that they can actually become women. This is an area where it is easy to slip from comedy to tragedy, and vice versa. But again, it is surely desirable that people know where they stand. Or in the case of some customers of the Red Lion in Thornby, Northamptonshire, where they can sit. In 2003 a party of five biological men, wearing frocks, went to the pub to have a drink. After a while, one went to the women's lavatory. This prompted complaints to the landlord from female customers who did not want people they perceived to be men sharing their facilities. The landlord asked the 'ladies' to desist; they left but in due course, with the assistance of the Equal Opportunities Commission, and £20,000 of public money, they sued the publican, alleging discrimination. He had been in an awkward position. Was he to allow any man in a dress into the ladies' lavatory? What if male student rugby players on a rag week came in dressed as nurses or St Trinian's schoolgirls? Was he to conduct a delicate discussion with his customers to discover to what extent they were, or considered themselves to be, transsexual, or in some other relevant category? What of the expectations of his conventional customers? Counsel had great difficulty in answering my question whether it was being alleged that there was discrimination against men or against women. It could hardly be discriminatory to expect men to use the men's lavatories, and the plaintiffs were not women, they were men dressed up as women. She submitted to me firmly that it was quite wrong to refer, as I had, to common sense. The claim failed. It was another good example of the law being insufficiently apt or clear to be applicable or readily understood by the litigants.

This area has been the subject of recent legislation, and is likely to lead to very great difficulty, peculiarity and confusion, not to say injustice. For a man may now declare himself, and 'identify,' as a woman, obtain a gender recognition certificate and then, for example, enter a women's tennis tournament. Rather more seriously, a woman has in this way 'transitioned' into legal recognition as a man, then become pregnant – as only a woman can - via a sperm donor, and had a child. Perhaps unsurprisingly she/he was registered as the mother of the child. 'He, or possibly 'she,' has now applied to the court to be re-registered as its father (The Times 27.4.19). Here lies utter absurdity.

It is elementary that a citizen should be able easily to find out what the law is upon any relevant subject, but this is becoming harder and harder to do. On 11th November 2006, at Cheltenham racecourse, an experienced jockey, Mr Hide, came off his horse as it fell at the first fence. In a manner quite unanticipated by any of the organisers or riders, he slid sideways for a several yards before coming into contact with an upright part of the course railings and breaking his pelvis. He waited three years, then started proceedings against the racecourse. The case came to trial before me in the summer of 2012. It was argued that there was a breach of a regulation regarding work equipment (the Use of Work Equipment Regulations 1998) which provided that such equipment – a term apt to include the railing – should be 'suitable'. Any interested person wanting to know what 'suitable' meant could read, in reg 4, that it had to be suitable 'in any respect in which it is reasonably foreseeable will affect the… safety of any person'. This highly unlikely accident was not 'reasonably foreseeable' by the long established and well understood standards of English Common Law. I dismissed the claim. But the Court of Appeal found differently. It did so on the basis that it was not sufficient to look at the regulation which had been passed into English law. You had also to look at something called a European Directive, pursuant to which it had been passed, and to notice that there was no mention there of reasonable foresight, and so, as the regulation did not truly reflect the directive, the latter must prevail, and the racecourse was liable for Mr Hide's injury. So, astonishingly, the course organisers could not discover what the law required of them by looking at the relevant regulation enacted by Parliament, and nor indeed could the judge. This is a situation such as that described by Lord Denning in Mr Fothergill's case: 'a confidence trick by Parliament and destructive of all legal certainty if the private citizen… was required to research through all that had happened before and in the course of the legislative process in order to see whether there was anything to be found from which it could be inferred that Parliament's real intention had not been accurately expressed by the actual words that Parliament had adopted to communicate it to those affected by the legislation'.

Next, easy access to the remedies of the law. During the latter part of the 20th century it was apparent that legal proceedings were sometimes slow; occasionally the parties and the court allowed cases to 'go to sleep' for years on end. And unless you could get legal aid, litigation was expensive. It was thought by some that what was largely to blame was the procedure – the steps which had to be gone through to get a case to court, and the rules governing the conduct of trials. Lord Woolf (later Master of the Rolls and Lord Chief Justice) was appointed by the Lord Chancellor in March 1994 to report upon how matters might be made simpler, quicker and cheaper. After consultations he produced an interim report called Access to Justice which suggested that the Rules of the Supreme Court (the RSC) should be modified so as to be comprehensible to the parties, not just to lawyers, and that to this end they should be 'shorter and more accessible'. His final, 370-page, report was published in July 1996. It stated: 'given the size of the existing rules, reducing the amount of material in them is obviously desirable', and it was important to 'reduce complexity and make the system more amenable to actual users and more acceptable to ordinary citizens'. This 'should reduce the... costs of courts and lawyers'. His proposals were accepted, and a committee was appointed to draft the new Rules.

Given the stated objectives, it was both surprising and alarming to note that as the new Rules (the Civil Procedure Rules, or CPR) began to emerge, they were not shorter at all. The 'bible' of English procedure is an expensive annual work known as the White Book. In its last edition under the old regime, in 1997, this extended to 3,933 pages. Those drafting the new rules had by the 2002 edition expanded it to 4,605 pages. There were annual supplements and revisions. By 2006 the CPR had reached 5,912 pages, almost 50% bigger than the rules it replaced. The authors of the rules did not stop there. By April 2018, after no fewer than 95 updates and alterations in 19 years, the Rules and associated material covered 6,488 pages – over 63% more than those they replaced. This is not simplification. On the contrary, there has been a deliberate and very substantial process of expansion and complication. Why were those writing the new rules permitted utterly to ignore the premise behind them? Why did they want to? These questions have never been answered.

Nor has litigation become any cheaper. Partly because the process is much more complicated than it was, it is much more expensive – because much more has to be done before you get to court. In 1997 the rules about costs occupied 128 pages. By 2016 the rules authors had increased this to 370 pages. Such has been the 'simplification' of the rules generally that it has also been thought necessary to include over 150 pages of 'guidance' so that they might be understood. But the whole idea was that they should in themselves be understandable.

Lord Woolf wrote in 1995 that one of the identified sources of unsatisfactory complexity was 'the multiplicity of practice directions issued with the object of explaining to litigants what particular courts or jurisdictions require them to do'. So were these avoided? They were not. On the contrary, they have been multiplied, magnified, and even given their own index. Every Rule now has its own Practice Direction, the text often repeating the rules to which it relates. Where it does more, it elaborates and complicates.

The very act of obtaining access to the courts to begin proceedings used simply to involve serving the appropriate originating document, commonly a writ, in which the plaintiff told the defendant what was being complained about and what damages or other remedy was sought. Now there is a tapestry of preliminary 'protocols' to absorb and comply with, and a variety of possible adverse consequences if you do not get it right. Everything is done to deter taking a case to trial, and pressures are put upon litigants to adopt methods of alternative dispute resolution, in short to settle and keep out of court. This is not facilitating access to justice, it is an attempt to inhibit it. Matters are made worse in some cases by arrangements under which even if a Defendant wins, he does not get his costs.

In 2004, at a conference in Millbank for the judges with special responsibility for civil law (the so called Designated Civil Judges, or DCJs) I spoke on this topic to an audience including most of the relevant senior judiciary, who were, directly or indirectly, responsible for this state of affairs. I made the general observation:

'For some reason intelligent contemporary minds do not operate in the way in which intelligent minds used to operate. In the C19 if you wanted a substantial and important piece of legislation to deal with commonplace transactions, you aimed for simplicity and compression with straightforward sentences and provisions. You got for example the Sale of Goods Act. Merchants as well as lawyers could understand it. Now, for no reason which is apparent or good, draftsmen do not draft, nor does Parliament enact, simple, easily-understood provisions. Instead you get measures like the Consumer Credit Act and its various offspring... It too is an act designed to govern very common everyday transactions for ordinary people. But it is written with great... complexity. Practical lawyers cannot say with confidence what it means. Academics browse contented in its thickets. The intelligent layman is not equipped prudently to explore it...'

I asked (in a manner humorous rather than Gladstonian) why the new rules were being elaborated rather than simplified. The senior and responsible people laughed heartily at the absurdities and did not disagree that what was happening did not seem to be what had been expected. They had presumably noticed this for themselves. But nothing was done. The prolixity of the authors of these new rules was out of control – everything was elaborated, specified, directed and particularized, nothing was simplified. There were even draft letters for solicitors to use, lest qualified solicitors might not be able to compose their own.

The Court of Appeal had itself in in October 2003 referred to the emergence of 'a cumbrous and confusing three-tier hierarchy of rules and guidance'. But still the process of adding complexity wherever possible has continued, like some exponentially replicating disease. Those at the top of the English Judiciary are people of high intellectual quality, and usually think with great clarity. It has to be accepted that they knew perfectly well what was happening, and allowed it to continue. The simplification of civil procedure which was promised by Lord Woolf has been replaced by a construction of forbidding complexity, far larger and more dense than that which it replaced. Indeed, the current rules are so far from being comprehensible to ordinary citizens that the Judicial College, in a paper in June 2018, wrote that litigants in person are 'operating in what is for them effectively a foreign language'. How can this have been permitted? Why is it not to be corrected?

In April 2018 Lord Justice Irwin, a member of the Court of Appeal, delivered the Peter Taylor memorial lecture. (Peter Taylor had been the future Lord Chief Justice whom I had watched when I was a Marshal forty years earlier). Its title was 'Complexity and obscurity in the law, and how we might mitigate them'. Speaking of the drafting of the new rules he said this:

> '...the process has been an expansion, with increasing particularity and increasing granularity: the process of expansion to avoid doubt has produced rules of a length and complexity exceeding that of the RSC. As we all know, litigants in person still flounder.'

In short, though he was careful not to say it explicitly, the reforms over which so much labour had been expended have failed. They are not easier for ordinary people, or even, as Irwin LJ remarked, 'the inexpert and inexperienced lawyer', to understand. What did he think should be done? Remarkably, he said 'any attempts to shorten them or make them accessible by generalised principle would seem to me simply to introduce doubt and difficulty. Therefore I am not recommending another rewrite... But the drafters and revisers should be constantly aware (as I'm sure they are) that the rules need to be operated by litigants in person, and therefore that the language must be as clear and straightforward as possible'. They have known this, of course, from the outset, but have ignored it. The Lord Justice added that there might be a place for 'introductory notes' to each part or subsections of parts, to set litigants 'on the right track'. In other words, more of the same – a fourth layer to add to the cumbrous and confusing three-tier hierarchy. It is astonishing.

The Swiss, not an unsophisticated race, contain their civil litigation rules (English version) on 102 pages of a pocket-sized paperback.

The more I watched the development of the new English rules over the 18 years during which I presided over trials as a civil judge, the more depressing it became. Day after day, in application after application, lawyers sought to exploit them and litigants without lawyers sought to survive them. The new rules have produced not simplicity, ease of understanding and cheapness, but complexity, uncertainty and expense.

A further obstacle which government has put in the way people wanting to use the courts has been huge increases in the fees payable in order to commence an action (for example, at the time of writing, 5% of the value of the claim for claims of between £10,000 and £200,000, so it costs £1,000 to initiate a £20,000 claim). This is said to be to defray the expense to the government of providing civil court facilities. But upholding the rights and remedies which enable commercial and other human intercourse to take place in a fair and predictable way is of course in the interests of the community as a whole, and the provision of public facilities for this should be just as much a public service as the maintenance of health or the defence of the realm. It is not clear why civil court users, in a nation based upon the rule of law, should have to pay, beyond general taxation, for the cost of provision of the Courts when they need to use them. Most legal aid has now been removed. Only the very poorest can get the assistance of the taxpayer to deal with what are often desperate legal predicaments.

This powerful combination of deterrent factors has produced a creeping necrosis in litigation. Often people can understand neither the law nor how to deploy it. And if they can, they are unable to afford to do so. Where there is no redress for wrongs, there is no value in rights.

It is a sad comparison with the National Health Service, where no 'user' is expected to contribute directly to the cost of hospitals. Outrage is commonly expressed should this be suggested. Currently enthusiasm is being expressed for 'on-line' solutions, the suggestion being that this will be cheap, efficacious and simple (much the same claims in fact as were made for the reforms twenty years ago). There may indeed be some place for a form of computer-based negotiation and settlement where the parties are both agreeable, and deft with their equipment. But what cannot be done through a computer is to conduct a trial involving the analysis of the credibility of live witnesses and, in particular, cross-examination. Cross-examination is an instrument of the greatest importance, fundamental to the discovery of truth and at the very heart of the judicial process. Any on-line arrangement will need its own set of rules, which will involve provisions different to those generally applicable. There will also need to be rules to convert on-line attempts at resolution into real trials where compromise is not possible or appropriate. This will mean yet a further layer of complication. It is hard to understand why a proper simplification of the rules of general application cannot be entertained.

Lest it should be forgotten, this drive for complexity is not limited to civil law. It is also very evident in crime. In an earlier chapter it was pointed out that some criminal legislation was so badly drafted that lawyers could not understand it. If it is thought that I might be exaggerating the difficulties introduced by our legislation, it should be remembered that Lord Phillips of Worth Maltravers – a top judge if ever there was one – observed in 2010 when he was President of the Supreme Court: 'Hell is a fair description of the problem of statutory interpretation caused by transitional provisions introduced when custody plus [an early release scheme] had to be put on hold because the resources needed to implement the scheme did not exist'. Hell. Senior legal figures in England are generally renowned for their calm understatement, but Lord Judge CJ, in the same case (R. v Governor of Drake Hall prison (2010 1 WLR 1743, 1769) said this: 'elementary principles of justice have come... to be buried in the legislative morass... it is outrageous that so much intellectual effort, as well as public time and resource, have had to be expended to discover a route... to what should be... the simplest and most certain of questions...'

The question which nobody appears keen to ask or answer is why, given the obvious undesirability of complexity in our law, nothing is done to achieve simplicity. This is something which ought to be a major concern of the government and in particular the Lord Chancellor. Instead, it is ignored.

Chapter 18

Judicial finale

My judicial position as so-called Designated Civil Judge, or DCJ, was one which did not automatically last forever. It was initially for four years, potentially renewable for another four. I had originally been appointed in 1998, was re-appointed upon Circuit changes in 2001, and after various discussions was appointed again in 2002, 2006, and 2010, each time for four more years. By 2012 I had been doing this work for 14 years. This was far longer than anyone else. On the whole I enjoyed the role, and I did not want to revert to being an ordinary Circuit Judge who would be expected to try whatever he was given to try, including crime. I engaged with the then Presiding Judge for a further extension from 2014, to last until retirement. He felt that he had little discretion in the matter, and anyway wanted to enlarge the Oxford group of three counties by adding another two, Bedfordshire and Hertfordshire. I did not think this at all a good idea, as these extra counties had not been running well, had poor performance figures, were distant from Oxford and inconvenient to get to. Establishing good working relationships, let alone efficiency and esprit de corps with another set of judges and court administrators, would not be easy. Amalgamation would dilute the excellent performance of Oxfordshire, Berkshire and Buckinghamshire, of which my existing group was quite proud, and whose timeliness was the best on the circuit. It would produce an enormous group of 3,400 square miles, coping with a population of some 3.5 million. There would be 14 courts instead of eight, about thirty DJs instead of 18, and a probable case load of 4,290 rather than our existing manageable 2,700.

All this I argued persuasively, I felt – but not persuasively enough. Other minds were made up, and it was decided to set up a new five-county group. The new group would be so large that it would qualify automatically for Senior Circuit Judge status, something I had long been seeking. But I felt from the indications I had been given that because of my existing length of service I would not be eligible, so I did not apply. Michael Kay QC, who had been the DCJ for Beds and Herts, did apply, and was appointed.

However, nothing much seemed to change. At Oxford, I continued to do the major civil work, and was treated by the staff as though I was still in charge. The new DCJ came to Oxford one day and indicated over lunch that his journey had been long and tedious, and that he would rather sit in Luton or Bedford, close to where he lived. This suited me, but gave rise to some dissention between him and a new Senior Presiding Judge (SPJ) who had understood that he would indeed sit at Oxford, where most of the substantial work was. After a few weeks Kay resigned his position, and was promptly re-allocated to crime. I then indicated that I would be happy to be the DCJ for the five counties but was told that there would have to be a competition, open to all. A number of people applied, some from the Bar, some existing judges; though nobody was prepared to tell me precisely who. We went for interview at the Ministry of Justice in Petty France, a large modern building constructed round an atrium, whose extensive ground floor at lunchtimes is given over to a crowd of civil servants in labelled lanyards, assiduously and simultaneously browsing both food and their mobile devices.

My interview, late in life for a job application, went well. I was able to point out that perhaps I understood the job of a DCJ better than anyone in England, since I was the only one of the original 1998 judges still in the field. After a day or two of mild anxiety, because it is never a good idea to count on judicial appointments until they are actually made, I was told that I had got the position, and would be promoted forthwith to Senior Circuit Judge. As this had been an ambition since 2004, it was gratifying to have achieved this rather modest eminence after only ten years of trying. The pleasure was not wholly undiluted however, since I had agreed to go from time to time to sit in Bedford, and for a few days a year, in Luton.

Bedford was in fact fine. I found a pleasant, swift, 50-mile cross-country route via Milton Keynes; and it generally took an hour and a quarter to the gates of the Bedford County Court, a huge, rambling Victorian building resembling a decayed minor public school unexpectedly equipped with several large courtrooms, mostly unused. It was in fact the Shire Hall, completed in 1883. It stood upon the north bank of the river Ouse. Nearby was the Swan Hotel, also on the river bank, where I repaired on my first day for breakfast. As I left the dining room I asked the head waiter what I owed. He looked at me, smiled, and said: 'There will be no charge, it is very pleasant to have someone eating here who wears a suit and a tie'. Naturally I went back the next day, but my benefactor was not on duty. A small waitress, not a native of the county, or indeed the country, said 'If you are not a resident, that will be £17 please'. I did not feel that I could explain to her that men in suits dined free.

After some unsatisfactory experimentation in coffee shop chains, I settled for breakfasts upon a café where egg and tomato sandwiches were made on request. Each day I asked for the same. Each day the waitress said 'white or brown?' Each day I replied 'brown'. After perhaps ten visits I said 'The usual please'. 'What's that then?' came the reply. Clearly, I was not memorable.

My room at the Bedford court was small, and largely filled with a big elm desk and a water dispensing machine, which I did not want.

The windows looked over the river, on which rowers pulled by in the drizzle, alone or in crews, responding to shouted instructions from the bank. Surly swans patrolled the grey water, ignoring the occasional duck. After about a year, work began nearby on the construction of a new footbridge. I hoped for something elegant, for bridges can easily be made elegant, and sometimes are. But not in Bedford. Eventually a prefabricated tubular thing, like a cheap, scaled up child's railway bridge, was lowered into position. Not only was it crude and unimaginative, its ends were not set at the same height, so it sat, ugly and unhappy in its sloping disposition, almost as though it knew something was wrong.

The ushers in Bedford were sent up from Luton and were assiduous. One in particular took a caring, matriarchal attitude, and brought me a large box file containing a stapler, treasury tags, elastic bands, ink, several ball-point pens, biscuits, envelopes, tea bags and a notebook. She took a mirror from some distant cloakroom so that I could tie my bands neatly. (By this time few Circuit Judges robed, but I still did, as it adds something to the judicial atmosphere.) The mirror vanished every night, but she would retrieve it. At two minutes to ten she would bring in a big mug of very hot coffee. This I could never drink as we sat at ten and always started punctually. (Punctuality is extremely important when running a court: the parties should not feel that they are in charge of the timetable rather than the judge, or that they can arrive late with impunity, expecting to be indulged. If ten or fifteen minutes are lost at the beginning of each day, and another five or so after lunch, this amounts to 100 minutes a week – more than an hour and a half – which over a year is 15 working days or three weeks).

The courtroom I used at Bedford, though shabby and old fashioned, had the advantages of morning sunshine and its own views of the river. But its acoustics were poor and for the first time I occasionally had difficulty making out what some people said. Low voices with strong accents came over badly.

Luton was a very different place. It was difficult to get to without being stuck in traffic at several points. When I arrived there on my first day, I found myself driving down a wide street almost entirely filled with scores of men, presumably of Pakistani origin, wearing flowing white robes. I slowed to a bemused amble while the Asian tide walked by, moving like a football crowd to some common Mecca, or its occidental substitute.

I found the county court eventually, in an ugly modern office building in a nest of small streets named after the battles of the Crimean war: Inkerman, Alma, Sevastopol. I was at first given the room of an absent judge, Gavyn Arthur, a large unmarried man, who when at the Bar had concentrated more upon the City than upon the law, and become Lord Mayor of London, and a knight. An ancestor had been Governor of Bombay. He liked the company of diplomats at lower ambassadorial level. It appeared, judging by a cabinet of invitations both current and spent that he displayed in his room, that every count, baron, princeling or pretender from what had once been the Austro-Hungarian Empire sought the attendance of Sir Gavyn at their receptions, dinners, soirées and investitures. He told me that he spoke German very well and was a good friend of Princess Michael of Kent. Sadly he died suddenly, in 2016, when an analysis of his caseload revealed that social engagements may sometimes have taken priority over his work. But he inspired considerable affection.

The civil court at Luton was in a desperate condition. Office administration had to a large extent broken down, morale was rock bottom (though the ushers were cheerful), listing was lamentable, there was a shortage of staff, and many of the litigants were, justifiably or unjustifiably, in a state of open warfare with the court office. The staff was the responsibility of a person called the 'cluster manager' and I had no power to do anything about these problems save complain. I did not go to Luton very often. It was a depressing court in a depressing town.

Back in Oxford, by contrast, all ran smoothly. Sue Hearn, the remarkable head manager, was indefatigable, imaginative, supportive and sometimes flattering. She always came with solutions, sometimes to problems I had not known about. The District Judges worked hard, patiently and efficiently. The ushers were cheerful and varied. One was an excellent photographer and energetic mountain walker, one a cricketer of some ability, one specialised in useful intelligence about the parties, counsel and witnesses, one always wore strong fragrant scent, and for a few delightful weeks I had the services of a spirited, well-dressed and amusing Nigerian princess called Uloma, on work experience before beginning a career as a solicitor. Whatever my mood, it only took seconds of her talk to make me feel cheerful. Ushers are important people in the lives of mild tedium led by many judges.

I still had a varied diet of interesting cases. It was satisfying occasionally to be able to uphold the meritorious modest litigant against big business. One of these was a chocolatier who had a contract with the Mandarin Oriental hotel chain to provide 150, 000 boxes of chocolates for their bedrooms. But after a few thousand had been supplied Mandarin said that it did not want any more, and told the chocolate maker to cease production. It did not offer to pay compensation for his loss of profit. As a very large enterprise it was accustomed to getting its way with small suppliers. I was happy to award damages of £73,166.

Since I had arrived in 1993 the judicial personalities had changed. Two judges, Tom Corrie and Patrick Eccles QC, came from the chambers which had been next to mine in Middle Temple Lane. Tom, an Eton scholar, disguised his high intelligence with a pretence of innocent self-deprecation, as though he was at sea at the mercy of the currents of life, blown into various vicissitudes by the court administrators, the senior judiciary, the parties, fate, or his wife, whom he called the Memsahib. As a child he had lived in East Africa, and travelled on Empire flying boats. He was an amusing, kind and perceptive man, who always knew the details of the private lives of the staff, the Bar and his colleagues, and commonly expressed himself with mordant scorn, especially towards those far to the left. He affected to loathe people with beards, and especially those who wore both beards and sandals. It was galling for him when his son, a barrister, decided not to shave for a while.

Tom did every kind of work. He grappled with the sad and sometimes ghastly complexities of hopeless families and their unfortunate children, he dealt with criminals, and – perhaps by way of a holiday – with some civil work, perhaps a car collision, a sub-standard house or a boundary dispute. He bore personal tribulations with a resigned metaphorical shrug, and was an excellent tribunal. He was not above falling out occasionally though, and was removed unwillingly from sitting at Northampton, apparently after some disagreement with the resident judge there. At the time I was President of the Council of HM Circuit judges, and was recruited, unavailingly, to his cause.

Ever since Oxford had been taken from the Midland Circuit in 2001, I had continued to enjoy an arrangement whereby I sat at three courts in the Midlands and two in the South East. As time went by I voluntarily abandoned Birmingham but continued at Warwick and Northampton. Tom pointed out in his dispute that his sitting pattern on two circuits was not in fact unique. Some months later, on 14th June 2010, I received out of the blue an email from the Presiding Judge asking if I wished 'to make representations as to continuing to sit on this circuit'. This was, I felt, rather a bleak way to proceed. I emailed back at some length to point out that I did wish to continue, that nobody had ever suggested that I should not, and that perhaps I might be told what was in her mind. We were able in due course to agree that I should continue. But a year or two later her successor refused point blank to retreat from a diktat that I should leave the circuit on which I had always practised. This was contrary to the normally accepted convention that a judge's sitting pattern should, initially at all events, be subject to discussion and agreement. I complained to higher judicial authority, but received no support.

Patrick Eccles QC, head of his chambers for many years, who had initially sat at Coventry and Northampton, also came to Oxford; a relief from a travel point of view as he lived near Abingdon. An old friend of Tom, with a head of very white hair, he was of a more erudite nature than most of us, with a remarkable recall of recondite legislation and authority. His approach to trials was careful and meticulous and he found himself engaged in some very lengthy pieces of criminal litigation. He had some Latin, and even a little Greek – unusual in the modern judiciary – and the ability to make a speech about a departing judge who had been little liked, but without offence either to the judge or to the truth. On one occasion he had the awkward task of coping with a defendant who was walking down England without clothes and insisted on appearing in court naked. Patrick relaxed by playing tennis.

A third arrival was Christopher Compston, a Holy Trinity Brompton enthusiast who had already been a judge for a long time (since 1986) before he came to Oxford. He did all kinds of work, sometimes with surprising despatch, but seemed happiest when setting off for the Isle of Wight in good time in colourful unstructured clothes. Somewhat resembling a stockier version of Michael Heseltine, he was fluent and amusing in conversation and anecdote. He also liked books, and conceived a particular affection for one of my volumes of Who's Who.

Anthony King, appointed in 1993, was a cheerful, well-built Wykehamist, born on the eve of the Dieppe raid in 1942. He sat until 2012, exclusively and reliably in crime, and was a firm sentencer. His favourite lunch at court was baked potatoes and prawns. He once bravely grappled in the street with a violent criminal whom he helped to apprehend, and then had the unusual experience of appearing in court as a witness to be cross-examined by the defendant's counsel. His favourite recreation was, I believe, fishing.

In 2002 Julian Hall had become Resident (senior criminal) Judge at Oxford. He came to this role a short time after having assumed and then relinquished the same position in Northampton. He was a man of some stamina who had commuted to Northampton from North London, but he settled very comfortably in Oxford, where he had been an undergraduate, and where his Norwegian wife, Ingrid, was a leading academic.

Julian is a person with many attributes. He had trained and worked as a chemist, and was also a musician, accomplished on the flute. Sometimes he wore a beard, sometimes not. He had a colourful taste in clothes. As a judge he was happy with most kinds of work, but at Oxford he normally sat in crime, where he soon got a reputation for imposing light punishments. On occasion it is entirely proper to sentence in a way in which those who know nothing of the detail of a case think is too lenient. (I have done this myself, notably with a sensitive young student who, after a drink, had been bullied by his friends into driving them home in his mother's car. He went slowly, but the night was frosty, he hit a tree and two of the passengers were killed. The father of one came to court and said the last thing he wanted was for the defendant to go to prison. I did not send him to prison, but the Court of Criminal Appeal did). Julian Hall was, perhaps habitually, lenient and was often criticised for it. But he did not mind, and did what he felt was right – which is what a judge should do. He was and is a friendly and avuncular man, who came to be thought of, like Harold Wilson before him, as the Headmaster.

It was during his reign that I had to go to some lengths to ensure that civil litigation got its fair share of courtroom allocation, as the administration was keen to improve criminal throughput at the expense of civil. Since then the volume of civil work rose and the amount of crime fell. Sometimes there have been empty courtrooms.

Julian's successor, from 2010, was Gordon Risius, an ex-soldier who had never been an advocate at the Bar, perhaps a disadvantage, but he had risen high in the army legal service, and then managed to transfer to become a Circuit Judge. He had sat in Reading. It appears that whoever was responsible for appointing resident judges had thought that there was much to be said for importing someone fresh to Oxford. My first sight of him, when with a diffident tap on the door I entered his room, was of a large pair of brown corduroy trousers standing, apparently unoccupied, in a corner. A closer look revealed that he was bent over, tidying the floor. I did not think that I could say 'General Risius, I presume' to the back of a pair of corduroys, so I withdrew. Gordon was a friendly and pleasant man, handicapped by deafness, who took his work extremely carefully. After a while he had a domestic accident which meant that he could not sit for a long period. This left rather a gap. Eventually, with commendable determination, he returned to court, but retired soon after.

All these judges came to Oxford after I did, and all retired while I was still sitting. By 2015 I had been there for longer than the total of all the other then current circuit judges. This, for someone who has always considered himself youthful – although then approaching 70 – was a curious feeling. Risius's replacement was Ian Pringle QC, a cheerful Scot who had been in practice in Bristol, and is an expert in Hibernian football. Joanna Vincent, young and very capable, was promoted from the District to the Circuit Bench, and proved good at administration. Michael Payne , until his retirement shortly before mine, still ruled the DJ corridor with enigmatic distinction, and Richard Matthews, a hardworking and reliable long-serving DJ remained in post. His recreation was football refereeing. Peter Ross, a highly effective judge, with a strong and entertaining personality, and an unusually varied career behind him, came to sit in crime, where he took on a mighty workload while generally managing to maintain good humour. Melissa Clarke arrived, able and keen, to replace me. This mix of judges meant that Oxford remained a pleasant place to work.

I was going to have to retire at 72, and gave a little thought to the manner of it. What commonly happens to a Circuit Judge is that on his or her last day there is a gathering of those at court, the senior judge present says a few pleasant things, followed probably by a member of the Bar and a solicitor. The retiring judge then delivers some remarks – often critical of something, with a view to getting his or her name in the papers – and thereafter, at Oxford, those present normally gathered on the gloomy landing outside the courts to drink a little farewell wine amidst the fixed metal seating.

I was keen on something slightly different, and very kindly Igor Judge, the former Lord Chief Justice, whom I had known and watched moving steadily upwards throughout my career, came to Oxford to say a few generous words. He was followed by Ben Williams QC, who made a deft and amusing speech, perfectly delivered. I had invited a selection of Sheriffs with whom I had become friendly to embellish the occasion (sadly a few invitations went astray), the Lord Lieutenant came, and we had a reception in the penthouse judicial dining room. It was a satisfactory departure.

Apart from a couple of months with the Judicial Appointments

Commission, interviewing scores of would-be Recorders over the telephone, with the assistance of a charming and talented person from Sheffield, that was the end of my legal career. I had, on the whole, enjoyed it quite a lot. My particular combination of talent and diffident ambition had not led me to a very great height upon the judicial ladder, but the rung on which I sat had been of some modest significance, and agreeable to occupy. I hope that I had some reputation as a capable lawyer and a pleasant and effective tribunal.

Chapter 19

Family, friends and animals

Writing about one's family and friends, many of whom have already been mentioned, is not of course entirely straightforward. Who and what to include, or to omit, are potentially delicate matters. My daughter for example, learning that I was writing a memoir, said that she did not wish to appear in it at all, though I might mention the fact of her birth. (She had not wanted a speech made about her at her wedding either, but responded pretty well with one of her own). My wife, by nature attractively reticent, also thinks that on the whole the less said probably the better. Neither has complete confidence that all my observations will be sedative.

We married in Norfolk on 25th July 1970, in the Norman church opposite Carol's parents' home, South Lopham Hall. We were both 25. Her father, Jim – who like mine had been in the RAF – was a distinguished farmer and a pioneering importer of Canadian Holsteins. He had five enterprises – cattle, pigs, sugar beet, peas and wheat – and said that so long as three ran profitably all was well, but if only two did then he would be anxious. He sat as a magistrate in Thetford, chaired the National Plant Breeding Institute for some time and, briefly, Norwich City Football Club. As a young man he had learned to fly and enjoyed fast cars and tennis. He was of middle size, with shrewd eyes, and always wore a jacket and tie, even to read cowboy novels while lying on a sofa. His clothes were tailor made, but not obviously so. When I first met him, he took me 'farming' by driving silently in his Bentley round the lanes to field gates and pausing in the purring car while a tractor driver or other employee would come over to report. At that time he employed over 100 people, housed many of them and provided retired workers with cottages. He was a wise man, save only that he did not believe in university for his daughters. He gave a lunch party for the workforce to celebrate our engagement, and they assembled around long trestle tables. Carol made an apt speech with confident diffidence which went down very well, with much gruff rustic cheering. Some of those there remembered her as a small child occasionally put on the back of a shire horse.

Her mother, always called Gale, although this was not her real name, was a stylish Canadian with six brothers and a tough upbringing in Manitoba, where the snow lay deep each winter. She spoke with a slight transatlantic accent, dressed with elegance, and was very popular. Her hobbies were gardening, her grandchildren, and collecting antique furniture – at some expense. This she justified on the basis that her husband's main pastime was shooting, which also cost money. Although both were energetic people, I never saw either of them run. Carol's parents were both most generous to me; her father with shooting invitations, often to Suffolk, where he had a gun with John Henniker Major (who had served in Yugoslavia with Fitzroy MacLean and Tito).

Carol had a younger sister, Wendy, thoughtful, good looking and business-like, to whom I introduced both Richard Barr, the balloonist, and then Philip Vallance, a barrister with a considerable intellect, whom she married. We once went to Sicily together, where his German was more use than my Italian. He took Silk the same year as I did, and later became chairman of the Travellers Club (perhaps surprisingly, as social intercourse had never been his forte, but he was most successful in the role). Carol's younger brother, James, in due course took over the farming, and periodically exhausts himself walking at high altitudes, cycling long distances and modifying his house. Another brother, Bill, sadly suffers from Downs syndrome and has led an institutionalised life. Until recently he exhibited periodic bursts of humour and insight.

The day of our wedding was windy. The marquee strained like sails in a fair breeze as the line of guests made their way past bride and groom. Most made some smiling innocuous remark, though one, the generously built industrialist Lord Netherthorpe, gave a sentence or two of sage advice, which I have forgotten. The first speech was made by Jim Prior, then Minister of Agriculture, for whom Carol worked. My best man, former flatmate Nigel Copeland, rose well to the occasion, as the canvas surged and relapsed disconcertingly above his head. In those days a wedding reception was an afternoon event with sandwiches, cake, tea, champagne and speeches, and then the married couple 'went away' to start their honeymoon, with the guests departing soon after. We got into a vintage car with Sedanca de Ville bodywork (which meant that the driver sat in the open while the passengers were comfortably enclosed) and were driven to Claridge's in light rain. The whole wedding and reception took about three hours. When our would-be-anonymous daughter got married nearly 40 years later in 2008, the reception, in a marquee filled with large Christmas trees, extended to about seven hours with a drinks party, speeches, dinner, dancing and a few fireworks to mark a midnight departure. This is now normal, the newly married being keener to spend time with their friends than alone with each other.

For our honeymoon we went first to the Costa Smeralda, a picturesque stretch of Sardinian coastline set in blue translucent sea, then becoming fashionable with Europeans with large boats. I rented a tiny outboard to ski behind, which alarmingly broke down about half a mile off – shore. Happily, the wind or tide delivered us to a beach, and when we walked over a spit of land behind it there was another strand on the other side, with a launch to return us to our hotel. Sardinia, or the bit we saw, was not a notably interesting island, but it had an agreeable, placid, antique atmosphere. I rather wished we had been at a dramatic hotel on stilts over the water called the Calla de Volpe, but it was too expensive, even for a honeymoon. While on Sardinia we bumped into a Suffolk MP, John Hill, who knew Carol and was staying in a villa which belonged to the artist Edward Seago. He gave us dinner one evening and, for pudding, cooked bananas. A fruit better kept out of the oven.

After the Mediterranean I felt we should go to Switzerland, to stride among Alpine hills to the background murmur of cow bells. These always remind me of a steel band tuning up in the distance, but must drive the cattle themselves mad with annoyance. I did not know that country very well then, and had simply asked a travel agent to find us an atmospheric little mountain village. We arrived in Grindelwald, which though undeniably Alpine was not little, but quite a substantial resort, full of big hotels. There were rolling meadows and fine mountains and it rained a lot, but Carol remained agreeably smiling and cheerful. One day we walked a few miles up a Western slope to a ridge. We looked over, upon chalets below. 'Ah' said Carol, 'I know where we are. That is Wengen, where the family came to learn to ski when we were little'. This slightly dimmed my sense of hardy adventure.

We took to going by little train to Kleine Scheideigg, which had cafes where one could sit watching climbers on the North Face of the Eiger. This had a fearsome reputation, and people spent a long time getting up, if they got up at all. Some fell off, some froze to death. I bought a book about it by Heinrich Harrer, who in July 1938 with three others – Kasperak, Heckmair and Vorg, was the first to climb this route. They took almost four days, bivouacking on the cliff face each night. Seventy-seven years later, in 2015, it was climbed by an Italian, Ueli Steck, in two hours and 23 minutes. Thus has mountaineering progressed in a lifetime. There is a film of his ascent. He more or less ran up the 5,900 ft face, with an ice axe in each hand and crampons on his feet. Harrer had no crampons because he could not afford them.

Steck died in 2017 when he fell on Nuptse, not far from Everest, in curious circumstances, climbing alone without basic equipment.

We have often been back to that part of Switzerland, the Bernese Oberland, sometimes to ski and sometimes to hike. On one occasion, we walked with naturalist Bruce Tremayne, and his vivacious and academic Iranian wife Soraya, from Kandersteg to Gstaad. Each morning we ascended to a mountain ridge, to be stirred by distant views, and each afternoon descended, at some cost to our knees, to a hotel in the next valley. I have also, on different occasions, walked from Mürren to Kandersteg (a quite remarkably exhausting day, involving a 5 a.m. start and two passes), and have climbed from Wengen to Männlichen. It now remains only to walk from Wengen to Mürren to have covered a gratifying 300 miles or so on foot across western Switzerland. A better achievement than 70 miles of Hadrian's bleak wall, done when I was 19, or the sixty-mile width of Wales, from Hay on Wye to Aberystwyth, completed some twenty years ago.

In 2014 I retained a Scottish guide to lead four of us up Monte Rosa, at 15,000ft the second highest mountain in Europe if you don't count one in Georgia. On the first day after our arrival he took us, without breakfast or acclimatisation, up a 14,000ft mountain, and then, as we panted at the top, said we were insufficiently fit. I found this annoying. One member of the party – Christopher Woodhead, who really was fit – found it infuriating, but concealed it well. We climbed instead four 14,000 ft peaks. I roped up with Miles Tuely – who had trained on a bicycle – in authentic Alpine style, carrying a redundant ice axe, and found trudging over the approach snow fields rather tiring, but the actual climbing very satisfying. There was not enough of the latter. There was much less traffic on our modest mountains than there is now on Everest.

We returned from honeymoon to the comfortable flat at Elvaston Place. Carol had given up her political job, which was a pity because she would have had a more interesting time working in Parliament than looking after me. My first day on returning was spent conducting a motoring prosecution in Chertsey – for which the Metropolitan Police solicitor never paid – while she shopped for and prepared the first of over 14,000 dinners or suppers, to date, something which has given her limited enjoyment, but at which she is very good. I have not calculated the number of shirts she has laundered. Possibly marriage vows should say something about domestic work.

In 1972 I was introduced by her uncle Don Alston to membership of the Worshipful Company of Glaziers, and began to attend its many dinners. I once had a stimulating evening next to Dennis Silk, Warden of Radley, but frequently these events were unexciting and the speeches formulaic. Everyone was much older than me. After a few years I decided to resign, something which apparently had never happened before and was said to be impossible. The only time I spoke to a Livery audience was in 2004 when Richard Lay invited me to address the Armourers and Braziers, of which he was then Master. Founded in 1346 they have a remarkable hall, laden with glinting armour, fierce weapons and many martial embellishments. It was an act of faith of him to ask me, for we were social friends through his attractive wife Veronica (an elegant and charming Samaritan and horse racing enthusiast), but he had never heard me speak. I mentioned the little-known English invasion of Tibet in 1904, when it was found that the local soldiers wore armour made of quilting, more efficacious against sabres than bullets. (As soon as the country had been subjugated, instructions came from London to leave, and give it back.)

Our elder son, born on 13th February 1973, was named after Roger de Hautville, ruler of Sicily in the late 11th Century and star of John Julius Norwich's *Normans in the South*. He was also called Charles, after me, and James, after his maternal grandfather. RCJ seemed mellifluous initials, and corresponded with those of the Royal Courts of Justice in the Strand, which I thought, when older, he might perhaps bestride. He has indeed become a successful barrister.

His birth was at the Westminster Hospital. Though all ended well it was not a satisfactory process, for Carol was in labour and considerable distress for a day and a half, and only then was it determined that a caesarean was necessary. She had an incompetent junior anaesthetist, whose notes I saw and later commented on. The hospital was more annoyed that I had read his notes than apologetic for his failures. I collected an exhausted but cheerful wife about ten days later (in a new car, a Fiat 132, the worst vehicle I have ever owned, which I only kept for a month) and we went home to our new house in Pimlico, into the experienced hands of Sister Bartram, who had looked after me when I was a baby.

In 1975 we moved to Oxfordshire. This coincided with the arrival of our second son, Hugh, born on 18th July that year, in Norwich. Carol had one or two miscarriages before his conception, and much of that pregnancy she spent quietly at her parents' house in Norfolk. His name, another Norman one, which foreigners have difficulty pronouncing, was combined with James and with my mother's maiden name of Wesson.

Almost the only person we knew in Oxfordshire when we moved there was Pam Berriman, who had been a teenage friend in Wolverhampton. She had married one of the Axtell brothers, from an Oxfordshire family best known for the high-quality specialist building work of their company, Symm and Co. (We were to become friends with his brother Malcolm, a tall and meticulous man with a fine house). Pam kindly invited us to a party. There we met Chris and Sue Burton, who lived near us, and through them we rapidly got to know many of our fairly close neighbours. Christopher is an entertaining and formidable man. Stockily handsome, and with three successful sons, it is not clear whether he should be thought of as a large small man, or a small large one. He has an urge for constant travel and regular domestic change. Few airlines or airports have not received his custom. He acquired a small portfolio of foreign houses, including a villa near the traffic jams of Saint Tropez, a place in the emptier Gers and a ski chalet near Val d'Isère, where he and Sue – a keen and hospitable conversationalist – have entertained us generously. In Oxfordshire they moved away from us to the alarmingly entitled Woeful Lake House near Burford. No sooner was that fettled up and embellished by some vivid pictures by Josephine Trotter than they went further away, to Northleach, to a smaller, very comfortable place, good for retirement. But soon they were off again, this time to Woodstock. He has periodically been a keen shot and skier, though, like me, not quite world class at either. We have been friends for over 40 years.

We saw a good deal of Von and Robert Parsons too, who were near neighbours: she, kindly, indefatigable, and an astute magistrate; he a quiet, tolerant, interesting and hospitable farmer, who recently died, without prior notice, in his sleep. They lived initially beside a mill race, in which I always felt children were likely to drown. Robert ran a friendly family shoot, and kept peacocks, to the irritation of their neighbours. Their younger daughter, known as Mole, was to became in due course a close friend of our daughter Kate, who was born on 10th July 1979 at the Radcliffe hospital in Oxford, and given the additional names Victoria, which I have always liked for various associations, and Hardy, after my father, who called himself Hardy Harris. At one point, being a good actress, she fleetingly considered the stage, and might have acted as Victoria Hardy. We once saw her perform at the Edinburgh Festival Fringe, where she played a blind woman who had to pour afternoon tea – a remarkable slow-motion depiction. Her brother Hugh has also acted there, and was a confident performer, looking well in one of my Morris-made suits in Prince of Wales check.

Soon after our arrival in Oxfordshire we found ourselves hospitably entertained from time to time by horse people. They were generally hunting enthusiasts, mainly with the Heythrop. Every dinner party seemed to include some casualties of recklessness or misfortune – in a wheelchair or neck brace, a splint or a sling. Conversation was primarily about horses, hunting, steeplechasing or racing. This was engaging, but after an hour or two I might find myself making efforts to move to another subject, perhaps of more general interest: for example, why were longbows replaced by muskets, which were inferior weapons in every respect? (The long bow had greater accuracy, longer range, better penetration, a five times faster rate of fire – ten shots a minute rather than two – and did not produce smoke which inhibited aim. It was silent, a great advantage in surprise attack, and you could, if on the winning side, pick up and re-use your ammunition). Such fascinating topics as this might last a few minutes before, catching the eye of someone on the opposite side of the table, my impatient neighbour would interject: 'but didn't Timothy do well on Asparagus Tips at the team chase the other day?' Astonishing', would chime another, 'and his brother's horse at Warwick too'. These people had tremendous range and stamina. Some had an interest (absolute or fractional) in a racehorse, and would think nothing of driving to Doncaster, York or Fakenham, hundreds of miles, to watch their possession run for a few minutes. A few days ago I met one who was keen to fly in a friend's light plane to watch her steed put in some furlongs in France.

At one of these dinners, years later, an elegant neighbour struggled to find anything of interest in me, but eventually she politely inquired, 'Well, what do you do?' 'I am a judge'. Instantly she turned towards me, a shine in her eye and an enthusiastic smile on her face. 'A judge, how fascinating – dogs or horses?'

Sometimes I tried a different approach. 'Why don't racehorses get faster and faster, like human athletes?' I might ask. This fact had not occurred to some. Others knew it, but thought it of no interest whatsoever that specially bred animals whose only desired quality was speed do not very often break records, whereas humans, randomly bred, get faster with every year. Nor could they explain very well why it was necessary to handicap horses, but not human runners. 'For the betting, I suppose.' 'Why do you have to have betting?' 'There would be no racing without it.' 'Why not, if it is such fun?'

We are lucky enough to have quite a wide spectrum of friends with a big span of interests. Some enjoy fine old cars – John Sword takes pride in classic Lagondas of supreme elegance, Nick Lees likes to race a snappy, characterful vintage Riley, Miles Tuely has a sedate grey Bentley. Some are gardening experts, some read unusually extensively. Many play golf, others play bridge – often, seriously and well. Several work estimably hard for charities. Norman Hudson is one of England's leading experts on fine houses. But we are never far from sociable people who enjoy horses, spend time and money on them, and clearly find them of equal interest to humans. A close friend largely devotes her life to dressage. Daily she exercises her mighty and valuable animals, for hours at a time, and feeds, cleans and grooms them. A demanding regime.

The children, skilfully cherished by Carol (who does not much like horses, though trained as a child to ride a pony by a Major Bugg), naturally dominated our household for some years. I enjoyed watching them became mobile: first in supine little spasms, then rolling over, then sitting unsteadily upright. They might crawl, like small seals, but finally and generally with an expression of some triumph, they propped themselves upright on chubby curved legs as a precursor to a first step, often a lunge which carried them down again. All this done with considerable dignity. Later they stand up exactly as a gorilla does, first with legs and bottom in the air, followed by raising their body upright. But learning to walk is as nothing to learning to talk. From a vocabulary which consisted of eloquent arm gestures and the odd grimace, they quickly graduated to a small armoury of key words like 'more', 'hot', and 'again'. Soon two words are combined: 'hot fire' (our children and grandchildren always seemed fascinated by open fires). But their greatest leap is understanding the pronoun 'I'. Infants are always addressed either by their names, or as 'you'. They are never called 'I'. How then do they manage to say, as sooner or later they do, 'I want it', when trying to get a toy, garment or piece of food, rather than 'You want it', meaning themselves?

The children's first schools were mildly unconventional. The boys went to a little establishment near the village of Great Tew (now overwhelmed by a country club called Soho House) run singlehandedly by a widow, Mrs Eyre. She was keen on school photographs with her pupils arranged in height order, and maths – but not spelling. Everyone appeared quite happy and Roger and Hugh seemed to read and do simple sums with some facility. We entered them for Summer Fields, a good prep school in North Oxford. There was an entrance exam, which I regarded as a formality.

I was wrong, and a day or two after the exam we were telephoned by the headmaster, Nigel Talbot Rice. 'I am sorry to say', he said, 'that

Roger has not passed his exam.' Alarming news. But he continued 'It may be that he has not been very well taught. I would like to see him myself. Can you come in on Saturday'? Naturally, cancelling everything, we could. For over an hour Nigel – as we grew to know him – tested and evaluated our six-year-old. Both eventually emerged from his study smiling. 'His instruction has been poor. But he is an intelligent boy, and will do quite well. I would expect him just to fail an Eton Scholarship. We will certainly take him.' This was remarkable. Summer Fields was a leading prep school, patronised by some very successful families, with national reach and not short of pupils. I have always been both surprised and extremely grateful that its headmaster should have noticed or bothered to re-consider anyone who had not passed its exam. It was a mark of his remarkable qualities, which were complemented by those of his wife, Jo, who cared for the small boarders with great kindness. Both Roger and Hugh (allowed in without a hitch), thrived and enjoyed it. They were excellently taught, especially by Nick Aldridge, made good friends and duly failed scholarships to Eton. When they got there, they found they were a year or more ahead of their peers, and had to tread water for some time.

One feature of Summer Fields was its annual school ski trip, when a group of 30 or 40 children and their parents went to stay in a rather basic hotel in Val d'Isère. These holidays were led by a schoolmaster called Charles Churchill, sociable, amusing and unflappable, though I believe a better golfer than skier. Discipline was limited, abilities varied from negligible to excellent, and a sense of gay amusement pervaded every activity. Lavinia Perry – farmer, sailor and sometime Sheriff of Northamptonshire, organised similar parties. Occasionally a child would get lost or left behind, but would always reappear cheerful and none the worse. Merlin Swire once missed the bus back to the airport, and thus his flight. But since his father owned Cathay Pacific his return to England did not present a problem. One or two adults usually became casualties, but their slings or crutches were treated not as signs of incompetence but as badges of enterprise, or the manifestations of a puckish fate.

Our daughter first went to school at Kitebrook, near Moreton in Marsh. Run by Anne McDermott in an eccentric and bravura manner, this was an establishment of a rare kind. I believe the school was solely her possession and that there were no governors. When you met Mrs McDermott she looked deep into the backs of your eyes. This was not hostile, but it was certainly a challenge. You were lost if you did not hold her slightly intimidating gaze. She did what she thought it appropriate to do, and though prepared to listen to parents was not to be led by them. She wrote in June 1986: 'Kitebrook... is so very different from the conventional vision! So full of life and humour, joy and also frustration and interest, achievement and development tempered by the occasional disaster! Every week contains something new, because of the marvellous basic ingredients – the individuality and potential of young children and their enthusiasm'. On the whole I think she got things right, and her pupils emerged self-confident and fluent, and with good friends. Not all were academically outstanding but most managed to get into the next school of their parents' choice. In Kate's case, this was Downe House, in pine woods on high ground near Newbury.

Roger and Hugh went to the same house at Eton, worked pretty well and thrived in different ways. Roger had two years in the football first eleven, known as The Association. We once watched with suitable pride as he scored the winning goal in a house match final too, an unimaginably heroic feat. Hugh was rather less athletic, but won prizes and trophies for declamation and acted fairly seriously. Both became President of the Political Society, in 1991 and 1993 respectively.

In 1981 I happened into the Royal Society of Portrait Painters' exhibition in The Mall. Taken with the contents, I thought it would be agreeable to have some family pictures painted. I liked the work of Norman Hepple, but not his prices. I asked if anyone in similar style might be suggested, and was recommended to Peter Walborne. Early in his career he had painted several Allied Generals in Italy, but the pictures had been stolen from a castle and never recovered. A bad blow for a young artist. Later, after a spell turning photographs taken in Harrods into portraits, he was asked to paint the Queen Mother (this hangs in the Middle Temple). He was much cheaper than Hepple. It was not the first time Carol had been painted: her father had commissioned Douglas Anderson in 1974, and he had produced a fine old-masterly picture, in which she looked a little severe. So severe that her mother would not hang it in her house, and gave it to us. It shows the faintest hint of a stubborn lower lip, about which I commented to the artist. I suggested it was not quite correct, and as I was her husband, I should know. He looked at me with rather more than mild professional scorn, asked if I was a painter too, and said he was quite content with the accuracy of his work. On reflection, he was right. But like my mother-in-law, I wanted something a trace happier and I looked for this to Walborne. He did indeed produce a most friendly depiction, in which, beside the sitter's happy disposition, one can detect faint traces both of the Queen Mother and Angela Rippon. My father was so pleased with his picture of Kate that he asked if he could have one too. The artist swiftly produced another, completely indistinguishable from the first.

In the 1990s I thought there was something to be said for an update and Roger asked a schoolfriend, Dick Smyly – who paints everything from wild boar to country houses – if he would paint our family. He duly attended at home, and first painted me, also looking perhaps a touch severe. This picture, unlike the others which followed it, has a somewhat rough texture, which Dick explained by saying that he forgot, under the influence of a little claret, to prepare the canvas the night before. However, I like it.

The only other art I have commissioned has been a few of the stylishly distorted architectural pictures of Ian Weatherhead, to whom I was introduced by a friend. The best of these are of Palladio's Villa Rotunda, and Cockerell's Sezincote.

In due course Roger went enjoyably to Exeter to read history, and there met Tania Stewart (who now operates at some altitude in insurance at Lloyds). Some years later, after he had been to City University to read law and then been called to the Bar (an event I have always been ashamed that I missed, as we were in Scotland at the time), they married. He joined a good set of chambers, quite close to where

I had been in Middle Temple Lane, and is now a leading specialist in clinical negligence, personal injury, and animal litigation. He has also become a Recorder.

Both Hugh and Kate applied to Worcester College, Oxford. Both were turned down. Hugh re-applied the following year to Magdalen, was accepted and got a First in PPE. Feeling the need for further education, he then won a Kennedy scholarship to Harvard. We went to Boston to attend the degree ceremony in Harvard yard. This was an entertaining event. Scores of chairs had been set up in the open air, but after the international audience of parents had assembled, it began to rain; gently at first, then harder. Initially all sat stoical, beneath umbrellas which dripped companionably upon their neighbours. But this soon broke down. The Americans fled indoors first, to be followed by a discreet scurry of proud, carefully-dressed families from Japan, China and South East Asia. Next to go, more noisily, were the Mediterranean Europeans – Italian, French and Spanish. This left a few sturdy Germans, and a contingent of English who mostly had Barbour type coats and a variety of hats. We stayed on as though at a football match, summer picnic, or wet Trooping the Colour. In the end we got pretty damp before tall helpful youths came to direct us inside.

Refreshments at Harvard were rather disappointing. I saw a tent marked 'Beverages', entered and asked for two glasses of wine. 'We have no wine, sir'. 'Then beer, perhaps, or gin'? 'No sir, we serve no alcohol whatsoever'. Why this should have been so, at a celebratory function, was unexplained, but was consistent with my attempt to get a drink in a hotel in the Bryce Canyon National Park. It stocked only two wines: red or white, and both were non-alcoholic. In the Hotel Irma in Cody, Wyoming (named after Buffalo Bill's daughter, who established it) they had wine, but refused to serve any because we were eating with two children, whom they presumably feared might absorb it by osmosis. The American attitude to alcohol is bizarre.

Kate also re-applied to Oxford, this time to St Hugh's, was accepted to read history, and in due course captained the university at mixed lacrosse. Her successful team consisted of five skilful girls who knew the rules and could cradle and shoot, with a balance of strong men who if they got the ball were hard to stop. Half blues were not available.

Both subsequently spent time abroad: Hugh in Delhi and Hong Kong (thereafter he joined the civil service and rose fast); Kate in Nepal, Washington and Kabul, where she worked with Rory Stewart after his Asian walk but before he became an unconventional candidate to lead the Conservative party. She has also worked for the *Economist*, *Financial Times*, Clinton's Global Initiative in Asia and English Heritage. So much for the admissions tutors at Worcester.

Both Hugh and Kate have also found delightful and very talented partners, Gaucho Rasmussen and Hamish Laing. Hugh has a son and a daughter, Kate two sons and a daughter. All are bright, interesting and affectionate children. Roger started his family a little before his siblings, and his trio of daughters operate as a wonderfully happy, versatile and self-contained unit, putting on a play, dance or gymnastic display at the drop of a hat.

For many years we enjoyed family summer holidays. I spent too much on some of these, as I certainly did upon cars (24 in 57 years) but generally found – in a happy variation of Parkinson's law – that income expanded to meet the strains put upon it. If one had only ever done what one could clearly afford, life would have been duller than it has been. The holidays with the children were either conventional Devon or Cornwall – initially as guests of Charles and Sally Villiers (a most tactful, kind and stylish person, very rarely dishevelled), or with the mildly eccentric Vanessa Davis and her amiable baritone City-expert husband, Peter – or to places like Crete, Corsica or Cephalonia.

Things sometimes went wrong in the Mediterranean. One year, surreptitiously and nocturnally, I had to disconnect the electricity powering the White Rocks Hotel's noisy Greek island dance floor so that we could sleep. Another time saw us putting to sea in a little launch until it became so choppy that I was begged, and then ordered, by my wife back to the harbour. I then hired a jeep which I thought the children would like riding in the back of, but they hated the dust and got sunburnt. Windsurfing was fine so long as there was little wind, and no surf. Polzeath with its English beaches was generally more fun, there were usually people there we knew, and no airports were involved.

One year we made a family trip to the Florida Disneyland, where my favourite memory is of Hugh, aged about ten, standing at a deck rail as our paddle-steamer crossed the lake on its approach to the Magic Kingdom. Just as the turrets and spires came into exciting distant focus, there shot out of the heavy morning mist three water-skiers: Mickey Mouse, Goofy and Donald Duck. They sped towards us, waved and zoomed around the boat. Hugh's look of fulfilled ecstasy as he waved back was worth the transatlantic fare alone. He had dreamed of this for years, and it was coming true. Roger was beginning to become more sophisticated and independent at that time, and liked to go off on his own on the monorail.

Sometimes Carol and I went on more ambitious trips. One to Zimbabwe stands out. It had been organised by the daughter of Laurens Van der Post, but in the end she did not come. We were in the hands of John Stevens and Gavin Ford, ex-Selous scouts who had fought for Rhodesia after UDI. They were formidably competent in the bush, but in quite different ways. Stevens, powerfully built, blond and a little above middle size, always carried a double-barrelled heavy calibre rifle, a revolver and a Bowie knife. His confident personality seemed to communicate itself adversely to the wildlife. Elephants would trumpet crossly at him at a range of a quarter of a mile. Hyenas would snarl under his gaze and leopards slink rapidly away. Once, out walking with him soon after dawn, we noticed vultures circling. From a range of about two hundred yards we saw a dead baby elephant, round which were crouching a lion and two lionesses, trying to eat it.

'Let's have a closer look' said Stevens, and I imagined we might crawl a few yards and study the savage scene through our binoculars. But no. 'Come on', he said, and we followed nervously behind as he strode towards the lions. They stopped eating and looked at us. Stevens marched on. They stood up and gazed steadily, tails slightly twitching. Stevens still went forward, until. when some thirty yards from them, he picked up and threw a stone.

'Bugger off' he shouted. 'John,' I said, rather anxiously, 'are we going any closer'?

'Oh yes. We will have a look at the elephant. Lion are all piss and wind... bugger off.' and he threw another stone. 'Keep together,' he ordered, and tramped forward.

I became very anxious indeed. We were facing three wild animals and he had only two rounds in his rifle. Finally, when we were about ten yards from the lions, they sprang back to some nearby mopani trees, under which they crouched alertly.

Stevens drew our attention to the hide of the dead baby elephant. It was scarred in various ways from the attempts of different animals to get through to the meat. It appeared that leopards could not manage this, hyena made limited progress, and vultures concentrated their attentions upon the animal's orifices, which they could penetrate and tear. Lions, once there had been a start, could begin to bite off mouthfuls. All this was explained to us, together with the age of the unfortunate calf, and for how long it had been dead. But I kept my eye on the lions, who were growling gently.

'I think we will move now' said John after a few minutes. 'Keep close together, move slowly backwards. Do not turn your back on the lion.' With him the word lion was both singular and plural, as with sheep. Very cautiously we retreated, and he unslung his rifle. We had gone perhaps twenty yards when the lions sprang forward – but fortunately only as far as the elephant corpse. This was a safari experience far removed from driving about in the back of a big Jeep. With John you felt that the animals regarded him as a threat and a challenge, but that if it came to a fight he could probably win. He had certainly had to shoot several charging elephants in the recent past, and explained to me the necessary points of aim. He had also, tragically, once had to shoot a lion which had carried off from camp his little daughter, whom he rescued from its jaws. But a fang had penetrated her spine, rendering her permanently paraplegic.

Gavin Ford was different. A smaller man of modest build, and with one leg slightly slimmer than the other, he was part of nature. The animals simply accepted him and those he was with. On one occasion he had us sit down near a large herd of buffalo. The great heavy-horned beasts mooched over to have a look at us and surrounded our little party, tossing their dripping fly-girt muzzles like Hereford cattle. Gavin said that we would not be gored or trampled, and that soon they would move on, as indeed they did.

On another, we were walking through light bush and saw an extended family of elephants. They were facing us, moving slowly our way, with the wind from them to us. Again, we were told to sit down in a group, and leave a rucksack or two in front. Slowly the herd grazed towards us. There were three calves, two suckling from the teats between their mothers' front legs, seeming somehow human. They came closer and closer, and paused to investigate the packs with their trunks, one of which was holding some just-cropped flowers. At this Ford began to ululate softly, and then with greater volume. 'Elley, elley, elley …' The nearest animal, a large cow, quested around with her trunk, turned her head left and right, stood over her calf, and tried to focus upon us. She produced a series of low digestive rumbles, without menace. We stayed like this in a kind of trance for several minutes before the elephant families moved gently past, guiding the calves with taps upon their flanks or shoulders, their huge feet silent on the dusty ground.

A few days later three of us, a psychiatrist, a schoolteacher, and a barrister, walked into the Matusadona hills with Gavin Ford, food and sleeping bags – but no tents. The idea was to range a little over the territory, watch elephants and anything else we might find, and bivouac at nights. It was so hot during the day that a bush hat seemed the most valuable possession one could ever have, but it cooled fast in the evening, when we sat round a fire drinking sweet tea and eating heated meat and rice. All round us lions and hyenas roared and screamed, and we discussed the post-UDI conflict, in which Ford had played an adventurous part, sometimes parachuting at minimum level out of Dakotas to attack ZANU or ZIPRA camps. He had despatched a number of people in personal combat. You would never have thought this to look at him. I went to sleep anxious lest some animal would select me for a nocturnal snack, but woke at dawn unconsumed.

Quite why one should seek fear for pleasure I do not know, but it was decided that we should take a raft down the Zambezi. This, at first mention, sounded innocuous enough. I pictured us floating gently past hippo and giraffe, admiring zebra drinking, and perhaps noting – at a suitable distance – a basking crocodile or two. But it soon emerged that this was to be white-water rafting, and grade six at that – an extreme kind. A crowd of about sixty attended at the launch point, where a team of sturdy, bronzed South Africans told some they could ride, and some – too fat, too young or too old – that they could not. We were six to a rubber dinghy, with a transverse seat in the middle, upon which sat our captain/guide, of mighty physique, plying two oars. We customers were distributed around the boat, and each was given a life jacket and a paddle. We were living ballast, our task to throw our weight forward when the zodiac hit a wave. And hit waves we did, initially modest ones in a predictable direction, but soon we were racing at, I suppose 15 or 20 mph, between huge rocks, down steep green slopes into the base of 'stoppers', waves anywhere between four and ten feet high.

If one had sufficient forward weight the idea was that the boat would penetrate the wave, not be picked up by it. For a while this worked, but then, at an apparently well-known spot with a name like Death Point, though deaths were rare, the wave came at an angle and really looked very frightening indeed. We hit this aquatic wall sideways, and the next thing I was aware of was being underwater, thumping painfully against rocks, and with darkness above. There was a grim feeling as I kicked upwards, but saw no light. Perhaps I was dead. In a last pellucid moment I realised I was underneath the upturned boat, pulled my way to the side, put my head above water, and breathed. This was better than drowning, but not much, as we continued to be hit and swirled by rocks and waves which from so low a viewpoint seemed very formidable.

I held on to a rope around the edge of the boat and after a while we came into an area of calm water. Two powerful arms appeared and our guide dragged me onto the upturned bottom of his boat. Quickly we were all accounted for. There was a drill for turning the zodiac back upright. We all sat looking chastened and fearful, as the guide announced that we would be encountering the next rapid soon. 'Do you want to try Hell's Alley, or the Twisted Chimney?'

I quite wanted to get out, but that was not an option. There was still an hour to go. There were crocodiles resting on the shore below the cliffs, but we were told that they never attack in rough water. On we went. I have never been so continuously frightened (though I did have a bad moment once in Times Square when I thought I was going to be attacked by muggers). Eventually we pulled out onto a bit of beach below a steep cliff. I was amazed to see Stevens and Ford shivering, and not, they said, from cold. The intrepid couple had felt anxious too. I shot off up the vestigial cliff path with the schoolmaster, looking for our wives, and feeling that I was back in an environment I understood. I also understood why fat people were forbidden, for though they would float satisfactorily they could not manage the climb out at the end.

If we were frightened in Africa we were charmed in Bhutan, when finally we got there, with Peter and Sally Cadbury. The Druk Air flight from Delhi took off four hours early, without us. Druk was quite possibly the most unsatisfactory airline in the world. With only one, or occasionally two aircraft, it was booked up years in advance, and anyway the next flight was not for a week. So (not assisted by our travel agent) we flew by an Indian airline to Assam and went in by Jeep, thus missing close aerial views of Everest but seeing the mediaeval road to Paro, and a castle where the King, a generally mild man whose aim was national happiness and whose hobby was archery, had for a time imprisoned the leader of the opposition. We commenced a trek, which carried us past chalets decorated with a profusion of carved wooden phalluses, farms with biblical ploughs, gentle jungle, deciduous and then pine woodlands, to mountains of some altitude.

At around 10,000ft we began to have headaches, and at 14,000 they got worse. Peter had hurt his back and felt he could not carry anything.

Sally's desire to walk evaporated. The Bhutanese guide, a tough, compact and well-educated man, was not impressed with the party's progress. None of us felt much like eating. Soon Carol acclimatised, and then walked many miles with great determination, paced by a slender Sherpa with an umbrella. We saw exotic forests and mighty hills, but sadly no yetis, about which, having read widely, I considered myself an authority.

In Bhutan there were sumptuary laws (to specify personal clothing). Men, all stocky and about 5ft 6in tall, wore knee-length tweed togas, with woollen stockings and sturdy brown shoes. They might have been Roman golfers. Some carried both sword and mobile phone. The women wore national dress of an indeterminate kind. The children, clad in miniature versions of these, were all taught English and were delightful. We visited a school one morning to watch assembly. 'Good morning Madam', one said to me with careful politeness, and then turned and bowed towards my wife: 'And good morning sir'. The children stood beside a flagpole up which was run the banner of their nation, and then they sang. I assumed they were singing 'Glory to the sunlit mountains and the icy crystal streams', or something of that sort. I inquired. They were singing 'Death to the Chinese', a race which they dislike and fear, probably with good reason, as China has a claim, via Tibet, to their country.

On several occasions we almost came across the King, since we stayed, in the absence of hotels, in his regional rest houses, and indeed sometimes occupied his royal bed. He travelled in a white Toyota Land Cruiser, followed by a second which carried the three sisters who were his wives. No doubt an excellent family arrangement. The current King of Bhutan is a fellow Bencher of the Inner Temple, though not, I think, a lawyer. I have never met him.

A major feature of Bhutan are Tzongs, huge old buildings, largely timber, in strategic places, which seem to blend local government centre, police station, fort, boarding school and Buddhist seminary. They are populated by large numbers of small, undernourished youths, with grubby saffron robes and shaved heads, who peered out like sad imprisoned rooks to inspect their western visitors. There are a few tigers in the countryside, but we did not come across them, though we did meet one unhappy man carrying the remains of a sheep killed by a leopard.

I long had an ambition to find a tiger in India, but several attempts, including in lesser known places with good reputations like Khana and Pench, failed. Daily, for over two weeks Carol and I set off in extremely chilly conditions before dawn to drive in a Jeep around the tracks and paths of these various reservations, but saw nothing save the odd deer and some giant cows, like aurochs, said to be dangerous, but of limited interest to look at. There were indeed tigers, proved when we ran into the distinguished and amusing wildlife sculptor Mark Coreth, who had just spent forty minutes sketching one. But we were unlucky. We did however have an entertaining night in a decayed palace called Kawardha, which was occupied by a mildly gloomy Maharajah and his reserved but delightful wife. She had never left India. His elephant stables stood empty, their only occupant an old Morris Minor. I thought, being in a palace, that I should dress for dinner, and put on my white suit, but the Maharajah turned up rather informally in an old anorak and sandals.

We were offered, as novel after-dinner entertainment, a walk along a dam to see hyenas, but decided instead to engage with the plumbing. Our bathroom was a converted hall, perhaps 40 ft square, with a double door in each wall, and in the centre, surrounded by a convolution of tarnished silver pipes, tubes and taps, was a huge bath cum shower, made in Newcastle. Instructions read: 'Hot waters have dangers to beware, carefully please to operate the controls with requisite precautions or very scaldy. Thank you gratefully'. At breakfast, where we had a waiter each, the butler confided in my ear 'You will not be forgetting the tippings, sir? We long for your soon return'. I felt just like Michael Palin.

Next year, 2007, we went to Nepal, where after a modest trek in the Annapurna foothills, it was possible, in Chitwan, to ride out to seek tigers on the back of an elephant. This was more authentic, more fun, and more successful. In three days of dawn jungle sweeps, with four elephants walking in extended line about 100 yards apart, we found two tigers, which growled theatrically and bounded about in appropriate fashion, baring their mighty canine teeth. (Why do cats – and us – have 'canine' teeth, rather than feline ones, which are much larger?) These were fine moments. Elephants are excellent cross-country vehicles. Solicitous, they sweep branches aside which might strike their passengers, they ford substantial rivers without hesitation, and no grove, bush or tree impedes their relentless path. On one, you have excellent visibility and feel intrepid and immune from danger, though I do know a chap called Andrew Mitchell, a wildlife expert, who tells of a Nepalese tiger jumping up at him, and how he was only saved by the gait of the elephant carrying him a couple of yards beyond the trajectory of the leap.

There was one great, long term sadness in my family, which was that my sister Elizabeth – blonde, not tall, with a good business sense, artistic, amusing, cheerful and friendly – became a serious diabetic when aged about twelve. Thereafter, every day of her life she had to inject herself to remain in suitable balance. She coped with this with serene bravery, went to school at Malvern, which she much enjoyed and then after a spell at the Oxford and County secretarial college, did a course at the Inchbald School of Design. She was a good draughtsman, and having excellent flair for colour and texture, set herself up as an interior decorator, operating with a girlfriend and business partner from premises in Bridgnorth. They did well for some years, obtaining many substantial contracts, often of a commercial nature. Eventually however they were brought down by a major customer who failed to pay a very large bill. My father offered to re-establish the business, but she felt that she would rather move on.

By this time she had married Michael Kirk, who was remarkable in his solicitude and care. A tallish man, closely resembling Eric Morecambe in appearance, and with unusual syntax, he retired early from his family insurance business and nobly devoted himself to Isa, golf, charity, and the affairs of the parish church at Enville. She needed his help, because her health grew slowly worse, though she remained full of gusts of animated, eye-narrowing laughter, and very sociable. Her sight gradually deteriorated, she required a kidney transplant, and many visits to hospital for one complication or another. They never had children because she believed that her condition might be congenital. Insofar as she could, which for a long time was considerably, she led a normal life, doing some writing, travelling and entertaining at their pleasant Shropshire cottage – marred only by its close proximity to a power cable pylon, which hummed audibly in a manner which I doubt was beneficial. They were very fond of, popular with, and kind to our children, and, as my father began to decline in his late seventies and early eighties, my mother having died quite suddenly when he was 69, they carried most of the burden of helping him.

Isa died of a heart attack aged only 58. I had spoken at her wedding, and did so at her funeral, and it was clear from everyone who talked to me, as from my own conviction, that her qualities of kindness, concern, character and courage far surpassed the normal, and most certainly any of my own.

I was not present when my sister or my father died (abruptly in 1994 after having been told that he had to go to hospital) but I was when my mother did. I was 33, and she thirty years older. She had been taken to the Royal Infirmary in Worcester with a subarachnoid haemorrhage, unconscious after an energetic game one Christmas. I suspect she was not properly treated, as nothing appeared to have been done to relieve the internal pressure of the blood upon the brain. By the time I arrived from Norfolk she had been in a coma for two days, and was breathing with a disagreeable rasp. I was sitting by her bed when this stopped. She and I had always been on the same wavelength, and though not religious or psychic, I felt perhaps that there would be some mental or spiritual indication of her departing soul or spirit. Indeed, I expected it. But there was not. One moment she was alive, though asleep, and the next she had gone. I cut a lock from her dark brown hair, and after a few minutes' contemplation left the room. I have spoken at four funerals, and have referred to spirits lingering to enjoy for one last time the affection of their friends. I still have some faint instinct this may be so, but it is not strong.

After the death of one's second parent there is a definite feeling of stepping into the front line, the next to confront the end of life. This is enhanced by the arrival of grandchildren – we have eight – who occasionally inquire how old you are. When I look at Carol she often appears about 50, and still has dark hair. Mine, once dark and prolific, has turned a shade between grey and white, and lost coverage. We are the same age. For some years we used to play tennis, generally mixed doubles at relaxed and amusing local tournaments, but at 74 she still plays tennis twice a week, and I do not.

The children are now sometimes our holiday hosts, rather than the other way around, and we have had some entertaining, energetic summer weeks in the French Alps in chalets they have organised.

Most people, I suppose, have a more or less wide range of acquaintances, whom they call friends, people they recognise, greet, and talk to with various degrees of enthusiasm. But this may be without much understanding of their nature, wisdom, foibles, vices or talents. Then there are those with whom over the years – or perhaps intensively over a few weeks – there grows real rapport, with insight into their thought and nature. You know what they are thinking beyond analysis of what they say. Some individuals have a portcullis round their nature through which, though you might think you can see, there is no progress. You do not need to agree with friends, though congruence of thought may help to form a bond. There is no doubt that the quality called chemistry is significant, consciously or unconsciously appreciated; perhaps too a turn of phrase, a tone, an accent, gesture, a grace of movement or a laugh. All these ingredients can blend into an affection or companionship which can properly be called friendship. These relationships, however, wax and wane, though rarely as a result of any conscious decision.

A few weeks ago, Carol came upon a list of those we had invited to a drinks party in London in 1972. There were eighty people on the list. We could only remember who about three quarters of these guests were, and she is very good at people. This is some indictment, even over a span of over 40 years. With a friend you can usually resume naturally where you left off, whether thirty days or thirty years before, and do so without thinking 'this is not the person I knew'. I had that sensation with someone with whom I had been at university fifty years ago, when we met again last year. Our conversation simply picked up without hesitation, and all nuances resumed as though never interrupted.

One good way to establish or confirm friendship is to go on holiday with people. This we have done with about seventy individuals, and with one exception it has always proved a success. I think normally because there has been some primary activity – walking, skiing, travel, investigation, culture – rather than simply hanging about in the sunshine wondering what next to eat or drink.

Another kind of friend does things for you. A day or two after I emerged from hospital recently the doorbell rang and there was Sally Browne holding a cake, to restore my weight and morale. She had made it, driven quite a long way to deliver it, and was all solicitude and encouragement. She did it a second time too. Others wrote, or called in, often with food or books. Hugh Brett arrived with a cunning small teapot, which turned out to be broken, so he went away and fetched another. David Morton Jack, now in his mid-eighties but still impeccably turned out and distinguished, came to see me in hospital despite parking frustrations sufficient to deter a saint. I did not feel my best in a hospital chemise.

One cannot write about all those who have been one's friends, and not comprehensively about others. Carol and I have been in more or less continuous contact with Nigel and April Copeland for about 50 years. We have lived in North Oxfordshire, they near Henley. He was my best man, and I was his. I knew April when I was twelve. Nigel had a long business career, not always to his entire satisfaction until he got a highly congenial job with the Royal Ballet School, but always overcame his frustrations. They are tireless in their consumption of culture, at home and abroad, and we have enjoyed many family highlights and various holidays together. April has been a valuable confidante and advisor. Their elder daughter Camilla, my goddaughter, became a City solicitor, retired very young and is now a magistrate.

Richard Barr is a slightly abrupt person with whom I have kept in touch for about 60 years. A prep school companion, vegetarian, and as earlier mentioned, adventurer, he retired to Shropshire. There he and his wife Caroline have restored a huge rambling manor house, where they held a reception after their daughter's wedding. It was a chilly day, almost raining, and the guests were driven out inexplicably onto a long terrace with views to the west. We stood there shivering, then heard the distant sound of an aircraft, which grew rapidly louder and then resolved into the wonderful roar of a Rolls Royce Merlin engine belonging to a Spitfire, flown by a friend of the groom. Eyes began to water, and throats to swell, as this glorious machine swept towards us at a height of about a hundred feet. As it passed over it curled and climbed and rolled, hanging for a moment in the air at the apex of its ascent, then swept down towards the fields below. For several minutes the pilot exercised this masterpiece of fierce and evocative grace, the very essence of English flair and courage. Then, with a final pass just above a huge carved hedge, he waved a jaunty salute to the weeping, cheering crowd and vanished to the south.

It is sometimes said that no real friends are made after one's twenties. We have not found this so, and have made many since we came to Oxfordshire aged thirty. We both enjoy walking in mountains – though I like them steeper than Carol does. This is a pastime for which, like skiing, it becomes harder, as one slowly gets older, to find satisfactory companions. They need to be fit enough to embark on sequential energetic days, intrepid enough to enjoy – or not to mind – heights, and companionable for lunches and dinners. They should have the same idea about extravagance or parsimony, and ideally speak several languages – as I do not. One man who meets all these criteria save the last is Jamie Chilton, an ex-soldier and retired property wizard, whose enthusiasms are not limited to creating gardens, building houses, photography, travel writing, and founding schools in Burma.

His dog-loving, psychotherapist wife, Maggie, now closer to eighty than seventy, recently walked a nocturnal urban marathon. With them, often accompanied by other pedestrians of respectable calibre, like the Charnocks, the Lees (a handsome, witty, fit and affectionate couple most at home storming a pass in a sporting car), or the Tuelys, we have covered a lot of high country in Italy, Switzerland and France. Another who meets many of the criteria is Charles Powell, a tea and gin expert and remarkable church fundraiser, who can slip effortlessly between French, Spanish, Italian and German – a facility I would love to have in order to appear intelligent abroad. Powell was disappointed in Romania though, for he had specially learned the language only to discover that where we went, they spoke only Hungarian.

We have had two educational Italian walks with John and Gabriella Magnay. He is an ex-guardsman and she an attractively outspoken Prussian, whom I once heard say to a friend, over dinner in Urbino: 'You and I have something in common; You are Jewish, I am German. So not everybody likes us'. We have been slowly up the Nile with Peter Kyte, an unconventional Silk and an Oxfordshire neighbour, who likes big motorcycles, literature and travel, and seemed able to prepare complex criminal cases in fifty minutes while on the train between Bicester and Marylebone. We have wandered in Andalucía under the auspices of the incomparably amusing and hospitable Hugh Arbuthnot – and, with Christopher and Mareyka Seel went to sad Cambodia, still in recovery from the barbarisms of the Khymer Rouge. It is a country with no old people.

Some friends are keen on culture, and this can be awkward. Stratford on Avon is handy for us and there are many excellent productions there, several of which we have seen with the Gray-Cheapes (Fiona books for everything) or the Brownes. But the Royal Shakespeare theatre also puts on some plays which are not enjoyable, and until you are settled in your seat, you simply don't know what is in store. I once left a performance at the Swan Theatre, which Shakespeare had set in Italy, but which the director had decided to stage in Oriental costume and setting, with the actors mincing about with their hands in their sleeves. A ridiculous approach which made complete nonsense of much of the dialogue. I went next door to the RSC's main theatre and asked the house manager if I might come in to watch *The Lion, the Witch and the Wardrobe*. She was most understanding.

Sadly, the new Stratford theatre provides overall a much worse experience than the old one. It used to be possible to park right outside, pass through heavy art deco doors into an attractive foyer, order a tray of turkey or smoked salmon sandwiches to be served in the interval in a stylish first floor bar, dine in a restaurant furnished with carpets, table cloths and a vestige of modest style, and watch a performance in a theatre which did not look like the entrails of an industrial building, with every girder, cable, strut and metal beam all messily exposed. The new theatre, now hideously embellished with an external flashing neon sign, is a dreadful mélange. When we first visited after its transformation, its most prominent feature was the whining roar of hand driers in the men's lavatory, which permeated the whole foyer.

We used sometimes to drive to Covent Garden for ballet or opera, in a little over an hour. But now the coagulation and arbitrary closures of the roads into and about London mean that the journey lasts two hours, and it takes 15 minutes to pay a parking meter by telephone (it was 15 seconds with coins). So we go less often (though Ian and Caroline Laing – our daughter's parents in law – have generously several times given us their box). The summer theatre at Garsington remains accessible and most agreeable, though sometimes a trace highbrow for my taste. I live in hope that those who put on country house operas might just occasionally put on some classic musicals instead. Especially My Fair Lady.

In retrospect, though without any very substantial achievements, I have had much to be grateful for. I have not – yet – known poverty, have never had to fight in war, have been fortunate to enjoy an interesting career which has been of some use to others besides myself, have rarely troubled a hospital, and been blessed with an enviable wife and children. These children have thrived very well in their various fields, all have very satisfactory and capable partners and delightful children of their own, of whom we see quite a lot. One cannot reasonably complain or repine, though sometimes, when in contemplative mood I raise my eyes from a book, it does occur to me that perhaps I might have gone a little further in life had I been ambitious to try slightly harder.

Index